THE ANGLICAN CHURCH IN BURMA

WORLD CHRISTIANITY

Dale T. Irvin and Peter Phan, Series Editors

ADVISORY BOARD:
Akintunde E. Akinade
Adrian Hermann
Leo D. Lefebure
Elaine Padilla
Yolanda Pierce

Moving beyond descriptions of European-derived norms that have existed for hundreds of years, books in the World Christianity series reflect an understanding of global Christianity that embodies the wide diversity of its identity and expression. The series seeks to expand the scholarly field of world Christianity by interrogating boundary lines in church history, mission studies, ecumenical dialogue, and inter-religious dialogue among Christians and non-Christians across geographic, geopolitical, and confessional divides. Beyond a mere history of missions to the world, books in the series examine local Christianity, how Christianity has been acculturated, and how its expression interacts with the world at large. Issues under investigation include how Christianity has been received and transformed in various countries; how migration has changed the nature and practice of Christianity and the new forms of the faith that result; and how seminary and theological education responds to the challenges of world Christianity.

OTHER BOOKS IN THE SERIES:
Krista E. Hughes, Dhawn B. Martin, and Elaine Padilla, eds., *Ecological Solidarities: Mobilizing Faith and Justice for an Entangled World*

Aminta Arrington, *Hymns of the Everlasting Hills: Practicing Faith in Southwest China*

Arun W. Jones, ed., *Christian Interculture: Texts and Voices from Colonial and Postcolonial Worlds*

THE ANGLICAN CHURCH IN BURMA

From Colonial Past to Global Future

Edward Jarvis

The Pennsylvania State University Press
University Park, Pennsylvania

Library of Congress Cataloging-in-Publication Data

Names: Jarvis, Edward, 1975– author.
Title: The Anglican Church in Burma : from colonial past to global
    future / Edward Jarvis.
Other titles: World Christianity (University Park, Pa.)
Description: University Park, Pennsylvania : The Pennsylvania State
    University Press, [2021] | Series: World Christianity | Includes
    bibliographical references and index.
Summary: "Examines the history of the Anglican Church in Burma
    (Myanmar) and explores its complexities, and its future, in the
    context of world Christianity"—Provided by publisher.
Identifiers: LCCN 2021024434 | ISBN 9780271091563 (hardback)
Subjects: LCSH: Anglican Communion—Burma—History. |
    Burma—Church history.
Classification: LCC BX5671.B93 J37 2021 | DDC 264/.03009591—dc23
LC record available at https://lccn.loc.gov/2021024434

Copyright © 2021 Edward Jarvis
All rights reserved
Printed in the United States of America
Published by The Pennsylvania State University Press,
University Park, PA 16802–1003

The Pennsylvania State University Press is a member of the
Association of University Presses.

It is the policy of The Pennsylvania State University Press to use
acid-free paper. Publications on uncoated stock satisfy the minimum
requirements of American National Standard for Information
Sciences—Permanence of Paper for Printed Library Material,
ANSI Z39.48–1992.

Contents

Foreword by Archbishop Stephen
Than Myint Oo   VII
Acknowledgments   IX
List of Abbreviations   XI

Introduction   1

chapter 1   "The Only Natural Soil Available": Burma
and the Arrival of Christianity   8

chapter 2   "A Devout Individual Churchman Here and
There": The Church in Colonial Burma   24

chapter 3   "Fellow-Subjects of Our Gracious Empress":
Peoples and Missions of the Colonial Church   43

chapter 4   "Where There Ain't No Ten Commandments":
The Church in the Early Twentieth Century   62

chapter 5   "Patient in Tribulation but Resolute in Faith":
The Church and the Second World War   85

chapter 6   "This Last Step in the Historic Task": Independence
and the Challenges of Postcolonial Burma   103

chapter 7 "A Land and People of Promise": Intercultural
Theology in a Southeast Asian Context 123

chapter 8 "Carrying the Cross": Perspectives on
the Church in Burma Today 147

Afterword 173
Appendix 1: Chronology of the Anglican
Church in Burma 181
Appendix 2: List of Bishops Having Leadership
of the Church in Burma 188
Appendix 3: List of Ethnic Groups and
Subgroups in Burma 192
Notes 195
Bibliography 207
Index 211

Foreword

It is my special privilege to write the foreword for the book *The Anglican Church in Burma*, written by Edward Jarvis, and to present some aspects of the Church of the Province of Myanmar (CPM).

It seems to me that the members of the CPM, including her leadership, are rather like footballers playing on the pitch who cannot just stop playing while the match is still in progress. If they pause to reflect on the match they will surely lose. Likewise, as a tiny church, if we pause in the mission that God entrusted to us to carry out in Myanmar, we will lose. The church could easily melt away in the face of the conflicts, disasters, and poverty surrounding her, and she could evaporate among the competing forces of secularism, liberalism, modernism, and postmodernism that gradually seep into Myanmar.

Nonstop struggling amid challenges and suffering, holding fast to the maxim "actions speak louder than words" throughout her history, from her genesis and across the different eras, therefore, has become one of the key identifying marks of the CPM (Anglican).

This means that the church has very little chance to reflect on herself— to know, understand, and realize who we are, where we are, and thence where and how we go forward. To know and understand, therefore, the history of the Anglican Church in Burma, founded on layers of our struggles, has become crucial for the CPM.

Now, by writing *The Anglican Church in Burma*, Edward Jarvis has filled this crucial gap that the CPM could not herself fill at this stage. Thus, the CPM is extremely grateful to him for this great work.

I too am personally and deeply indebted to Edward and his passionate work, because he has in a roundabout way completed my own unfinished work, my dissertation, titled "The Shaping of Myanmar Anglican Identity," which explored the forces shaping the identity of Myanmar Anglicans amid the interplay of missionaries and local communities in the context of the religious, social, and political challenges present throughout the history of Myanmar.

In the pages of his book, with its eight chapters, covering about two hundred years of Myanmar's history (and the mission history of Southeast

FOREWORD

Asia at certain points), as a historian and an academic, by digging out a range of cultural, social, political, and ethnic factors, the author aims to help us grasp the mind and spirit of the CPM, the forces shaping her identity, her dynamism, and her "DNA" as the Church of Jesus Christ to accomplish God's will in Myanmar.

Indeed, the CPM today is a church that is still able to maintain the Anglican ethos, such as in her orthodox faith and practices (one, holy, catholic, and apostolic), in her liturgy, in her spirit (unity and diversity), and in her threefold ministry (the orders of bishops, priests, and deacons). Together, these have been the binding forces of the CPM, preserving her as an Anglican church and the Church of Jesus Christ amid unmentionable sufferings and unavoidable challenges throughout her history.

All of these factors combined to imbue the CPM with a DNA that allows her to adapt to all situations and circumstances, and an "immune system" that enables her to resist all pressures without losing her Anglican essence. I think that such a DNA and immune system are vital for all Christians and Christian churches if they are to remain faithful to Christ, the founder of the Church, and devoted to God's mission, in this day and age, which can feel overshadowed by forces of darkness.

I am sure that the reader of this book will discover exactly how this DNA and immune system, the dynamism of the CPM, have emerged at key points in history.

This is my wish: that the CPM may become as a bird that flies with the strength of its own wings, freely, along with other birds, toward the destination that God set for us to reach. It is my hope that those who read this book may feel what I feel, for the Church of Christ.

To God be the glory.

THE MOST REVEREND STEPHEN THAN MYINT OO

ARCHBISHOP PRIMATE

CHURCH OF THE PROVINCE OF MYANMAR (ANGLICAN)

Acknowledgments

Huge thanks are due to the many individuals and organizations who have generously shared their time and effort to assist me in the preparation of this book. As gladly as I seize the opportunity to thank them all, I hope it will not appear evasive to thank entire organizations and an entire church, rather than composing a long and inevitably incomplete list of individual names. In some of those individual cases, anonymity is necessary for one reason or another, so a complete list would not be possible. By way of compensation, this book is not only about the people of this church but also respectfully dedicated to them.

Thanks go first and foremost, therefore, to all the members of the Anglican Church in Burma—the Church of the Province of Myanmar (CPM)—especially their faithful shepherd, Archbishop Stephen Than Myint Oo, and his devoted college of bishops. Of the latter I must particularly thank Bishop Samuel San Myat Shwe (assistant bishop of Yangon) and Bishop Noel Nay Lin for their encouragement, and Bishop Mark Saw Maung Doe, whose historical research is a great gift to future scholars. I am also indebted to the kind clergy, particularly my patient and supportive friends Rev. Canon Dr. Paul Myint Htet Htin Ya of Holy Cross Theological College (HCTC), provincial secretary, and Rev. Dr. John Thet Lwin, formerly of HCTC and now rector at Mawlamyine, for an abundance of advice, information, and guidance. Thanks also to Rev. Dr. Moses Tun Aye and Mr. Samuel Tun for their kind words of encouragement, and to Rev. Reginald Bennett for his assistance. I am very grateful to the eminent Dr. Wilfred Aung Hla Tun for his insights and advice. An especially big thank-you goes to Margaret Mai Ra for her invaluable assistance.

In the wider (and dispersed) community of Burma and Southeast Asia, for many and varied types of assistance and encouragement, I am eager to thank (in alphabetical order), Green Globe Travel, Mel Hepworth, Tim Houghton and Crosslinks (BCMS), Nanda Kyaw of the Aung Si (Ocean Pearl II) Guest House, Lum Pan Hpaulu, Mahkaw Naw La, and Ian Richmond. Special thanks to Thomas Yeutter for generously and patiently sharing his incisive and insightful observations. Beyond Burma, I am very

ACKNOWLEDGMENTS

grateful to Bishop Ng Moon Hing and Benedict Rogers for their encouragement. I would like to express my appreciation for the support and work of L'Osservatorio—Research Center on Civilian Victims of Conflicts—part of the Associazione Nazionale Vittime Civili di Guerra (Italian National Association for Civilian Victims of War), especially for their exceptional commitment to Burma and to threatened peoples everywhere, and to L'Osservatorio's director, Sara Gorelli, for allowing me to be part of the team.

It is an extraordinary honor to be associated with Penn State University Press's World Christianity series and the series editors Dale T. Irvin and Peter C. Phan, along with Kathryn Yahner and Laura Reed-Morrisson—sincere thanks to you all. Thanks also (in alphabetical order) to the Bodleian Library, Oxford; the Borthwick Institute at the University of York (home of the Mirfield Collection); the British Library; the Christian Leadership Training Centre (CLTC) in Waing Maw; Holy Cross Theological College; the nonprofit Internet Archive (www.archive.org); the Mirfield Fathers; the Royal Anthropological Institute of Great Britain and Ireland; the Royal Asiatic Society of Great Britain and Ireland; and the School of Oriental and African Studies, University of London. For their precious contributions to the historical record of the Church, I would like to mention here, in memoriam, the late Ven. Charles Henry Chard, the late Rev. Alfred Thomas (Tim) Houghton, the late Rev. Dr. John Ebenezer Marks, the late Rev. William Charles Bertrand Purser, the late Bishop Jonathan Holt Titcomb, and the late Bishop George Algernon West. To all of these remarkable authors and organizations, and for the preservation and distribution of so many wonderful resources, I owe a huge debt of gratitude.

My thoughts turn inevitably to those individuals who have shaped and inspired my own modest scholarly output, especially my dissertation tutor, who then briefly became my colleague and subsequently became my friend, Gerard Mannion, who passed away long before his time in 2019. I would be glad for this book to be considered among the many tributes to him. In closing I would like to express my heartfelt thanks and love to all my friends and family, especially Rachanee Surintharat, for supporting and encouraging me in so many ways. Having failed miserably in the past I will not attempt to comprehensively list them all, but they are always in my thoughts.

Abbreviations

ACNA	Anglican Church in North America
ACS	Additional Clergy Society
BCC	Burma Christian Council / Burma Council of Churches
BCMS	Bible Churchmen's Missionary Society
BEIC	British East India Company
BIA	Burma Independence Army
BNA	Burma National Army
CCR	Constitution, Canons, and Rules (Anglican Church)
CF	Chaplain to the Forces (in the British Armed Forces)
CIBC	Church of India, Burma and Ceylon (1930-47)
CIPBC	Church of India, Pakistan, Burma and Ceylon (1947-70)
CMS	Church Missionary Society (1812-1995), Church Mission Society (since 1995)
CNI	Church of North India
CPB	Church of the Province of Burma (1970-89)
CPC	Country of Particular Concern (see USCIRF)
CPM	Church of the Province of Myanmar (since 1989)
CR	Community of the Resurrection
CSW	Christian Solidarity Worldwide
FCA	Fellowship of Confessing Anglicans
GAFCON	Global Anglican Future Conference
GCBA	General Council of Burmese Associations
HCTC	Holy Cross Theological College
KIO	Kachin Independence Organization
KNDO	Karen National Defense Organization
KNU	Karen National Union
MBE	Member of the Order of the British Empire
MC	Military Cross
MCC	Myanmar Council of Churches
MEP	Société des Missions Étrangères de Paris
MIT	Myanmar Institute of Theology
MM	Military Medal
NCO	noncommissioned officer
RDA	Rangoon Diocesan Association
SPCK	Society for Promoting Christian Knowledge
SPG	Society for the Propagation of the Gospel in Foreign Parts, renamed United Society for the Propagation of the Gospel (USPG) in 1965 and United Society Partners in the Gospel (USPG) in 2016

ABBREVIATIONS

USCIRF	United States Commission on International Religious Freedom
USPG	*See* SPG
VJ	Victory over Japan
WASH	Water, Sanitation and Hygiene
WMA	Women's Mission Association
YMBA	Young Men's Buddhist Association
YMCA	Young Men's Christian Association
YWCA	Young Women's Christian Association

INTRODUCTION

"I want to tell you something about Burma, a country which, though one of the most interesting and beautiful in the world, is comparatively little known to the majority of people."[1] So wrote the painter and illustrator Robert Talbot Kelly more than one hundred years ago, words that are as true today as they were then. Modern-day Burma, or the Republic of the Union of Myanmar, is still a most interesting and beautiful country, and really getting to know it is still a challenge. It is a notoriously complex country from the points of view of history, politics, culture, ethnicity, and linguistics. Ancient clichés such as mysterious, enchanting, bewitching, colorful, and intriguing are all truisms when applied to Burma, but the country's complexity utterly defies lazy descriptions. The often daunting and confusing sociology of Burma is matched not only by an equally foreboding geography but also by an extraordinarily complex religious landscape.

Burma's estimated total population of somewhere between fifty-four and sixty million people presents an intricate and overlapping patchwork (definitely *not* a so-called melting pot) of many different ethnic groups that, broadly speaking, each have their own traditional homeland area located within the national territory. While there is a long history of violence and internal conflict, it must not be assumed that the ethnic groups are all at war with one another; there is, in general, a high degree of mutual respect and solidarity among Burma's constituent peoples. Some of these peoples are united by a common religion, and when this is not the case they are often united at least by a common desire for self-determination and by shared experiences of oppression and hardship.[2] Few of the peoples of Burma are united by a common first language, though Burmese serves as a lingua franca, and many of Burma's people are at least bilingual or trilingual. This all adds to the wonder and complexity of Burma.

To Burma's multiplicity of ethnic groups, most with their own independence movements, historic alliances, and historic rivalries, is added the inevitable complexity of great religious diversity.[3] Christians, though a minority, are more widely spread, more visible, and more vocal than many people would imagine. As is well known, British empire builders—first the military, then the civilians—took the Church of England with them wherever they went, including Burma. Privileged as they once were in many ways, Anglicans have only ever been the third-largest group among the Christian denominations in Burma, losing out to Baptists and Roman Catholics, who, for a variety of reasons, enjoyed more missionary success. Even with the might of the British Empire behind it, Anglicanism in Burma never vied, bullied, coerced, or conspired for first place among the denominations, and later generations of Anglicans have wondered why the colonial government did not do more to promote their church. It was destined to be a modest and unassuming church, begun as a simple extension of the one back home in Britain, which George Orwell, who spent six years in Burma, half-affectionately and half-sarcastically called "the poor, unoffending old Church of England."[4] It is no small credit to subsequent generations of Anglicans over the past two hundred years that their church is still to be found all over the country.

The present-day Anglican Church in Burma may sometimes be presumed to be a mere relic of the British Empire, a thing discarded and left behind by the departing colonists. It may be considered an oddity, an anomaly, a focal point for the nostalgia of a dwindling Anglophile clique—perhaps catering to the last surviving nonagenarian handful of former functionaries of the Raj and their descendants. But the reality is not nearly so bleak, arcane, or pathetic as this, and although it was indeed originally a church of empire, the Anglican Church in Burma, both before and since national independence in 1948, has enjoyed a rich history and identity all its own.[5] This book sets out to explore what became of that "poor, unoffending" Victorian colonial church, to uncover its often surprising part in the dramatic history of the twentieth century, and to chart its survival in the face of suppression and persecution. This book aims to explain the Church's current role in a rapidly evolving regional and global Christianity and a rapidly realigning global Anglicanism by carefully looking into the key issues and contexts involved. This book reveals that far from being a decaying relic of empire, the Anglican Church in Burma has found and continues to nourish its own unique and vibrant identity.

Contrasts run throughout every aspect of the Church's history. The bringers of the supposed salvation of British colonialism may have conveyed some lasting benefits to Burma; this is difficult to dispute. Among the most enduring of such benefits, culturally speaking, would be the high value placed on education and the virtue of expanding access to it. Another lasting benefit, practically speaking, would be the railways, which to this day interconnect the vast and daunting territory at a low cost to the passenger. But colonialism also institutionalized certain types of prejudice, condoned daily injustices, and forged deep inequalities. During the Second World War, triumph was wrested from adversity at enormous cost, and the hoped-for liberation of national independence also brought with it new lows of division, discrimination, and violence.

In recent years, the world has become aware of situations apparently devoid of hope emerging from Burma's Rakhine state, where the Rohingya ethnic group and others continue to face a dire human rights and humanitarian catastrophe. The crisis has provided a window onto the complex and confusing situation inside Burma and has facilitated a growing realization that the Rohingya case is just one of many cases of systematic state violence. This is in stark contrast to the declared democratic aspirations of recent elected governments and invites the conclusion that the military never truly relinquished power.[6] This situation has not left the country's Christian population untouched, and the Church has been forced to craft both its own defense mechanisms and cautious responses to the surrounding persecutions. But clear answers and compact solutions are not readily available, so it is important to set correspondingly realistic expectations when investigating any one aspect of the country.

Being a Christian in Burma is not one single definable experience, of course. The population of Burma is composed of many different peoples, and Christians, though present among nearly all of these peoples, are not evenly distributed. Christians are most present, however, among peoples who have undeniably suffered the highest levels of oppression and discrimination. Both previous and current governments of Burma have presided over some of the most unconscionable and atrocious human rights violations and humanitarian crises.[7] Anglicans as a specific body have never been openly branded as targets for special persecution solely on account of being Anglican, but Anglicans have nearly always been present among the most persecuted peoples. However, to overidentify the Anglican Church with one people or to overidentify any one people with oppression would be a grave mistake. It can sometimes be difficult to ascertain whether Christians have been targeted for being Christians or for other ethnic or political reasons, and care must always be exercised when talking about generalizations. Human rights activists and observers have argued for the need to approach Burma holistically and see all the pieces of the interlocking patchwork as a whole. All the peoples of Burma, in fact, have been oppressed by the same regime(s), and they all aspire to the same basic ideals of peace, justice, freedom, and human rights.[8]

It used to be said that all the best writing about Burma was a hundred years out of date. This has been remedied in the first two decades of this century by a small number of dedicated authors who have embraced the challenge and controversy of Burma. Prominent among these authors, with his fearless dedication to exposing injustice, is Benedict Rogers. For Rogers, reporting on Burma is part of his wider commitment to human rights activism, illustrated by his involvement in the Christian Solidarity Worldwide organization. With a similarly well-informed sensitivity for the difficult issues involved, David Eimer's recent book *A Savage Dreamland: Journeys in Burma* portrays Burma and its people vividly. It is indeed about a hundred years, however, since the story of the Anglican Church in Burma has been properly brought up to date in book form. An inestimable wealth of archival material has been lost or deliberately destroyed in the multiple tragedies of the Second World War and the various large and small postwar anti-religious campaigns, combining with other adverse factors to leave a lamentably permanent void for the inquirer, researcher, and scholar. This constitutes the most obvious and glaring limitation to doing this type of research. It particularly means that much of the very early story of the Church in Burma throws up questions that, as far as we can know, are to remain in want of a conclusive answer. For instance, the exact course of negotiations and correspondence involved in organizing and establishing the first presence of the Church in Burma cannot be comprehensively traced.

Among the older available sources, of special interest are Bishop Jonathan Holt Titcomb's *Personal Recollections of British Burma and Its Church Mission Work* (1880), Rev. W. C. B. Purser's *Christian Missions in Burma* (1911), and Rev. Dr. John Ebenezer Marks's *Forty Years in Burma* (1917). These titles and others are now freely available in digital format online, the nonprofit Internet Archive (http://www.archive.org) being the ideal place to start looking. A little later on, in the 1930s and 1940s, Bishop George A. West's several books added much to the record of day-to-day life in the Church, as did Rev. Canon A. T. Houghton's fascinating *Dense Jungle Green: The First Twelve Years of the B.C.M.S. Burma Mission* (1937). Details of all of these titles and many more can be found in the bibliography. I must also mention the full digitalized collection of editions of the journal of the Rangoon Diocesan Association (RDA)—called *Quarterly Paper* from 1897 to 1927 and *Burma News* from 1928 to 1970—which are all available online courtesy of the School of Oriental and African Studies, University of London (the Burma/Myanmar Collection). To all of these remarkable authors, and for the preservation and availability of these wonderful resources, I owe a huge debt of gratitude.

Along with all the other issues to consider when studying Burma is the question of the name—is it Myanmar or Burma? The official name of the country, according to the current political administration, is Myanmar. The renaming of Burma as Myanmar in 1989, and of Rangoon as Yangon, without consulting the populace, remains a controversial topic.[9] Alongside this move came the amended spellings of numerous cities, towns, rivers, and street names in a sweeping (and some would argue belated) rejection of the spellings and pronunciations introduced by the British. Although seen by many as political opportunism without a mandate, both the decision to rename the country and the name Myanmar itself have their defenders and detractors in all walks of Burmese life. One camp maintains that "Myanmar" is not a new name at all but just a more faithful spelling of the country's "old" name—better than the British transliteration "Burma"—and that it reflects the true Burmese pronunciation more accurately.[10] It can be near impossible for Western, Anglophone ears to perceive any commonality between the two spellings, but this relationship between a B and an M is not unique; a similar effort is needed to connect "Bombay" and "Mumbai," the old and new spellings of the great Indian city. The British name Burma is said by some to evoke the long history of colonial subjugation, while the name Myanmar is defended as being intrinsically correct, historically accurate, and universally acceptable.[11] The name "Myanmar" purports to mean "land of many peoples," though its etymology, as well as the concept's sincerity and desirability, is widely contested. It is not the aim of this book to resolve or much less add to this controversy; the use of the name Burma rather than Myanmar here reflects the fact that for most of this story that was the name used, and it is therefore the name used by the institutions, organizations, political entities, and people in the story. For consistency with the contemporary texts and documents used, therefore, Burma, Rangoon, and the old names and spellings of locations in Burma have been employed, except, of course, where post-1989 documents and texts refer to Myanmar.

When it comes to the story of the Anglicans of Burma, it may be true that written sources are ancient and scarce, but history has not stood still for the Church. This will be especially clear to those readers who have been following developments in the Anglican Communion at the world level. In recent years the Church of the Province of Myanmar (CPM), to give it its official name since the changes of 1989, has reached a worldwide audience as one of the voices vigorously debating the future of global Anglicanism, with much to say about the orientation of global Christianity in general.[12] That voice has begun to be heard loudly and clearly, well out of proportion with this Church's small size. It has joined the chorus of radical, challenging, and even rebellious voices coming from the global south of the world, as one of the cornerstones of GAFCON, the Global Anglican Future Conference. GAFCON is a conservative movement within worldwide Anglicanism calling for a return to Bible-based orthodoxy, out of concern for what it sees as the Anglican Communion leadership's attempts to meet the world halfway and adapt to liberal secular values. In its slightly less than two-hundred-year history, the Anglican Church in Burma has thus gone from a collection of scattered outposts and a handful of wandering missionaries to being a significant player in the campaign to preserve orthodox Anglicanism. Some would call it a bastion of a conservative brand of Christianity that is arguably ancient history in Anglicanism's country of origin, from which, ironically, it was exported to Burma in the first place.

The future of the Church in Burma is therefore not only open-ended and somewhat difficult to predict but is being made on a daily basis in ongoing debates and developing regional and international relationships. The issues are far from trivial, and they go to the heart of organized global Christianity and what it will mean to be a twenty-first-century Christian. The coming years will prompt many types of reflection for a developing country like Burma. Against the backdrop of multiform challenges and realizations brought about by the coronavirus pandemic, in 2020 the Church in Burma celebrated fifty years as an autonomous provincial and primatial Church, and in just three years' time the Church will celebrate two hundred years of Anglican presence in Burma. Despite evident difficulties, there is no better time to encourage further study in this area, and with the support, openness, and optimism of the current Church leadership, there is much scope for future scholarship from both inside and outside Burma. As far as the history is concerned, there are many valid and appealing reasons to delve into this fascinating story. This book reconstructs the two-hundred-year history from archival materials but also benefits from new field research with fresh perspectives from the ground. It draws on the insights and viewpoints of Anglicans from many different backgrounds who have graciously welcomed me into their midst and patiently answered my interminable questions, and the end product is humbly dedicated to all of them. The story of the Anglican Church in Burma is a crucial aid to a complete understanding of World Christianity in general and Christianity in Southeast Asia in particular.

Chapter 1

"THE ONLY NATURAL SOIL AVAILABLE"
Burma and the Arrival of Christianity

Burma, officially the Republic of the Union of Myanmar (Pyidaunzu Than-mǎda Myǎma Nainngandaw) but often still referred to as Burma, consists of a flat central heartland surrounded by mountain ranges to the north, east, and west. The country is strung roughly north to south by four rivers: the Irrawaddy (now called the Ayeyarwaddy), the Sittaung, the Salween (now called the Thanlwin), and the Chindwin. They all flow into the Gulf of Martaban in the south, while the Bay of Bengal lies to the west of Burma. The Irrawaddy delta has been populated by rice farmers for countless generations, the fertility of its soil giving rise to several variations on a proverb that says: "the cultivator tickles the ground and it laughs out a rich harvest."[1] Burma borders China in the northeast, Laos in the east, Thailand in the east and southeast, Bangladesh in the west, and India in the northwest. The territory stretches 1,280 miles (2,000 kilometers) from north to south and 578 miles (930 kilometers) from east to west at the widest points. Burma's total area is almost 262,000 square miles (678,500 square kilometers), with 1,200 miles (1,930 kilometers) of continuous coastline, along the Bay of Bengal and the Andaman Sea to the southwest and the south, this coastline forming one-third of the country's total perimeter. Burma is therefore quite surprisingly large. Superimposed on a map of Europe, Putao in the far north of Burma would be in the middle of the North Sea, Mandalay near Paris, Rangoon at the Pyrenees, and Moulmein near Marseilles. Victoria

Point, at the southern end of the Tenasserim isthmus, would be three-quarters of the way across the Mediterranean.[2]

In the latter part of the first millennium, south-heading migrants from China-Tibet settled in the valleys of Burma's four rivers. Then came the Mon, the Tibeto-Burman, and the Tai-Shan peoples. The first main identifiable ethnic groups to clearly emerge were the Mon, the Burman (also called Bamar), the Shan (who still refer to themselves as Tai), and the Rakhine (in the Arakan region), each establishing their own kingdoms, with the first three vying for supremacy. The Burmans eventually unified and expanded their kingdoms, establishing the first, second, and third Burmese Empires. The ancient Mon kingdom in the south would finally be overwhelmed by the Burmans only in the mid-eighteenth century, followed by the annexation of Arakan, thus establishing a Burman-dominated nation-state approximately within the boundaries of modern Burma. However, the vast Shan lands in the east and the newer states of the Karen (Kayin) and Karenni (Kayah) peoples were never under direct Burman control but only under their suzerainty. The descendants of those Burman nation builders are today's majority Bamar ethnic group, which for clarity should properly be called Burman in English, rather than Burmese. "Burmese" nowadays refers to *all* citizens of Burma, regardless of ethnic group, as well as referring to the main language of Burma. The word "Burmese" was for some time widely used to refer solely to the Bamar ethnic group, a usage that unfortunately implied that those outside the Bamar ethnic group were not true citizens of Burma, the homonymous country. This confusion was often not intended and did not usually reflect ethnic bias, but in other cases the confusion was politically calculated. For these reasons, it is preferable to adhere to the more precise use of "Burman" to refer to the Bamar ethnic group and "Burmese" to refer to all citizens of the country.

The current population of Burma is officially about fifty-four million, though the real figure may be higher. The largest population groups in the plains areas are still the Burman, the Karen, the Mon, and the Rakhine (also known as Arakanese), as in ancient times. The Shan live primarily in their large state in the east and the Shan plateau. Conventional reckoning counts 135 ethnic groups and subgroups (see appendix 3). A good number of ethnic groups and subgroups live in the mountainous regions of the country—for example, the Chin people (including the Naga people), the Kachin, the Karenni, and some Shan subgroup peoples (the Pa-Oh, the Palaung, and the Wa) as well as many other smaller subgroups—giving rise to the colonial-era designation of "hill tribes" or "hill peoples." The British would come to hold the so-called hill tribes in high esteem, and their loyalty to the British, up to and including the Second World War, became legendary. Also, it was among the hill tribes that most converts to Christianity would eventually be found, and their members still make up the majority of Anglicans today. This applies especially to the often-persecuted Karen people, who would be considered the most responsive to Christian teaching out of all the peoples of the entire British Empire.[3]

Since antiquity, most of the populations of both the plains and the mountains of Burma have been farmers, and those living along the main rivers and along the seacoast have been fishermen. While Burma has never had a caste system like neighboring India, high social status could be conferred by advanced age, Buddhist monastic ordination, or royal appointment. Such high status came to regulate social relationships across all walks of life and occupations, with the senior person in the relationship expecting to be heeded by the junior person. This outline of ancient Burmese society is what the first Christian missionaries found still intact and largely unaltered upon their arrival in the early seventeenth century. The ethnic composition of the population and the precise local structure of society can be complex, even by the standards of Southeast Asia, and it is not for naught that Burma has often been described as an anthropologist's paradise.[4]

The Introduction of Christianity to Southeast Asia

Southeast Asia consists of eleven nations lying to the east and southeast of the Indian subcontinent and to the south and southwest of mainland China. The region is made up of the modern-day states (in alphabetical order) of Brunei, Burma (or Myanmar), Cambodia, East Timor, Indonesia, Laos, Malaysia, the Philippines, Singapore, Thailand, and Vietnam. These nations have a number of things in common, not least that they have all been profoundly influenced and shaped by their interactions with the old Western colonial powers. Nearly all of the Southeast Asian countries were once colonies. All of the colonizing powers brought Christianity with them, beginning in the early sixteenth century with the Portuguese in modern-day peninsular Malaysia and the Spanish in the Philippines. Another common inheritance of the Southeast Asian nations is that prior to their encounters with the colonial powers and Christianity, they were exposed to two strong regional cultural, philosophical, and religious influences—from the west, India left its mark with Hinduism and Buddhism, and from the north, China had a lasting impact, importing Daoism and Confucianism.

In addition, each nation of the region developed its own traditions and beliefs so successfully that the incoming religions and philosophies never superseded local customs but fused with them. The result of this, still observable today, is that the practice of the same religion or belief system—for example, Buddhism—may be noticeably different even in neighboring countries. This is often remarked on most readily by local adepts of the religion itself when visiting their regional neighbors. This phenomenon can be observed in Burma, where society may initially seem uniform and united in its overt, public Buddhist devotions, and the religion appears seamlessly interwoven with the life of the people.[5] But as impressive as this public spectacle may be, the Buddhism encountered in Burma is no monolith; early visitors to Burma realized that the tenets of Buddhism were not maintained in some imagined pure form at all and that they were mixed up with preexisting local superstitions and spirit beliefs.[6] This did not mean that people's attachment to either Buddhism or the preexisting belief systems was weak or easy to supplant; on the contrary, the added complexity of this religious fusion would increase the challenge for those seeking to introduce Christianity. Many would be the cases in which powerful and deep-rooted beliefs and superstitions would defy the teachings of both Buddhism and Christianity altogether. Some missionaries would arrive at the conclusion that for the people of Southeast Asia, the world was more densely populated with spirits than it was with living people and that their beliefs in "giants, omens, soothsayings and necromancings" were impervious to evangelization.[7]

Successful colonization, however, was not primarily about converting people to Christianity, and the Church's missionaries were not just sent along to spearhead the arrival of the colonists, as may sometimes be imagined. The main motivations for colonizing were economic and commercial, not spiritual, nor even ideological. The Western powers became interested in Southeast Asia for its natural products, especially spices initially and later rubber, teak, and valuable metals and gems. The economic importance of the region meant that control over it was hotly contested both internally and externally, and retaining that control meant achieving a more thorough cultural domination of the chosen lands. The importance of Southeast Asia would, of course, eventually outlive the colonial period, and the region would go on to alternate between ideological playground and proxy battlefield of the Cold War.[8] But when colonial rule was the name of the game, cultural domination relied on the successful establishment of Western religion, or at least the dissemination and normalization of its values. Upon arrival in the region, and faced with a complex tapestry of local religions, the spiritual representatives of the Western powers tended toward a dismissive attitude at best, while at worst they were openly hostile. They tended to write off the local religions as idolatry and polytheism, but in time it would become clear that Christianity could only ever achieve a foothold when presented as being not in conflict with, and even potentially harmonious with, the previously established local beliefs.

To some extent Christianity would have to tolerate and accommodate local traditions, customs, and superstitions, just as previous incoming major religions had had to do, and in most cases Christian practice would have to accept a degree of fusion with them. This may sound syncretistic and unacceptable to the monotheistic Christian mindset, but this was already a familiar and well-established phenomenon, as Christianity had moved successfully across cultural borders since its beginnings. Even today, in the Western world, all faith communities tend to be discussed in primarily Christian terms such as "congregation," "worship," and "ministry," even when these terms are not proper to non-Christian religions and are often not completely appropriate. Similarly, non-Christian theologies are often evaluated according to Christian concepts such as revelation, discipleship, and salvation, whether these are technically applicable or not, and other religions' holy books are generally presumed to have the same kind of role and centrality as the Bible has for Christians.[9] In a similar way, popular forms of the major world religions in Southeast Asia are usually perceived through a locally produced lens.[10] Christianity in a supposed pure form, whatever that might mean, is therefore not to be found, but the result is arguably no less authentic for its interface with other beliefs. Christianity, it may be said, does not compete with other religions in the region but complements them, as the Indian Jesuit Aloysius Pieris wrote.[11]

Importing Political Models

Once the primary economic and commercial goals of colonial expansion were achieved, developing a lasting and influential presence in the region required political strategies that frequently utilized religion. The establishment of Roman Catholicism in Southeast Asia, in particular, was loaded with ulterior political motives, or at least its facilitation by the ruling powers was. The persecution of early Roman Catholic converts in Vietnam, for example, served as a very useful pretext for the creeping colonization of what became French Indochina, with the French deploying extra forces ostensibly in order to protect their coreligionists.[12] The continental European colonizers of Southeast Asia, whether personally devout, indifferent, or even anticlerical, could not deny religion's potential as a way of importing their social, cultural, and moral values and as a justification for enforcing their economic, civil, and military presence. The rigid hierarchy of the Roman Catholic Church, the unquestionable God-given authority of its prelates, and its impressive symbols of wealth and power were all useful models to export to new lands. This partnership of an authoritarian moral code and pragmatic empire-building ambitions reflected the ideal of Catholic Europe—Christendom—with society being seen as one organic whole, governed by two perfectly parallel and all-embracing spiritual and secular powers.[13]

Toleration of local ways and beliefs, such as was required in Southeast Asia, has not necessarily been considered an impediment to the spread of Christianity. Instead, it has often been regarded as something that could itself be utilized for the dissemination of Christian values in locally acceptable forms. What has often resulted is a kind of symbiosis of religions rather than one religion supplanting the other.[14] Although, theoretically, this need not have been seen as a cause of conflict, both the Roman Catholic hierarchy and their local converts have historically had difficulty reconciling local and imported beliefs. Much of the difficulty lay in relating to alien institutions of power based in faraway lands—Italy, Spain, France—accentuated by the fact that the Roman Catholicism of the colonial period, from the sixteenth century onward, was marked by increasing centralization and consolidation of papal control. Centralized thinking led to what some senior Southeast Asian Roman Catholics would later describe as the leveling of inherent local characteristics, considering this an abuse of power by the Vatican. They would argue that they had no problem giving obedience to the Church in dogmatic questions requiring unanimity, as long as this was accompanied by diversity in matters that do not strictly concern dogma.[15]

Confessional Comparisons

From the religious point of view, the colonial experience in Burma, Malaya, and the Dutch East Indies was somewhat different from the colonial experience in regions that were under Roman Catholic colonizers. The confessional differences between Protestant Holland and Britain and the Roman Catholic powers of Spain, Portugal, and France were reflected in political rivalry and also in the powers' differing attitudes to colonization. The Protestant Dutch, and especially the British, prioritized trade and subjugated all other evangelistic and ideological objectives to it; good trading relations meant keeping the peace, and consequently they aimed not to clash with local religions. The presence of missionaries in the colonies was, of course, allowed, but under quite rigorously imposed conditions, such as those set by the all-powerful British East India Company (BEIC) in the late eighteenth and early nineteenth centuries. Subsequent generations of missionaries would generally appraise these limitations as having been overly restrictive, blaming them for smothering the early development of the local Church. This reality contrasts with a popular perception of Christian missionaries as mere accomplices of the colonizers, an unholy alliance between Christianity and colonialism.[16] There certainly were many instances of Christian missionaries cooperating too closely with the colonial masters; some of them enjoyed excessive material and other privileges, and some were overly reliant on military protection in the face of local hostility, but it is erroneous to conclude that all Christian missionary activity was just part and parcel of Western colonialism.[17]

Acutely aware of being late starters on the Christian scene in Southeast Asia, some senior Anglicans would be critical of what they perceived as their Church's lackluster approach to evangelization, complaining that its leaders, lulled into indifference by comfortable lives back home, fundamentally lacked passion for the divine mission.[18] Most senior Anglicans in Southeast Asia, newcomers to the region as they were, were at least equally critical of the heavy-handed tactics of some of their Roman Catholic forerunners they heard about, who had baptized the natives wholesale and driven converts into church at the point of the bayonet.[19] They did also admit that some Roman Catholic trailblazers, such as Francis Xavier, had been motivated by unparalleled zeal and devotion, while others, lacking grace and tact, resorted to extraordinary coercive methods.[20] The BEIC's prohibition of aggressive missionary work in its territories was seen as a naturally cautious reaction to so many forced conversions by the Roman Catholics rather than just being a policy that was good for business. The Anglican Church more than anyone would bear the brunt of the BEIC's prohibitions, as the two organizations were effectively both representatives of the same empire and were under each other's watch. Even when the

"THE ONLY NATURAL SOIL AVAILABLE"

BEIC's ban began to be relaxed, the ethos remained in the form of sometimes unhelpful, indifferent, or even hostile official attitudes to spreading
the Word of God and a pervasive belief that robust missionary work was
simply bad for business. This may have been at the heart of many senior
Anglicans' ire toward the Roman Catholics.

Missionary Adventures and Misadventures

The first Christian missionary in Burma was a French Franciscan who
arrived in about 1554. The first rudimentary church of sorts was built by
Jesuits in about 1613, while the first brick-built church, ruins of which still
survive, was established in Syriam in 1750. Members of the Armenian Apostolic Church were also present in Burma as early as 1612.[21] Early attempts
at missionary work in Burma brought mixed results. The year 1692 saw
the first priests of the Society of Foreign Missions of Paris (MEP) arrive
at Pegu (Bago), but they were arrested on the king's orders the following year, exposed naked to the bites of mosquitoes, and finally sewn up in
sacks and thrown into the Pegu River.[22] In 1719, Pope Clement XI had more
luck in securing permission from the Chinese emperor to minister to the
friendly kingdom of Ava and in Pegu and Martaban. A diocesan priest and a
Barnabite missionary (the precursor of a long involvement in Burma by the
Barnabite order) were dispatched to Syriam, then the main river port serving
Pegu. Upon arrival they were surprised to meet two Portuguese-speaking
priests already living with a small community of descendants of the earlier
expeditions.[23] The first church was eventually erected, and another priest
and a missionary bishop arrived to oversee matters, but in 1745 raiders overran and plundered the port of Syriam, and the bishop and two missionaries
were murdered while traveling under a safe conduct permit granted by the
emperor. A few years later, in 1749, another Barnabite, Father Paolo Anto-
nio Nerini, who had escaped the sack of Syriam, returned from exile. Nerini
orchestrated the building of the big brick church at Syriam, an Armenian
gentleman being the main donor. Nerini (1710–1756) was appointed bishop
but was never consecrated. He succeeded in building churches and bringing in more priests, but more of them were killed in attacks on Martaban
and a further sacking of Syriam.

This largely was the pattern for the following century of Roman Catholic missions in Burma—three steps forward and two steps back—but with
increasing diligence and genuine evangelical commitment, the Roman

Catholic religion gradually established its presence.[24] Hostility eventually gave way to some official toleration of Roman Catholic missionaries, as long as their work remained restricted to serving Europeans, under pain of further terrible penalties. This was the situation in Burma before the advent of British colonization, in the days when foreign missionaries were very few and entirely at the mercy of local law. Although there was liberty for all foreigners in Burma to worship according to their own customs, it was generally understood that no Burman would be allowed to change his religion or to be anything other than a Buddhist.[25] It was said that in around 1820, there were still only about four Roman Catholic priests in the whole country and that they had a very limited remit that ruled out any evangelization.[26] Until at least the early 1850s, the Roman Catholic missions were almost entirely in the hands of Italian missionaries.[27] Political upheavals at home gradually saw the Italians give way to French missionaries from the MEP once more.

The levels of freedom and safety experienced by all these missionaries were predictably transformed by the presence of the British, especially after the prohibitive and purely mercantile BEIC control gave way to direct British government rule. In Southeast Asia as a whole, British government policy in its various colonies was not uniform, varying from complete freedom of missionary activity to strict controls on which sectors of the population could be preached to—for example, only to expatriate British or imported Indian workers. In Burma, the policy that began to evolve was one of effective freedom of religion and missionary endeavor, with the government remaining religiously neutral, neither facilitating nor hindering the expansion of one religion over another. This neutrality—or perhaps indifference—was the basic policy in the rest of the Indian Empire.[28]

Resistance and Rivalry

Despite the willingness of some early missionaries to present Christianity in ways that were harmonious with local beliefs, it would soon become apparent that substantial numbers of conversions from Buddhism were not going to materialize. This would become the received wisdom in the whole Christian community, but Church leaders did not accept it without a struggle.[29] They would blame what they called "Buddhistic atheism" and the "clinging atmosphere of heathenism" for "paralyzing" the religious sensibilities of the people.[30] For Anglican bishop John Miller Strachan, who actually

"THE ONLY NATURAL SOIL AVAILABLE"

took a greater interest than most in local religion, it was a clear face-off between the Gospel of Hope (the benign, life-giving "Light of the World" brought by the Church) and the Doctrine of Despair (or the heathen, atheistic "Light of Asia").[31] And yet the local populations effortlessly resisted the Church's generous offer. These positive and negative references to "light" were not without strong connotations for the Anglican clergy. One of the most popular hymns during the Victorian era was Thomas Ken's "All Praise to Thee, My God, This Night," beginning with the lines "All praise to Thee my God this night / For all the blessings of the light." This was, or is, one of the "Great Four" English, or Anglican, hymns, according to Rev. James King's *Anglican Hymnology*, and it had additional significance for Burma. The author, Thomas Ken, a nonjuring bishop, was closely associated with Winchester, the sponsoring diocese of the Church in Burma.[32]

This symbolism of the blessings of the light—faith, goodness, and Christ Himself as *lux mundi*, the light of the world—spoke particularly clearly to the Anglican missionaries in Burma. The colonial missionary, it was generally felt, heralded "the triumph of light over darkness—of Christianity over idolatry; while at the same time [viewing] with pride and patriotism the glory of his country."[33] The overcoming of such prejudices would be a protracted and complicated process, and the Church soon learned that the symbolism of light was not exclusive to Christianity. Kawthoolei, the Karen people's name for their homeland within Burma, can also be translated as "Land of Light."[34] The increasingly large and important Indian community in Burma also put great energy into the festival of Deepavali (or Divali, Diwali—spellings vary), celebrating the victory of light over darkness, good over evil, and knowledge over ignorance. On all sides, the clergy saw robust and healthy traditions that were not especially conducive to the introduction of an equally robust Christian teaching, however tolerant and accommodating it may have been prepared to be.

Buddhism in particular, Bishop Strachan concluded, had a kind of soporific power to induce spiritual sloth and indifference, suppress the natural inclination to religious wonderment, and blunt the moral faculties and sense of duty, as he saw it.[35] It was Buddhism, rather than the government's religious neutrality, that was to blame for Christianity's lack of progress, Church leaders like Strachan felt. Even up to the 1960s, Anglicans promoted the following Prayer for Burma: "O Christ, Who art the Light of the world, shed Thy Light over the land of Burma and grant that those who are following the Buddha in his search for true light may find the fulfillment of their hopes in Thee, the Savior and Redeemer of all mankind."[36] This continued conflict of "lights" hints at a standoff that was never resolved, but early Anglican clergy also pointed the finger at their own institution, which they believed had received nothing less than a divine mandate and which had so far failed to step up to the task.[37] Buddhism's hold over the people was not always seen as a truly religious phenomenon, however, but as having more to do with honoring the traditional social status of the Buddhist monks. Were it not for this, Strachan thought, Buddhism in Burma would have died out. There were reasons to genuinely admire the monks themselves, he conceded, as they really tried to live the austere life prescribed by their doctrine, while being, in Strachan's opinion, absolutely wrong in their conception of holiness and the way to attain it.[38] Buddhist resistance to Christian evangelization would perhaps never be fully comprehended, and as we will see this has remained a topic for debate for Christians in Burma and all across Southeast Asia.

Anglican and Protestant missionaries across Southeast Asia remained conscious of the fact that they were not the first ones to arrive there professing the Gospel, even in the case of remote and impenetrable Burma. There would continue to be clear elements of competitiveness in the face of the Church of England's implacable adversaries, the Roman Catholics. There were a good number of Catholic-leaning Anglicans, especially back in England, who begrudgingly admired the Romans' many illustrious and intrepid missionary societies, such as the Jesuits and the MEP, and these Anglicans resolved to replicate the Romans' success.[39] As a result, the type of Anglican who felt compelled to accept the missionary challenge tended to come from a Church tradition that was sympathetic to Roman Catholic ecclesiology, with an emphasis on church order, apostolic succession, sacraments, and liturgy. This is usually known within Anglicanism as the High Church tradition, which has both Catholic and Evangelical expressions, and Anglican organizations such as the Society for the Propagation of the Gospel in Foreign Parts (SPG) and the Society for Promoting Christian Knowledge (SPCK) were flagships of it.[40] This tradition within the Anglican Church continues to exist today, of course, but its focus and priorities have been replaced; the main issue today is the perception that fundamental biblical values are under threat both inside and outside of the Church. These Anglicans generally tend to identify with what is now described as traditionalism or orthodoxy within Anglicanism, embracing both Catholic and Evangelical traditions, as the High Church identity did. In evaluating the influence of the High Church missionary organizations in Southeast Asia, it is interesting to observe that the most enduring character of Anglican churchmanship in the region today can still be described as traditional, orthodox Anglicanism and in many instances Anglo-Catholic.

The two main waves of missionary activity in Southeast Asia, the first one being Roman Catholic and the second one Protestant and Anglican, were always seen as distinct in spirit, even if generalizations, however veracious, do a disservice to exceptional individuals. Roman Catholic colonial missionary work in Asia, as in Latin America, would never completely escape the reputation for conducting forced baptisms en masse and driving natives into church at the point of the bayonet, as part of an aggressive and deeply ideological imposition of Christendom. Their defense would be that passion for the Gospel and the urge to save souls can sometimes lead to extremes of fanaticism, but it can also lead to extremes of humanity, heroism, and saintliness. Such aggressive proselytization can perhaps be selfless, even if misguided. Protestants in Southeast Asia were aware of and able to criticize their Roman Catholic forerunners, but they would become similarly susceptible to criticism. Though British Anglican missionaries did not start out as accomplices of the colonialists, their experience in Burma usually confirmed for them that the British Empire was ultimately a good thing, replacing what they saw as cruel and despotic local rulers and bestowing marvelous benefits, such as railways, law enforcement, agricultural methods, trade, and education.[41] Even some of colonialism's harshest critics conceded that with all its benefits, the British Empire, out of all the empires, was probably the lesser evil. Anglican missionaries were able to feel that they were in the right place and take a certain amount of pride in the enterprise they were involved with; many of them settled in Burma for decades, raised their families there, and felt a profound sense of belonging to the country. The Anglicans' close association with the imperial powers ultimately gave them a lot of license to work across social boundaries as well, including with poor and excluded sectors of colonial society; it is worth noting that non-Anglican missionaries, too, largely indistinguishable at first glance from the Anglicans, enjoyed similar freedoms by proxy.[42]

Theological Contrasts and Conflicts

Over time, by a variety of strategies, and by accepting the need to set more modest expectations, European missionaries of different denominations did succeed in introducing Christianity to Southeast Asia. Local religions had initially been somewhat crudely referred to as polytheism and idolatry, but with the colonies safely established, Western anthropologists began to refer to them more diplomatically as animism and nature worship. This more generous approach would reach its fullness in the twentieth century, and the word "cosmic" would gradually come to be used not just as an umbrella term for tribal and clannic belief systems but also to describe the local forms taken by the major world religions in the Southeast Asian region.[43] Christianity had settled into a cosmic culture, and what is found as a result are popular and cosmic forms, rather than supposed pure forms, of what could be called the "metacosmic" religion of Christianity. These local forms of Christianity could either be rejected as cosmic deviations or appreciated as cosmic expressions of a metacosmic religion, but what do we mean by cosmic? The cosmic religious outlook views all the forces of nature as personal divine beings working alongside humans, and upon death all are absorbed into the cosmos together. The forces of the natural world are not instruments in the hands of people but rather their coworkers, jointly participating in the marvel of existence. This results in a widespread cultural appreciation of worldly things being sacred, and of the sacred being something of this world, resulting in a "sacred this-worldliness."[44]

Sacred this-worldliness is thought to partly explain the long tradition of active participation in revolutionary and independence struggles by clannic and tribal peoples throughout Southeast Asian history.[45] In this part of the world, there is no cultural equivalent of the peculiar strongly held Western maxim that religion and politics do not mix, because there is no equivalent of the Western philosophical dividing line between the worldly and the sacred or the sacred and the profane. This difference became evident with the arrival of the first Christian missionaries in Southeast Asia, especially considering that European thought during the same period had begun to reject the blurring of secular and spiritual power and to consign religion to the apolitical realm of values and ideals.[46] Without having to labor under this concept of separation between the sacred and the worldly, the religious development of Southeast Asian peoples and their attachment to world religions such as Christianity could take on unique features, reflecting local values and customs without conflict. Eventually, Anglican missionaries in the late nineteenth and early twentieth centuries would begin to actively encourage and seek to accommodate these local developments. They often recognized the flaws in colonial Christianity and promoted the idea of an indigenous Church to replace it. These contesting missionaries have been called "atheists of empire" because of their loss of faith in the British imperial ideal.[47] They objected to trying to impose the arbitrary dictates of autocratic church government on local people who already had their own cultural and spiritual traditions. In China, for example, atheists of empire argued for an openly and undeniably Chinese Church in which the fundamental principles of the Christian religion could be "grafted upon the sound stock of Confucian morality."[48]

The role of religion in fostering strong ethnic group identities, often with the politicization of religious ideals and a propensity to engage in activism and protest, which is characteristic of the cosmic religious outlook, has not always been to the benefit of minority peoples in Asia, Christians included. The drive for independence has sometimes taken the form of asserting the superiority of the majority religion over and above all the others, with it often being touted as the "true" religion of all the people and the best expression of the nation's core values. In several parts of Asia, Vietnam and Burma included, anti-colonialism would evolve into anti-Christianism, and both of those national movements had roots in Buddhist organizations.[49] The history of Christianity in Southeast Asia has certainly made it natural to associate Christianity with colonialism, but casting one religion as the sworn enemy overlooks the fact that any religion can be utilized by the unscrupulous for political ends. The purported Buddhism of Burma's ruling and military elite, which arguably pays only the most symbolic form of lip service to actual Buddhism, would be a case in point.[50]

Not every uniquely local process of religious development has sought to assert majority national control, of course, and the phenomenon is not synonymous with the instrumentalization of religion for political ends. Localized processes of religious development have seen world religions contribute to strong minority ethnic identities, whether these be in the Buddhist, Christian, or Islamic domain. This can also be a characteristic that helps communities to cross boundaries of faith, status, and caste, and in this way religion has played its part in the many occasions when Southeast Asian peoples have shown their tenacious fighting spirit to the world. In the Second World War, members of the most marginalized and excluded ethnic groups, many of them Christian, would play a vital part in defeating the Japanese. This experience brought forward the expectation that they would subsequently be rid of their colonial occupiers, too: the British in Burma and Malaya, the Dutch in the East Indies, and the French in Cambodia, Laos, and Vietnam. These aspirations would gradually find expression in theological shifts as well. Southeast Asian Christianity, for example, would eventually go from being a theology of domination, an instrument imported by the colonial masters, to a theology of liberation.[51]

THE ANGLICAN CHURCH IN BURMA

The former theology could be seen as fruit of that "unholy alliance" between the Christian missions and Western colonialism, which all in all was less a theology than a strategy for inculcating a Christian moral worldview to sit in harmony alongside the European economic worldview.[52] In Burma and other parts of Southeast Asia, Christianity would never completely rid itself of its negative association with the old colonial powers.

Summary

The Anglican Church entered a complex spiritual landscape when it ventured into Southeast Asia in general and Burma in particular. Four centuries ago, all of the European colonial powers had a major interest in Southeast Asia, but the Anglican Church did not just go along as an appendage of the British Empire, as may be assumed, and its missionaries did not always have a free pass to operate in the new lands. All of the colonizing powers saw it as politically advantageous or even imperative to bring religion with them, but they did so in different ways. There were two prevailing visions that translated into a variety of missionary methods. The vision of the Roman Catholic nations was built on an unreformed understanding of Christendom, a holistic societal model with spiritual and secular authority as undivided features of the same central power, sharing the same values and ends. This more absolute or totalitarian vision sometimes translated into aggressive missionary tactics, using incentives, coercion, persuasion, or bullying to convert people to Christianity. Colonizers from the Protestant nations, according to the second vision, wanted to keep religion in its proper, secondary place to commerce. They saw the benefits of having missionaries with them as ambassadors for their moral outlook and as representatives of their social and economic value system, but the priority was trade and nothing must endanger that. Missionary work in Burma and elsewhere was limited in scope as a result, and aggressive evangelization was not allowed. However, even modest and tactful missionary work sometimes met with a very hostile local reaction.

All missionaries across the whole of Southeast Asia met with preexisting religious diversity, a long-established feature of the region. To this day, incidentally, striving to ensure that this diversity is respected, and safeguarding against religious difference being misused as a political tool, is an enduring challenge in several parts of Southeast Asia.[53] The introduction of Christianity (and indeed other world religions) into Southeast Asia raises questions about why the day-to-day practice of the same religion can manifest itself very differently in different places. How do religions connect, interact, and dialogue with one another, especially with those religions, beliefs, rituals, and customs that were present before the arrival of the newcomer religion? In Burma, daily life was closely interwoven with long-preexisting beliefs and customs, belief systems that themselves could be interwoven with one another, with none of them existing in a "pure" form. Missionaries were frustrated in their efforts to bypass these overlapping beliefs, referring to them derogatorily as atheistic and heathen superstitions, and ultimately several generations of missionaries would mainly blame Buddhism for Christianity's lack of progress. The challenges facing the missionaries back then, the analogous challenges facing Christians in spreading the word today, and the merits or demerits of the various approaches employed all remain food for current debate.

Christian missionaries gradually realized that seeking to combat or eradicate local religions was generally either ineffective or counterproductive, and varying degrees of toleration, accommodation, and fusion were going to be inevitable. The contrast has been described in terms of a cosmic religion, such as Buddhism, and a metacosmic religion, such as Christianity. The cosmic religious outlook is deeply implanted in Southeast Asian culture, and Christianity, in the words of Aloysius Pieris, had to sink its roots into a cosmic culture because it was "the only natural soil available."[54] The difference in outlook goes far beyond theology, however, and the cosmic religious worldview of "sacred this-worldliness" has lent itself to activism in causes that would usually be seen as expressly secular political causes from a Western viewpoint. Such causes might include ethnic or national independence, freedom from domination by another group or country, and preserving ethnic identity, language, and nationhood. Variations on the phrase "religion and politics do not mix" can be found throughout Christian-influenced societies, especially where these have their roots in European culture. The values expressed by this motto point to some of the biggest and most pressing questions in contemporary Christianity. We may ask whether the phrase mirrors, loosely, the philosophy of the separation of church and state in the aftermath of the Christendom model, in which the division of secular and spiritual authority was considered baseless and illegitimate. We may also ask, looking at the history of Southeast Asia, whether colonialism was not the ultimate fusion of religion and politics.

Chapter 2

"A DEVOUT INDIVIDUAL CHURCHMAN HERE AND THERE"

The Church in Colonial Burma

Burma was colonized in distinct stages by the British, who were already Burma's powerful neighbors in India. Serious territorial disputes on the ill-defined Indian border had been a feature of the closing decade of the eighteenth century and the first two decades of the nineteenth century, culminating in the very costly two-year-long First Anglo-Burmese War (1824–26). Rangoon, then a fishing port of twenty thousand people, was first taken by the British in 1824, and the war ended with the return of the disputed states of Arakan, Manipur, and Assam to British India. During the subsequent sixty years and with two further major military campaigns in 1852–53 and 1885–87, Britain would colonize the whole of the country, putting an end to Burmese sovereignty and independence, and would declare Burma to be a province of India. A colonial administration was installed in Burma "at least possible cost"—to echo a possibly apocryphal phrase sometimes attributed to Lord Dufferin—in what was certainly viewed as the commercial coup of the century for Britain.[1] Throughout this long and arduous process of colonization, a distinction between the plains areas and the remote hills areas developed, which was formalized in the division of ministerial Burma, also referred to as Burma proper, and the frontier areas. Ministerial Burma was mostly flat plains and most of the frontier areas were mountainous and hilly. This led to a distinctive categorization of the inhabitants, and from this distinction come references to the plains peoples and the hill tribes.

The British viewed Burma as an extension of their Indian possessions, though its administration presented problems distinct from those in India. During the various phases of British annexation, there were incidences of armed resistance both from the majority Burman (Bamar) people on the plains and from the Shan, Chin, and Kachin people of the hill tribes, among others. But the trade-focused British wanted to avoid unnecessary wars, and out of sheer convenience the more remote areas inhabited by the Shan and Karen peoples were allowed to rule themselves, with the result that relations with these peoples became quite good. The preexisting independence of the small Karenni (Kayah) state to the south of the vast Shan state, on the Thai border, was acknowledged, and this state was never included within the official borders of British Burma. In parliament, some seats would later be reserved for the Karen, immigrant Chinese, Indian, and Anglo-Burmese minorities, an arrangement bitterly contested by many Burman representatives. The Mon people, neighbors of the Karen on the plains, and the Rakhine people, although included in ministerial Burma, had no representation at all.

As explained in the previous chapter, a tolerant or neutral attitude toward religion and religious diversity, regarded as a commercial necessity by some of the colonial powers, was the path generally chosen by the British. The priority was to do successful trade and accumulate wealth, not to achieve ideological or spiritual domination for its own sake.[2] This was already the position of the British in India, where maintaining a position of religious impartiality was considered to be a supreme duty, no less.[3] Few, if any, in the Anglican Church, thankfully, longed to enforce Christianity in the way some previous colonizers had done in other parts of Asia, with oppressive and abusive methods of coercion.[4] The British East India Company's insistence on refraining from doing missionary work in its territories was widely seen as a rejection of those undignified precedents, as well as being a policy genuinely more conducive to trade.[5] However, parliament in London also took seriously its other supreme duty, as it perceived it, to provide professedly Christian government to administer the non-Christian peoples who came under its influence.[6] In 1813, this took the form of ecclesiastical establishment in India, the officialization of the Anglican Church. A bishop of Calcutta, belonging to the Church of England, was appointed by the crown and paid from the public revenues of India. Therefore, when the British colonization of Burma began eleven years later, the new territories came under the ecclesiastical jurisdiction of the Diocese of Calcutta. In time there would be four other dioceses in India (covering the present-day nations of India, Pakistan, Bangladesh, and Sri Lanka): Madras, Bombay,

THE ANGLICAN CHURCH IN BURMA

Colombo, Lahore, and eventually Rangoon in Burma. But the Church in Burma would begin life as part of the vast territory of the bishop of Calcutta.

The First Missionaries in Burma

The earliest Christian missionary in Burma, as we have seen, was a Roman Catholic, a French Franciscan who arrived in about 1554.[7] The Roman Catholics were followed by the American Baptists 250 years later, in 1807; like the Roman Catholics, they were mere guests in the country and not always welcome ones. Whereas in some parts of the world the arrival of Christianity may have been met with indifference or disinterest, the reception in Burma was often very hostile. The earliest Anglican histories observed that there had been practically no converts up to then because those who did embrace Christianity were crucified or buried alive, and it quickly became common knowledge that it was not safe to even show a serious interest in Christianity.[8] Adoniram Judson, the pioneering American Baptist missionary, was eventually received by the Burmese king, and he pleaded for protection for his handful of Burmese converts. The king replied that he could not change the law, which was admittedly extremely harsh, but he pointed out that the power to enforce the rules or waive them was in the hands of the local magistrate. This noncommittal response, reminiscent of Pilate washing his hands, was what had already prevented the Roman Catholics from doing bolder missionary work.

Judson later recalled a story about a distinguished Burman teacher who had converted to Roman Catholicism thanks to the early missionaries, who then sent this talented teacher to do further studies in Rome. Upon his return to Burma, he was charged with having renounced the established religion, and the king ordered that he be forced to recant. The man was shackled and thrown into prison, where he was tortured and beaten from the ends of his feet up to his breast, until his whole body was reportedly "little else but one livid wound."[9] Some people were apparently so moved to pity by this case that they sought to bribe the torturers to go easy on the man, who throughout the torture loudly professed his commitment to Christ and declared afterward that he had felt little or no pain. Realizing that the poor man was at the point of death, however, his sympathizers protested to the king that the prisoner was clearly insane, as demonstrated by his cool behavior under torture, and could obviously not be held responsible for his wild claims about having converted; this tactic worked, and the king ordered the

"A DEVOUT INDIVIDUAL CHURCHMAN HERE AND THERE"

man's release. He was taken away by the missionaries to recover and was then taken to India, where he lived out his remaining days in peace. After that, Judson later recalled, the Roman Catholic priests, of whom there were only four in the country, completely refrained from proselytizing. Their ministry was confined to their own flocks, which consisted of the descendants of foreign settlers. The official establishment of the Christian Church as part of British colonization would mark a dramatic turnaround for the status of Christianity in Burma and for the freedom and safety of missionaries of all denominations. Even so, conditions in the first decades of the nineteenth century allowed for extremely limited development.

Anglican clergy were first present in Burma during the military campaign of 1824, in the specific role of chaplains to the British troops. As such they had no responsibilities for evangelizing or ministering to civilians, foreign or otherwise, nor to any of the native population, though ministering to local people did take place on some ministers' own initiative. With the first annexation campaign successfully concluded, the troops and their chaplains became a permanent presence. In addition to the military chaplains, six government chaplains were then appointed, assigned to the main colonial stations. The work of a government chaplain was unremarkable, consisting of regular services in the chapel, visiting classrooms and hospitals, and a little pastoral work, all carried out at the headquarters of military garrisons and civil administration stations. Some ministers, a later government chaplain recalled, did make attempts to launch real missionary activity for the salvation of the souls of the "heathens," but such mavericks simply could not count on institutional support or endorsement to carry this type of work forward. Second and third generations of clergy would be utterly scathing of the fact that the Church hierarchy at home in England, for whom missionary work in Burma may have seemed like a distant fantasy world, appeared largely indifferent to the urgent needs of the missions, with the exception of, in Archdeacon Charles H. Chard's words, "a devout individual Churchman here and there."[10]

This was the tenuous and unofficial nature of Anglican missionary work in Burma for the first thirty years or so, before the arrival of the missionary societies could be arranged. With very little support and no dedicated resources, a few government clergy would bravely venture out from the safety of their garrisons to remote areas once a month or once a quarter, or in some cases they could only manage twice a year. In these remote colonial outposts, ensuring religious observance was usually considered to be the responsibility of the deputy commissioner or assistant commissioner,

THE ANGLICAN CHURCH IN BURMA

the police chief or the doctor, or any other ranking official of the colonial administration who happened to be a regular churchgoer. At the request of the bishop of Calcutta or the government chaplain, he would read the service on Sundays to a small assembly of Christians, meeting in the courthouse or on the veranda of someone's official residence.[11] British control over the country was still only partial during the 1830s and 1840s, and even the most outgoing cleric met with many serious obstacles. Residual diffidence and hostility hanging over from previous times meant that pioneering Christian missionaries could still face derision, opposition, or expulsion from a village or district.[12]

Parish, Marks, and the Years of Expansion

After those unpromising early years, the 1850s and 1860s were to become a boom time for pioneers and pathfinders to make their mark. As much as the Anglicans may have wanted to distance themselves from the aggressive evangelization methods of times gone by, the military campaign of 1852 was received with rejoicing and renewed hope for the boost in resources and territorial expansion it brought.[13] British Burma was suddenly a lot bigger, richer, and of much more interest to the Church and general public back home. At this juncture, Rev. C. S. P. Parish, who was the government chaplain in Moulmein (Mawlamyine), began to raise funds and petition the Society for the Propagation of the Gospel in Foreign Parts (SPG) to consider sending missionaries to Burma.[14] Parish's initiative made this a turning point in the development of the Church of England's presence in the country. The SPG responded favorably to Parish's requests, sending out the first SPG missionary in 1854: Mr. T. A. Cockey, a Eurasian trained at Bishop's College in Calcutta. The first bishop of Calcutta, Thomas F. Middleton, had founded Bishop's College and opened its doors to Indian and Eurasian (mixed) students, including for ordination training, in clear defiance of racially discriminatory instructions given to him in England.[15] About a third of the SPG's missionaries over time would be Indians or Eurasians trained at Bishop's College, like Cockey, and their main focus was to launch mission schools.[16] In 1859, the SPG sent Rev. A. Shears from England.[17] In the same year, a talented educator, Mr. (later Rev. Dr.) John Ebenezer Marks, began his life's work in Burma, first in Moulmein (Mawlamyine) and later in Tavoy, Mergui, and Taungoo (also spelled Toungoo). Marks's achievements are detailed in his book called *Forty Years in Burma*, published, with a foreword by the archbishop of Canterbury, in 1917. In reality much of the writing credit was due to his friend and colleague Rev. W. C. B. Purser, who collated and edited Marks's articles, notes, and aides-mémoire.[18]

Marks arrived in Burma as a layman and an experienced teacher in 1859, was accepted as a candidate for ordination three years later, and was ordained deacon in 1863 and priest in 1866.[19] He was transferred to Rangoon, from which he opened mission stations all along the Irrawaddy, and established St. John's College, which, under his auspices, became the leading educational institution in Burma.[20] With Rev. A. Shears, Dr. Marks produced the first translations into Burmese of parts of the Prayer Book.[21] Marks went on to Mandalay in 1868, where he succeeded in establishing a good rapport with the then reigning King Mindon, who was generally open, though somewhat fickle, in his relations with foreign missionaries.[22] The king went so far as to build a church in his royal capital, Mandalay, a schoolhouse next to the church, and a residence for the missionaries, though he later grew wary of being seen to aid the increasing domination of the British. The core of the Church's mission was and would remain the provision of education, and no one had as much influence in this respect as John Ebenezer Marks.[23] To this day, his name and works are well known throughout the Church in Burma, and he is regarded as one of the great educational missionaries of the age.[24] Such was the impact of a few talented early missionaries, coupled with what had been lacking up to then: concrete support from an organization back home, namely, the SPG.[25] The SPG was founded in 1701, when the English Church's colonial outreach was mainly directed toward the Americas.[26] By the end of the nineteenth century, however, half of the society's work would be in India, with an emphasis on education and medical work.[27]

The structure of the Church back home had always been the model to follow in the colonies, and the first real Church of England *parish* as such in Burma was established in the relatively remote town of Sittwe, Arakan, as early as 1825. This rushed step was almost certainly not justified by the size of the local Christian community in Sittwe, and it was no doubt motivated by a desire to symbolically mark the British conquest of the Arakan region. St. Matthew's, Rev. C. S. P. Parish's government chaplaincy church in Moulmein, became a proper administrative parish in 1854, and Rangoon had its first real parish in 1866. Taungoo would receive parish status in 1893. The locations of the early parishes reflect the Church's history: Sittwe shows the British eagerness to demonstrate dominion and a stable base in Burma, Moulmein and Rangoon had the most significant concentrations of British personnel residing there, and Taungoo represented the most significant focal point of native expansion in the Anglican Church.[28] All of these key presences would foreshadow later episcopal jurisdictions (dioceses), followed by a permanent base in Myitkyina in the far northeast by the early 1900s.[29]

The first proper diocese to be established in Burma would be Rangoon in 1877. This decision was a huge step forward, as up to then all of Burma had been part of the Diocese of Calcutta. It was evidently impossible—as the Rangoon Diocesan Association (RDA) history later recalled—for the bishop of Calcutta to effectively oversee all of the work in Burma, and the arguments grew persuasive for separating Burma from the unwieldy Diocese of Calcutta.[30] This did not mean that Burma had been ignored up to then: the bishops of Calcutta, first Bishop George Edward Lynch Cotton and then especially Bishop Robert Milman, earned an enormous amount of respect for their efforts to serve Burma, making pastoral visits that brought hope and encouragement to clergy and laity.[31] These efforts only highlighted the need to divide up the huge diocese, especially after Bishop Cotton tragically drowned during a visit to Assam (his body was never found) and his successor Bishop Milman died of exhaustion.[32] The creation of the new diocese did not come in response to any significant increase in Burman converts, it is important to note, though there had been a large influx of formerly Baptist Karens. More influential was the huge growth of the British civil, commercial, and military establishment in the twenty years following the annexation of lower Burma in 1852–53.[33]

A Missionary Diocese

On 24 February 1877, the new Diocese of Rangoon was created, and the new bishop found himself with a vast jurisdiction that would eventually cover the whole of Burma. The new bishop of Rangoon was the London-born Rt. Rev. Jonathan Holt Titcomb, honorary canon of the Diocese of Winchester. On 21 December 1877, he was consecrated at Westminster Abbey, after which he departed for Burma, arriving in Rangoon on 28 February 1878. The bishop of Rangoon was appointed by the British secretary of state for India, with endorsement from the crown. Half of the bishop of Rangoon's salary was paid by the government and half was provided through an endowment raised by the Diocese of Winchester and the Society for Promoting Christian Knowledge (SPCK). By reducing the number of government chaplains, the government was able to pay the bishop the stipend of a senior chaplain— eight hundred rupees a month—and to allocate a house for his residence, for which, however, he was charged full rent.[34] But the bulk of the credit would always go to Winchester, with the Diocese of Rangoon being considered a daughter of the Winchester diocese and Bishop Titcomb himself having been provided by them.[35]

These developments would bring a welcome and dynamic change in outlook to the Church. The second bishop of Rangoon would later observe that, thanks to his predecessor, the Diocese of Rangoon was "emphatically a missionary diocese."[36] The team under Bishop Titcomb was very small—just one archdeacon and four chaplains—and its work was still officially limited to ministering to the British civil and commercial community, as well as some family and dependents of the military. Like the first army chaplains five decades before them, Bishop Titcomb's team was not expected to go around converting vast swaths of people, and certainly not evangelizing the whole of Burma, but even with their ostensibly limited role their number was insufficient. Furthermore, the strains, stresses, and dangers of working in Burma quickly became clear, and there would continue to be a pattern of tragedy, injury, and sickness that saw careers and lives cut short. Bishop Titcomb himself would be forced to resign in 1882 owing to a serious accident (the effects of which he died from some years later) in the Karen mountains when he was on visitation.[37]

The timing of the foundation of the diocese was fortuitous, because the comparative harmony enjoyed under the sympathetic King Mindon came to an end upon the king's death in 1878. His successor was King Thibaw, who was apparently seized by paranoid megalomania and quickly ordered the massacre of around seventy of his closest relatives. Thibaw's cull targeted the children of his family members as well as anyone who might soon produce a credible heir, as he aimed to remove any potential current or future rivals for the throne. Thibaw's tyranny sparked violent rebellions in several states and saw a quarter of a million refugees heading south to the comparative safety of British-ruled territory.[38] These events provided the perfect pretext and justification for the British to finally seize the rest of Burma, which they longed to do, but Thibaw's cruelty also lent weight to a popular image of Burma as a lawless, dangerous, and barbaric land.

Perceptions of Burma from Within and Without

The idea of church work in Burma always attracted a small number of undoubtedly brave individuals, but the local Church could never quite support enough of them. The SPG and the SPCK were steadfast in their support, but the ends could not be made to meet.[39] At the same time, recruiting missionaries who were actually ready and willing to make the trip was never easy, due to the widespread impression back home in England that Burma was a wild and dangerous place to work. "Don't go to Burma," Dr. Marks himself had been warned. "You'll die of malaria in a month, and if you do not die of that, those bloodthirsty Burmans will kill you. Their great delight is to kill white people."[40] Marks was not put off by this warning, but even he came to disparage the Burmese at times, calling them "the Irish of the East,"[41] believing that like the inhabitants of the emerald isle, in his view, the Burmese were a mass of contradictions. Marks contrasted what he saw as the energy and laziness of the Burmese, their diligence and carelessness, concluding that they were affectionate, unselfish, and kind but basically unreliable. His firm belief was that only an English Christian education could give them stability of character.[42]

Another factor hindering the arrival of prospective missionaries was simply the distance from England: there was no possibility of addressing an urgent need for a missionary, or capitalizing on mission opportunities as they arose, when it took months for a new missionary to get to Burma. The British government sent funds to the new metropolitan bishop of Calcutta (since 1832 the bishop of Calcutta had also been metropolitan of India and Ceylon), Rt. Rev. Ralph Johnson, so that he could provide more clergy for Burma. From this initiative, Bishop Titcomb founded the Additional Clergy Society (ACS), an increasingly necessary move because neither Titcomb nor his successor, Bishop Strachan, was willing to accept the idea of a limited role for the Church. Both of them subscribed to the ethos of a missionary diocese, though, without ignoring the Church's primary responsibility to colonial personnel and other expatriates. Even this main duty of ministering to the Europeans and Eurasians was massively complicated by the fact that the majority of them lived in small scattered communities, often at great distances from one another, and anything resembling permanent spiritual oversight was impossible.[43] This clearly went beyond the remit of normal diocesan clergy, but the bishop was pastorally responsible for the whole country, so it was with Rangoon's full encouragement that missionary societies—the SPCK, the SPG, and the CMS (Church Missionary Society)—continued to expand their operations in Burma. In addition to all of this, as the bishop of Rangoon was the only bishop in the country, all ordinations, whether of local natives (first among Karens and then among

Tamils) or British missionaries, had to be done by him. The same applied to all confirmations and the consecration of new churches, as they sprang up, which all came under his authority.

When missionary work finally began to bear a little fruit in terms of converts, the clergy shortages were felt even more strongly, but the Church rejoiced just the same. The way the Karen people, especially, seemed to embrace the Christian message compensated for the slower reaction from the general native populace. The Karen response to Christianity was the direct opposite of the Buddhist response, Bishop Strachan reflected, pointing out that both the Roman Catholic and Baptist missionaries also found great success among the Karens. Strachan lauded the Anglicans' Taungoo-based Karen mission as the most successful mission in the diocese, and the missionaries could barely contain their enthusiasm.[44] Some of them saw immense significance in the conversion of the Karens, whose legends of a single god (Y'wa), a Garden of Creation, and a Golden Book led some missionaries to conclude that, in the Karen people, they had discovered one of the lost tribes of Israel.[45] Bishop Titcomb himself noted that some Karen legends seemed to correspond to the early narratives in Christian scripture, except for the names and other details.[46] Decades later, Bishop George A. West would also remark that the original Karen conversions seemed to be heralded by prophesies and predicted by "curious traditions of a biblical flavor."[47] Bishop Strachan's explanation of the Karen mission's success was less fanciful, however, considering as he did that the "heathen" Karens were simply blessed with an open-minded and naturally receptive attitude; he believed that with a few more missionaries thousands more could have been converted.[48] The Karen people would become and remain arguably the most notable example of a positive response to Christianity of any ethnic group in the British Empire.[49] Missions directed toward the urban Tamils and Chinese also began to blossom at around the same time.[50] The Indian missions in Burma would always face a linguistic challenge in that the Indian community was largely made up of two groups, Tamils and Telugus, each with a completely different language. Added to this was the fact that the same mission had to be extended to cater to the Chinese as well, but despite these linguistic challenges, Bishop Strachan was able to describe these missions as flourishing.[51] At the same time, he lamented that there were no resources to go after the unreached hill tribes—the Shans, Chins, and Kachins—though much would eventually be achieved with them, especially the Chins and Kachins.[52]

THE ANGLICAN CHURCH IN BURMA

Working Among Buddhists and Other Faith Groups

It could be argued that the British government, through partly financing the bishop of Rangoon, was now contravening its own rule by actively promoting evangelization, rather than just "Christian government," among non-Christians; the bishop was, after all, a government-paid official in spiritual charge of the entire country.[53] The effect of the Church of England's strictly religious ministering at this stage, however, was not significant. Even by the end of the nineteenth century, there would still be only four towns whose European populations were sufficiently numerous to require the presence of permanent clergy: Rangoon, Moulmein, Mandalay, and Taungoo.[54] Neither Church nor government leaders favored an aggressive or coercive pursuit of converts, and there was no suggestion of utilizing Christianity as a tool for keeping the natives firmly under control. In any case, converts from Buddhism remained rare. Even the tentative approval of King Mindon, potentially far more impactful than government endorsement, and the various royal favors he had granted to the Church had never translated into an increase in conversions.[55] In the Church's assessment, it was always "Buddhistic atheism" more than anything else that presented a barrier to progress.[56] Burmese Buddhism, it was thought, was not so much spiritual enlightenment as sociocultural programming, with the "vast and all-pervading" monastic system being interwoven with the life of the people, suffocating any further spiritual curiosity they may otherwise have had. This attachment to Buddhism, Anglicans believed, was an effective barrier to discovering Christ because Buddhism purported to offer everything one needed, including a sort of "adumbration of Christ" in the story, teachings, example, and character of the Buddha.[57]

The complexity of this challenge had two predictable, alternating effects on the Anglican clergy: increased zeal and frequent frustration. Bishop Titcomb had initially shown himself to be a leader of enormous enthusiasm who heartily threw himself into the work of organization. As the diocese was new, this organizing constituted a large, urgent, and important task.[58] But the frustration was also evident, as senior Anglicans lamented Burmese indifference to the messengers of Christ who proposed the "Gospel of Hope" to replace the Burmese "Doctrine of Despair."[59] Bishop Titcomb, by reading and interacting with the locals, had made a commendable effort to understand the Buddhist mindset, but Buddhism was not the only pervasive and widespread belief system to deal with.[60] Predating Buddhism, the missionaries learned, was the lingering superstitious worship and dread of *nats*, or spirits.[61] *Nats* are a type of spirit attached to trees, rivers, mountains, and valleys who concoct blessings and misfortunes for people by night and out of sight. Dr. Marks described this belief as a very bad and exaggerated form of children's notions of fairies and boogeymen, with the major difference that belief in fairies, like belief in Santa Claus, tends to become naturally and easily dislodged with growing up. In dealing with potential converts or school entrants, Anglicans would generally face some combination of *nat* beliefs and superstitions, such as astrology or palmistry, as well as residual Buddhist teachings.[62]

The process of admitting non-Christian students to Anglican schools was uncompromising, however: "This is a Christian school—the parents would be told—If you put your boy here, he will be taught the Christian religion. No underhand method of fear or favor will be brought to bear upon him to make him change his religion, but he will be instructed openly and plainly in the doctrines of Christianity."[63] Dr. Marks stated that in the thousands of school admissions he oversaw, delivering this proviso, there were never any objections, whether from the native peoples of Burma (Burmans, Shans, Karens, etc.) or the immigrant worker peoples (Hindus, Bengalis, Madrassis, etc.).[64] As capable of accepting Christian instruction as they were, non-Christians could also be mystified by the faith that by the final decades of the century was present in Burma in at least five significant-sized denominations—Baptists, Roman Catholics, Anglicans, Presbyterians, and Methodists. The tolerant and welcoming King Mindon once famously summoned the French Roman Catholic bishop Paul Ambroise Bigandet MEP (1813–1894) and his friend the English Anglican Dr. Marks: "What is the difference between you two teachers of religion?" King Mindon asked. Both senior clerics were somewhat stumped, with the Anglican turning to the Roman Catholic for a response and the French bishop insisting that Dr. Marks answer: "The King noticed our difficulty—Marks recalled—and said 'You answer me, Bigandet.' With wonderful French readiness the Bishop replied: 'The English priest can get married but I cannot.' The King laughed and said: 'Is that all? And for that you want two churches to worship in!'" Then, turning to Marks, the king inquired: "English priest, why have you not married?" Marks replied: "Because, your Majesty, no lady has asked me," at which there was general laughter, with which His Majesty heartily joined in. "Then why not marry one of my daughters?" asked the king. "I had to confess—Marks recalled—that His Majesty did me too much honor, and I must remain single. What might have happened if I had been matrimonially ambitious I refrain from even contemplating!"[65]

Challenges, Setbacks, and Achievements

As noted previously, language was a challenge for all missionaries. An urban mission among the Indian community resident in Rangoon, for example, would usually involve working with speakers of multiple, very different Indian languages. Chinese Christians, also, were not necessarily native speakers of one and the same Chinese language or dialect. A more universal and primary challenge was obviously the need for missionaries to learn the difficult Burmese language. Dr. Marks was one of the first to appreciate the subtleties of Burmese: "What does *Nè nè ma sa hnin* mean?" Marks once quizzed Rev. W. C. B. Purser. "It means, 'Don't eat a little,'" Purser replied. "'No, it does not,' said the Doctor. 'It means, "Eat a good lot." I always used that expression when I went round the dining room to inspect the boys at their meals.'"[66] Purser later reflected on this exchange, saying: "My own translation was literal enough, but Burmese is pre-eminently a language of double entendre, and the interpretation put upon the words by the Doctor would certainly be the one which would be understood by the boys. At the same time, there would be sufficient trace of the opposite meaning for the boys to appreciate the joke."[67] On another occasion, a Karen convert presented her baby to the missionaries for baptism. The mother wanted to honor Bishop Titcomb by naming her daughter after him with the name "Bishop" (but with the Karen pronunciation "Bisher"). After some unsuccessful attempts to explain this linguistic gaffe and negotiate a happy solution, they eventually settled on a feminized version of the name—Nan Bisher—which could be loosely translated as "female bishop."[68] Therefore it could be said with some truth that the world's first Anglican female bishop was from Burma. In all seriousness, however, such stories illustrate the flexibility and generosity that were often shown in accommodating cultural and linguistic differences: "We all said the Lord's Prayer," recalled Dr. Marks, "asking, of course, not for our daily bread, for that is not the food of the country, but for our daily rice! In our school we had but two meals a day, rice and curry in the morning, and curry and rice in the evening!"[69]

What the Church was actually doing in practice often stood in contrast with the official nature of its presence and the government policy of being religiously neutral, and this situation was riddled with paradoxes and anomalies. Missionaries went to great lengths to learn the local language and culture, but the Church's influence did not extend far beyond the British civil and military community. This was still the situation after many decades of British rule. It was ironic, too, that the great concentration of Christian educational institutions in the capital actually hindered evangelization, because it tied down such a great deal of precious manpower. Meanwhile, the spread of Christianity in rural areas also depended on the provision of Christian educational institutions, village schools being the main point of contact with the local community and a launch pad for further missionary work.[70] Anglican schools were appreciated by government officials, who ensured that they received occasional bits of extra support in various forms. The Church's view was that their schools were demonstrably more efficient and therefore utterly deserving of preferential treatment from wise administrators.[71] But occasional government favoritism was not a solution to all the Church's problems, and such privileges could not extend to addressing the shortage of human resources. It is also worth noting that the government tolerated the bending of the rules in other directions, too: religion had been kept out of government-run schools altogether, in line with the policy of religious neutrality in public institutions, but in practice Buddhist instruction went on everywhere.[72]

Another area of activity to begin from an educational basis was the Church's work aimed at women. In 1866, the SPG had supported the launch of a Ladies Association for the Promotion of Female Education Among the Heathen that was later renamed the Women's Mission Association (WMA).[73] The WMA arrived in Burma by 1868 and grew rapidly, providing teachers and also training local teachers for women's education. The WMA presented a unique concept in many of the environments it worked in, being devoted to the education of women and championing their place in rapidly changing societies, and its impact and success were considerable throughout Asia.[74] The local Church itself made huge efforts to pioneer education provision for girls.[75] Rangoon boasted St. Mary's Girls' School, an SPG institution opened in 1865, which was soon followed by four other girls' schools in Burma. As a result of this, women began to play visibly more important roles in society and to take some positions of responsibility.[76] Around 1892, the Young Women's Christian Association (YWCA) also began work in Burma.[77]

The Church, Colonialism, and the Future

Missionary work undoubtedly had progressive and pioneering aspects, sometimes in defiance of the official guidelines, but at most levels the Church remained intertwined with that colonialism that some of its own functionaries would later describe as despotic.[78] At the time, however, the Church was widely seen as a benign socializing influence in contrast with the harsher context of the empire.[79] Church work continued to be mostly focused on civilian city-dwellers, and this audience included swaths of the poorest laboring classes. Troops and larger government enclaves had their own chaplains, but the myriad smaller stations and colonial outposts were meant to be cared for by the Church, sometimes, if at all, being visited by the ACS founded by Bishop Titcomb.[80] The tenure of Bishop Titcomb, first bishop of Rangoon, had been disappointing only for its brevity (1877–82), but compensation had come in the form of his successor, Bishop John Miller Strachan, and his impressive twenty-one year tenure (1882–1903).

The new bishop was a highly experienced missionary and also a medical doctor, skills that placed him in high demand throughout his career.[81] He would become known far and wide as "the Doctor Bishop."[82] Not long after Strachan's arrival, the Third Anglo-Burmese War saw the British finally annex the entire country. In 1886, construction began on a new cathedral in Rangoon, which would take the name Holy Trinity from the existing procathedral, now long gone, on Strand Road. The architect of the new building was the Madras-based Robert Fellowes Chisholm, renowned architect of the British Empire and pioneer of the Indo-Saracenic style of architecture.[83] In Madras, he had designed Presidency College and the Senate Buildings of the university, and one of his best-known later buildings is Cadogan Hall in London. The cathedral would be completed in 1894. Bishop Strachan had arrived in Burma after years of experience in India in the Diocese of Madras, from where he knew of Chisholm's architecture. In 1892, the bishop's eagerness to foster links with the Church back home in England supported the launch of the RDA.[84]

With the approach of the end of the century, many in the Church praised the growth and stability achieved under Titcomb and Strachan. After spending the final three decades of the century in Burma, Archdeacon Chard wrote that the Church had been completely transformed during his tenure, notwithstanding the many difficulties, and he gave Bishop Strachan much of the credit.[85] It was felt that the spirit of the missionary diocese was truly being kept alive, with active strictly missionary clergy alone numbering twenty around the country, already half of whom were natives. The Karen mission stood out under the direction of the evidently dedicated men in charge of it, Rev. Alexander Salmon and Rev. H. Kenney. Archdeacon Chard had seen the numbers of both clergy and churches in Rangoon more than double, as well as the construction of the beautiful cathedral.

Total clergy in the diocese numbered forty by the end of the century, with a vast network of outposts and stations serviced by members of the ACS, which left no significant settlement without the pastoral attentions of at least a visiting clergyman.[86]

Chard and Strachan were part of a generation of highly industrious missionary clergy who made no apology for their role in that empire that George Orwell, as a police officer in Burma, would later condemn as "a despotism with theft as its final object."[87] But just how complicit with the colonial regime were the Church's leaders? The written reminiscences of some senior missionaries can be seen as highly nationalistic and often reflecting distinct ethnic and racial prejudices.[88] Even the good lady emissaries of the YWCA could be quite disparaging of Burma, referring to it as "Pagoda Land" and describing it as being populated by "swarms" of yellow-garbed monks.[89] Elizabeth Wilson of the YWCA wrote that missionary work in Burma could only sound romantic to someone who had not visited the place.[90] The standard view across all classes of Westerners was that British colonization was something akin to salvation, bringing order out of chaos, freedom out of tyranny, knowledge out of ignorance, and wealth out of poverty.[91] The benefits of empire may truly have appeared to them to outweigh its failings, and while the clergy certainly subscribed to this standard view, they were not generally complacent, self-satisfied, or incapable of seeing the empire's faults as well. The Church was without question the only branch of the colonial apparatus to consistently seek to address the inequalities and privations of British-ruled society.

Summary

The Church's first seventy-five years in Burma were characterized by great challenges. Anglicans faced the challenge of being a missionary church despite wavering support, limited resources (including human resources), and lack of comprehension from home. They faced the challenge of trying to operate effectively without falling foul of the colonial administration, which insisted that missionary work remain low-key in accordance with the official government policy of religious neutrality. The Church also tackled the demanding tasks of learning multiple and varied local languages, cultures, and customs. Missionaries accepted considerable obstacles of distance and logistics, and they accepted that physical exertion and even exhaustion were necessary to overcome these obstacles. What motivated those undoubtedly courageous and committed individuals who ventured out as early British missionaries to Burma, knowing that they might return home with their health ruined, or might never return home at all? We might say that by virtue of their class, education, and background they were keen to support the whole British colonial package, including the exporting of Western values and religion, but this conclusion poses more questions than it answers: What did empire mean to them, anyway? Were they blind to colonialism's flaws, or did they just decide to live in denial of them? Or was empire viewed as an acceptable means to a justified end for them, and if so, what was that end?

The timing of the arrival of Bishop Strachan—the doctor-bishop—in Burma allowed him to assess the situation from the center of the action, when the change of local monarch threw society into chaos. It is no surprise that the defense of colonialism came easy to Strachan, since he arrived in time to witness the rise and fall of the soon-to-be-exiled tyrant King Thibaw and his violent, despotic reign. Strachan was adamant that the British Raj was a vast improvement on such barbarism, bringing not just wise and paternal laws to guard against such chaos but also marvelous benefits, such as railways, a justice system, law enforcement, cultivation techniques, trade, and education.[92] The colonial government provided some schools and encouraged and enabled the Anglican Church to create even more, but was this purely philanthropy and magnanimity? After all, the British needed large numbers of capable and literate local people to fill posts in the lower levels of colonial bureaucracy, so surely it was just very convenient if they were schooled in the British way and manner? The British promoted the provision of education ultimately in order to better control and run the colony in a civilized fashion, and this strategy worked, whereas the Church's strategy of using education as a pathway to Christian conversion generally did not. They were undeterred. The Church's schools were a source of great pride, being the most respected and efficient schools in Burma and among the best in Asia. Much was achieved in the field of education provision, which paradoxically devoured resources and tied down valuable manpower that could have been deployed to the missions.

It is evident that the Anglican Church did not always operate in the way the colonial masters would have liked. The SPG's work, in particular, tended to focus on the very poorest strata of society, addressing what was referred to as the "colonialism within colonialism" resulting from a rigid and unforgiving class system.[93] Anglicans generally made sure to keep the peace, however, at times even vigorously defending colonialism, or at least promoting the "lesser evil" argument. But there was clearly a contradiction between theory and action. Was this contradiction a case of internal disagreement, a few headstrong individuals going their own way, systemic hypocrisy, or just an ill-prepared Christian organization struggling to do the right thing? Intentionally or not, the Church's support for colonialism acted as a trade-off, giving missionaries a certain amount of proxy authority under which to operate more freely than before and thus extend their assistance to disadvantaged groups in society.[94]

The chief regret of Strachan's generation of missionaries was that the Church's spiritual achievements had not been greater, and Strachan placed the blame at the door of the institutional Church itself. He believed that God's main works were performed through the efforts of faithful agents, not through miracles, and that failure was to be ascribed to apathy, indifference, and absence of vigor within the Church.[95] The most glaring sign of failure at the end of the Victorian age was still the low level of success among the Buddhists. Only around twelve hundred Burmans had joined the Church by the turn of the century. The Buddhist heartlands of Mon, Rakhine, Shan, and the Karen plains still remained completely impassive to the Church's predications. Bishop Strachan pointed out that it was not just an Anglican problem and that the Roman Catholics and Baptists yielded similarly slender results, despite what were considered to be their more plentiful resources.[96] This prolonged experience of not getting anywhere may have helped to give rise to tendencies of ethnic bias and prejudice, and perhaps even a sense of dislike of the Buddhist majority.[97] Adherence to "atheistic" Buddhism was equated with an absence of religious sensibility, and this was considered to be the other main obstacle to missionary success in Burma.[98] This frustration with Buddhism would ultimately outlive the tension between government and Church, the disappointment with the lackluster Church hierarchy back home, the rivalry between denominations, and all the other causes of resentment for the Anglican Church. It remains a matter for debate to this day.

Thus, the Victorian age saw the beginnings of tensions that would last for more than a century, tensions both between religious groups and within religious groups. Some Burmese would come to see the Christians' preaching to ethnic minority groups as a divide-and-rule strategy, supposedly planned by the British, and the ethnic minorities' openness to Christianity was criticized for being servile and characteristic of "imperialist lackeys."[99] Decades later, Nu, the first prime minister of independent Burma, would explain that the missionaries had deliberately sown the seeds of racial and

THE ANGLICAN CHURCH IN BURMA

religious conflict; the ethnic minorities would, in turn, point the finger at what they alleged was Burman chauvinism and oppression.[100] These too are controversial topics still very ripe for debate. It is hard to deny the real, tangible, positive contributions of many missionaries, however, and against all the odds the Church did continue to grow steadily as the "emphatically missionary diocese" they envisaged. It was a time of selfless pioneers whose names live on in the Church they built: Parish, Cockey, Shears, Marks, Chard, Salmon, and, of course, the first bishops, Titcomb and Strachan. All of these individuals and many more constituted the Church's part in the complex and contradictory despotism—"benevolent, no doubt, but still a despotism"[101]—of Queen Victoria's empire.

Chapter 3

"FELLOW-SUBJECTS OF OUR GRACIOUS EMPRESS"

Peoples and Missions of the Colonial Church

A bewilderingly multifaceted job awaited those who did heed the call to depart as missionaries for the Anglican Church in colonial Burma. As we have seen, a mixture of historical, political, geographical, cultural, economic, and linguistic factors impinged upon and hindered the development of the Church and its work. It became common knowledge that missionary work in Burma was no easy ride and that only indomitable, deeply held convictions could sustain the willing few.[1] Missionaries were not paid nearly as well as colonial officials (who generally had less responsibility), and missionaries were more exposed than other public officials to the lurking natural hazards of Burma: malaria, typhoid, plague, cholera, dengue, and dysentery, along with the everyday assaults of insects, carbuncles, prickly heat, and white ants, not to mention occasional floods and earthquakes.[2] Professional frustrations awaited newly arrived missionaries, but there were also great satisfactions in store.

As mentioned previously, it was in expanding access to basic education and working among underserved and marginal groups in colonial society that the Church tended to have most success. Whether reaching out to the poorest urban classes of laborers, servants, and small traders, or doing pioneering work among women and girls, the Church distinguished itself as more than just another branch of the colonial apparatus. At its radical best, the missionaries' work was seen to break down barriers of race, religion, and social position.[3] But Church leaders were also aware that despite

THE ANGLICAN CHURCH IN BURMA

the prominence of its cities, Burma was almost entirely rural, and it was arguably in the jungle, in the mountains, and on the margins of the cities that the real life of the country went on.[4] The prospect of expanding its missionary work among minority ethnic groups in rural as well as urban areas was an engaging and exciting prospect for the Church, but one that prompted many difficult and perplexing questions.[5] This chapter focuses on this particular field of operations, surveying some of the most significant and successful missions in which the colonial Church would find the formula for its long-term survival, its lasting sense of purpose, and its missionary identity.

The Karen Mission

When the fledgling Church in Burma was still in the care of Bishop Milman, bishop of Calcutta, the soon-to-be-thriving mission to the Karen (Kayin) people was begun at Taungoo (also spelled Toungoo). The aim was to take over a large number of Karens—as many as six thousand—who had broken away from the flourishing Baptist mission there, and who, it was feared, would have been left "like sheep without a shepherd" and risk falling "back into heathendom" unless they were taken in by the Anglican Church.[6] But why had this large number of Karens left the Baptists? The case would long be considered a curious and instructive story, and it began around 1863 as the result of a schism.[7] The American Baptists had enjoyed great success in the Karen hills, and the Church of England had no intention of treading on their toes. The American Baptist Mission to the Karens had been founded by Francis Mason, DD, who was in fact English, not American. Dr. Mason, baptized in the Church of England, had emigrated to America as a young man, where he had joined the Baptists. He discovered his true vocation in Taungoo, where he found great success as a missionary among the Karens, assisted by Mrs. Ellen Mason, his wife. Thousands were, by their efforts, brought to Christianity and baptized. Over time, however, it was Mrs. Mason who began to develop religious ideas (and even receive visions) that the Baptist leadership judged to be at best eccentric and at worst heretical. While history unfortunately leaves us to speculate as to the precise nature, content, and theology of these visions and ideas, we do know that this development actually resulted in Mrs. Mason being excommunicated. Less dramatic versions of the story suggest a dispute over land ownership, the Baptist leadership's opposition to Mrs. Mason opening a Karen girls' school, and her "subversive" broader advocacy of local women and girls.[8] Dr. Mason, who refused to condemn his wife's actions, was excommunicated along with her, but he was later rehabilitated. Mrs. Mason was unrepentant, however, and whole villages of Karens stood by her, refusing to accept any other teacher.

Mrs. Mason pleaded with Bishop Cotton of Calcutta and then with his successor, Bishop Milman, to receive her, along with around six thousand Karen converts, their schools, and mission properties, into the Church of England. Mrs. Mason explained that she had always been sympathetically inclined toward the Church of England, to which she felt she already spiritually belonged, she said. Both Bishop Cotton and Bishop Milman rejected her requests, as Church policy was not to interfere with what was seen as a Baptist matter. Mrs. Mason, however, continued her petition with biblical tenacity, and eventually Bishop Milman decided to send an emissary from Rangoon, Rev. John Trew, to go among the Karen people and make inquiries. Trew reported back to the bishop his view that, if left to their own devices, Mrs. Mason's followers would probably drift back to the Baptist mission and the schism would die out. Consequently, nothing was done about Mrs. Mason's proposal. At the same time, however, Trew also suggested that a tentative Anglican mission could be started in Taungoo, but aimed at the Burmans, so as not to be in open competition with the Baptist mission to the Karens.[9] As a result, in 1873 Rev. Charles Warren was sent to Taungoo to begin a mission. This mission gained a handful of Burman converts, and in fact a small Burman mission has existed at Taungoo ever since, though it was quickly overshadowed by the importance of what was about to become the Anglican Karen mission.[10] As time went on, Trew's prediction about the Karen schism proved incorrect; far from returning to the Baptist mission, some of Mrs. Mason's Karen converts were going over to the Roman Catholics or lapsing into "heathenism."[11] This was again and again brought to Bishop Milman's attention by the persistent Mrs. Mason, and at this point the bishop hesitated no longer. He received them all into the fold of the Anglican Church, and they formed the nucleus of the Church of England mission among the Karen people.[12]

Warren's Taungoo mission, as already mentioned, was begun in response to Trew's suggestion of gaining a discreet foothold in Karen territory, and this had proven a clever strategy. Warren made a respectable start, but the conditions and workload were very demanding. In addition to his work as a missionary, he had been burdened with the role of local English chaplain, an arrangement that was forced on him since the military station at Taungoo had ceased to operate and therefore no longer provided a resident chaplain. The situation was so severe that in June 1875 Warren died from overexertion and anxiety, only two months after his own wife had also died.[13] He was replaced by Rev. T. W. Windley, assisted by Rev. W. E. Jones, and the mission continued to gain momentum.[14] The evidently gifted Windley was instrumental in producing the first Karen translation of the Prayer Book, which was printed in Rangoon by the publishing wing of the SPCK.[15] In 1884, the mission gained a dynamic and industrious new leader in Rev. Alexander Salmon, who would lead the mission successfully for fifteen years. No one was allowed to forget the Karen mission's origins, and the specter of schism still occasionally reared its head when confident groups of Karens asserted their influence, but minor conflicts were usually successfully resolved.[16] On 20 December 1896, the bishop ordained two young men to the diaconate—Mr. E. H. Day and Mr. P. R. L. Fisher—at Christ Church, the cantonment church in Rangoon. Day was working in the Burman mission in Shwebo, and Fisher was working under Rev. Alexander Salmon at the Karen mission in Taungoo. The bishop described Fisher as a promising young missionary with real zeal and devotion.[17] Just a few months later, however, on 3 May 1897, Fisher apparently died from epilepsy after a working visit to a remote village called Kotanee (also spelled Kootaney). A very sad event by any reckoning, but an air of mystery surrounded the story of young Fisher's death.

Another missionary setting out to Taungoo, Rev. John Hackney, was able to establish some details of the events surrounding Fisher's untimely death.[18] Visiting the "heathen" village of Kotanee for himself, Hackney noted that the journey between the railway station and the village was no less than a seven-hour hike, a truly murderous feat with a heavy kit. Fisher, it was known, had secured the services of three local men—a certain Morshah, Palah, and Tai Tai—to carry his bags and equipment, but the trek had been too much even for them. They apparently downed their load and just deserted the unlucky missionary, leaving him to carry his own heavy baggage for three miles through a boiling inferno of treeless, shadeless paddy fields in the glare of the tropical sun. Hackney concluded that this ordeal undoubtedly contributed to Fisher's death a week or so later. During his own visit, Hackney sat eating dinner in Kotanee when the village chief's son came to join the party and accidentally let slip the names of the three deserters. Hackney immediately produced his pocket notebook and entered their names, to the astonishment of the chief's son, who was then treated to Hackney's uncensored opinion of the miscreants. A few minutes later,

Hackney recalled, the young man rose and returned to the village. Hackney followed on about half an hour later to find that the three men in question—Morshah, Palah, and Tai Tai—had fled into the jungle.

The village chief's son had been sly in tipping off the three culprits, but Hackney soon gained a much more positive impression of the chief himself. Despite a reputation as a surly, uncivil man, the chief was very courteous and attentive to Hackney, offering him the best room in his house—a foul-smelling den over a crowded pigsty, as Hackney recalled. Hackney was also very pleased indeed to receive an unsolicited apology for the conduct of the three village men and an expression of sorrow for Fisher's death. Under the circumstances, the chief forgave Hackney, who expected the village food to be inedible, for bringing two chickens with him; under ordinary circumstances it was an unpardonable and dangerous offense to bring alien poultry into a village. Though he survived the visit, unlike poor Fisher, on the whole it was acknowledged that Hackney did not win over the village. One or two families attended the church service he held and stayed to converse until late, but it was clear, Hackney felt, that the general tone of the community was against the Church. There was another unfortunate precedent concerning this same village chief: around 1886, one of the Anglican Karen teachers, a widower named Kosee, married a girl called Naw Mookashar, with whom he had a daughter. A few months after Kosee himself died, the widowed Mookashar took up with this same Kotanee village chief and had a son, who then died along with the mother, Mookashar. Hackney believed that Mookashar had died of remorse for her sinful alliance with the heathen chief.[19]

Reaching a genuine understanding between very different peoples required a great deal of work. Under Rev. Alexander Salmon's leadership, an annual Karen Christians Conference began to be held "for the discussion and settlement of matters relating to native modes of life and the modifications and limitations necessarily introduced by Christianity."[20] By the late 1890s, the mission was divided into a north area and a south area, for the purposes of administration, and from 1898 each area held its own conference. Writing of the northern area conference, Salmon praised the enormous efforts of the people, who had specially erected a hall made of bamboo to accommodate no fewer than one thousand participants. The proceedings consisted of devotional services, addresses for Church workers, choral services, and Holy Communion for the general public. There were meetings at which resolutions were proposed and spoken upon, and at which letters detailing the work in each village were read out, as well as subcommittee meetings of various kinds, Church Council meetings, and exhibitions.[21] The resolutions referred to such varied matters as attendance at public worship, the authority of and respect due to village committees, proportionate giving, school fees, support for catechists, the importance of earnestness in their religious duties by Karens who have obtained government employment, Karen customs regarding evil and superstitions, gambling, and temperance. With regard to temperance, it was decided that each village would elect a committee devoted to discouraging the use of intoxicating liquors at marriages and burials.[22] From an inauspicious beginning, the union of the Karen people and the Anglican Church was proving to be an enduring and successful match.

Tamils and Telugus

As was to be expected, the importance of the port of Rangoon for the empire made it an extraordinarily multicultural and cosmopolitan place by the end of the Victorian age.[23] Colonial officials or business executives moving to Burma from other parts of the empire tended to bring their own locally recruited servants, staff, and workers with them, thus constantly adding to the ethnic mix. More significantly, the British authorities shipped workers around the empire in considerable numbers, according to need; they would bring in workers with particular skills, such as in laying railway track, from other colonies, rather than training the local workforce. It is also worth remembering that the British were not the only Europeans in Burma; a large portion of the "British" military personnel were Irish, and among the traders and merchants there were French, Italian, and Portuguese cohorts. There was also a well-established Armenian community, with a flourishing church of its own, and a thriving Jewish community with its synagogue. Alongside the many Europeans in Rangoon, all of Asia seemed to be at work there: Indians of darker skin color often filled the ranks of the so-called coolies, or unskilled laborers; Bengalis worked as clerks; Chinese could be found working in crafts such as carpentry. As in some other parts of the empire, Punjabis formed the backbone of the police, Indian Muslims worked as merchants, Tamils often staffed the hotels, and the sampans crisscrossing the river were propelled by Chittagonians as enthusiastically as their Venetian counterparts with their gondolas. Most aspects of daily life in Rangoon, whether railways, electric trams, hospitals, or post offices, were staffed by "anyone but Burmans."[24]

"FELLOW-SUBJECTS OF OUR GRACIOUS EMPRESS"

Vast numbers of Indians had migrated to Burma, often from parts of India whose economies were less stable than those Indian states with major ports and military bases. The peoples of the poorer hinterlands of southern India—Tamils and Telugus—came in great quantity, from areas most prone to unpredictable harvests and adverse weather. Of those Tamils and Telugus who arrived in Burma, the Christians among them were likely to be either Roman Catholics or Anglicans, mostly either first- or second-generation converts, the products of European missionaries' successful apostolates in India. Other peoples, such as the Chinese, made their way to Burma either as contracted labor in essentially the same way as the Indians or by their own means in the time-honored ways, in search of work and business. Under Bishop Titcomb, the first incarnation of St. Gabriel's, the Indian mission church on Pagoda Road, was built.[25] At various times up to the present day, it has been known as both the Tamil church and simply as the Indian church, because in addition to the Tamils it has also served as the spiritual home to the Telugu and Chinese missions.[26] It was first under the guidance of Rev. James Alfred Colbeck and later Rev. Thomas Ellis of the SPG.[27] It was a roaring success, and soon a Tamil clergyman was specially ordained to look after the growing number of Tamils.[28] Bishop Titcomb happily recalled the delight of the Tamil Christians in receiving a clergyman who shared their origins.[29] Later, Bishop Strachan also took great pride in the Rangoon mission among the Tamils and Telugus, as increasing numbers settled in Rangoon permanently toward the turn of the century.[30] Moulmein (Mawlamyine) was home to a more limited Tamil mission.[31] The original St. Gabriel's church building in Rangoon, which sat around two hundred people, quickly became inadequate, as the attendant congregation could reach twice that number, but it would not be replaced for many years.[32] The second church building, dating from 1926, still stands and is in use, with an outstanding original priest's house beside it. It is still the "Indian church" of Rangoon, and it provides a healthy number of ordination candidates to Holy Cross Theological College (HCTC).

Among the Chins, Kachins, and Shans

After the colonial war of 1885–87, Upper Burma became an official part of British Burma and an official part of the remit of the Anglican Church, but vast swaths of the country remained beyond the effective reach of the Church. As much as they might have celebrated the new mission opportunities, the Church had no resources to do anything about it. Bishop Strachan longed to start work among the remote Kachin people of north and northeastern Burma and the Chin people of northwestern Burma, and to increase work among the eastern Shan people. All of these people were now "fellow-subjects of our gracious Empress,"[33] as Strachan phrased it, but it would take the extraordinary efforts of a few brilliant and determined individuals, and the surprise input of a new missionary society, to make any of this work possible. The Church would also have to face a range of prejudices and fears conjured up by the reputations of the hill tribes in contrast to the tranquil Karens and Tamils they had already come to know so well. The mysterious Chins, especially, were considered a much wilder race, and word came from colonial officials that one missionary alone could not be sent to Chin country—even two men would live in constant danger. The new Chin state colonial government was prepared to provide a house and salary for the purpose, but Strachan was never able to find two suitable and available missionaries.[34]

Even when some brave missionaries did show willingness to go far north, they could not be replaced where they were already serving, and so they could not go. Furthermore, as these newly encountered peoples had completely different languages (bearing no similarity to Burmese and hardly ever any similarity to one another's languages, either), linguistic demands were going to play an increasingly important part in decision-making. It took such a long time for a missionary to learn a vernacular with something resembling the required fluency that to then move him to a different part of the country was regarded as a great waste, and thus the difficulty was much increased.[35] In terms of character, the Shans in the east-northeast were considered an analogous challenge to the Chins. They were rumored to be swarthy hill warriors who were constantly fighting and gambling, "straightforward though rough in their demeanor."[36] The Shans mostly inhabited high plateaus or belts of hills, far out of the easy reach of missionaries in terms of distance. The Shan people's vast territory surprised Bishop Strachan with its pleasant climate, though, which he believed would be agreeable for even the most delicate European, whose physical health might benefit from being there.[37] And yet, no missionaries were available.

The Chins' rugged homeland is in the northwest, between Burma and Manipur in India, though there were, it turned out, pockets of Chins who had internally migrated and settled farther south within Burma. A minority of them were scattered among Burman settlements and thus within reach of the missionaries. The Chins' religion was described as a mixture of theism,

Buddhism, and spirit (*nat*) worship.[38] These new southern Chin missions would present a host of new problems for the first time, including in the area of communication. Most of the minority ethnic groups had no written languages before the arrival of the missionaries. With the Karens, both the plains and hill branches of the people, the Baptist missionaries had already introduced written language before the Anglicans started work among them. A similar situation would be found with the Kachin people, once the Anglicans eventually began working with them. But in order to work with the Chins, the Anglican missionaries would have to devise a written language for them from nothing, using Roman letters. The joint driving forces behind this were the need to translate the Bible and Prayer Book into the vernacular and to teach the people, who were illiterate, to read and write.

To put it mildly, this must have been incredibly time-consuming work; meanwhile, the missionaries had enormous difficulty trying to impart the basic tenets of the Christian faith (their entire reason for appearing there unannounced, after all) through just oral instruction (in English, with whatever words of the local languages they could pick up) and improvisation. Burmese was well established as a written language, and the whole Bible had already been translated into Burmese by Adoniram Judson. As we know, however, few Burmans, the main speakers of the Burmese language, had converted to Christianity, and the majority of Christian converts came from minority ethnic groups who primarily spoke their own languages, not Burmese. They had widely varying knowledge of spoken Burmese, but most could not read Burmese at all. Very gradually, the Bible would be translated by missionaries into each of the minority ethnic languages, first the four Gospels, then the whole New Testament, followed by the Old Testament. Supplementary texts on Christian spirituality and education were practically nonexistent. In the short term, the Anglicans decided to concentrate their efforts on translating sections of the Prayer Book, which would at least provide a framework for essential daily and weekly worship. This was followed by the translation of the Hymn Book. The Anglican Church was institutionally hindered by the fact that it did not yet delegate tasks of any importance to local native evangelists and teachers and did not put much effort into training them, as the Baptists did. All of the potential for expansion described earlier remained reliant on an influx of educated, ordained, or at least ordainable personnel.[39] The further success or failure of the Church's efforts would be determined by the clergy's willingness or unwillingness to break with this institutional quirk.

THE ANGLICAN CHURCH IN BURMA

It was a layman, C. R. Torkington, who had begun working among the southern-dwelling Chin people in the days when the remote northern Chins were still far out of reach.[40] Torkington had arrived in Burma as a soldier, and he had resigned in order to devote himself to missionary work. In 1900, Rev. George Whitehead started a mission to the offshoot of the Chin people known as the Asho Chin, also called the "plains Chin." The mission focused on the area around Prome (Pyay) and along the "Riverine" area—that is, along both the east and west banks of the Irrawaddy (Ayeyarwaddy). The area of operations went from Rangoon up to Prome, with the mission's home base at St. Michael's Church, Kemmendine, which still functions today. The mission area was therefore very large, and Whitehead was one of those clergy who pioneered the training of local catechists in order to assist with the mission. There were converts at quite a number of villages up and down the river, such as Shar Pyu Kyin, Kyar Inn, Htantabin, Paunsabar, Myaynigone, Doe Nwe, Gyundaung, Pai Kya, and Tawma, to name a few, with most of the congregation being scattered in small pockets, except in one or two cases where the whole village became Anglican. Most of them were farmers and illiterate. Whitehead was instrumental in translating parts of the Prayer Book and later Luke's Gospel into Asho Chin while simultaneously teaching his new converts to read and write. At first the Bible was available in Burmese, so he and his local assistants decided to teach the converts how to read and write in Burmese first. The Kemmendine mission center, headed by Rev. W. C. B. Purser, took over the day-to-day running of the Asho Chin mission when Whitehead, with great regret, left to teach at the new Kemmendine Theological Institute.[41] Purser's protégé, Rev. Charles Randolph "Rand" Puner, was later stationed at Prome and put in charge of the Chin mission.[42] The vastness of the mission territory also encouraged the ordination of the first Asho Chin minister, Saya Tun, who began looking after the area under the supervision of the missionaries at Kemmendine.[43]

From 1924, the evangelical Bible Churchmen's Missionary Society (BCMS, today known as Crosslinks) extended its mission in Burma to the Kachin people in the far north, the Khumi Chin along the Kaladan River in the west, and, later, just before the Second World War, among the Shans in the east.[44] BCMS had been founded in 1922 as a result of a schism in the Church Missionary Society (CMS); some CMS missionaries and followers had become unhappy with what they perceived as the society's drift toward theological liberalism. BCMS was intended to be a continuation of CMS's original theological and missionary vision. The BCMS mission among the Kachins took Mohnyin as its base, and this would become the seat of Emmanuel Bible (or Divinity) School, the Church's northern institution of theological education. Central to the story of Kachin missionary work is the name of A. T. (Alfred Thomas, known as Tim) Houghton (1896–1993), a BCMS missionary. Houghton came from a family that has now been involved in missionary work for several generations. His own first glimpse of Burma came in December 1918 while he was serving as a wartime-commissioned army officer, and he felt drawn to return as a missionary, eventually dedicating his life to this endeavor.[45] Even as BCMS broke new ground in working among the Kachins, some people in the Church still assumed the worst of the hill tribes, though they invariably discovered their innumerable virtues through direct experience. The Kachins, like the Shan, had been considered a warlike race, supposedly known for extorting money and goods from those traveling between China and Burma.[46] In 1929, the BCMS mission opened new mission areas in the north, this time up the Kaladan River at Paletwa, Chin State, one of the westernmost townships of Burma, headed by the Rev. H. Hacking. The Khumi Chins have yet another language of their own, separate from the Asho Chin language, which is part of the Kuki-Chin group of languages. Once again, language formed one of the most significant elements of the challenge.

The Andaman and Nicobar Islands

Though it may seem incongruous now, the Andaman and Nicobar Islands, described as a string of beautiful jewels in the Indian Ocean inhabited by ancient, mysterious tribes, formed part of the Diocese of Rangoon, though they were a full two days and nights away from Rangoon, traveling by steamer.[47] Bishop Titcomb praised the natural beauty of the Andamans, but the luscious islands happened to be home to the Ross Island Penal Colony, established there in 1858. Its first inmates were rebels who had taken part in the Indian Mutiny of the previous year. Ross Island, as well as being the longest-surviving penal colony in the British Empire, was notorious for its savagery and inhumane cruelty, and the few prisoners who managed to escape fared no better against the hostile indigenous tribes. The islands continued to be home not only to current prisoners but also to those who had somehow avoided fatal clashes with the warders or other prisoners and had been granted a degree of freedom, provided they did not attempt to leave the islands and reported periodically to the prison administration.

These "self-supporters" survived by hawking goods, scavenging, or cultivating small plots of land.

Bishop Strachan was understandably wary of the people he met on his visits to the islands. There were about eleven thousand male and female convicts present on the islands in Strachan's day, nine thousand of whom were convicted for murder, so nearly every resident he met there was a murderer, he explained. Strachan wrote that he nevertheless enjoyed visiting the Andamans and concurred with his predecessor about the islands' beauty, considering them one of the fairest scenes on the face of the earth.[48] But there was little for the Church to be directly involved in, with only about forty-five to fifty native Christian convicts. A catechist held regular services for the Christian convicts but was not allowed to make any attempt to work among Hindus, Buddhists, or Muslims. By the late 1920s, the Church boasted a small but growing body of Christians on Car Nicobar Island, including a catechist, a teacher, and a doctor in charge of a small government-built hospital.[49] They were visited by the chaplain of Port Blair about six times a year. During the Second World War, the fate of this community would make for one of the most heartbreaking stories in the history of the Anglican Church in Burma.

Mixed and Varied Congregations

Burma's mix of peoples made it a "medley of Asia," and the major cities, especially Rangoon, provided great opportunities for multicultural missionary work in the latter part of the nineteenth century.[50] Since the establishment of the Diocese of Rangoon, the Church had gradually begun to see small numbers of Burman converts in Rangoon, Mandalay, Taungoo, and elsewhere. At the beginning of 1879, Bishop Titcomb held a confirmation service in Rangoon that had to be conducted in three languages—English, Chinese, and Burmese.[51] Bishop Titcomb played a leading role in securing a delivery of Bibles, prayer books, and other literature in Chinese, though his attempts to recruit a Chinese pastor from somewhere abroad did not succeed.[52] Bishop Strachan did later manage to provide a few catechists to work among the Chinese community.[53] Strachan credited the initial conversion of large numbers of Chinese in Rangoon to the work of Dr. Marks.[54]

Some time after the fall and exile of King Thibaw, when Strachan was visiting Mandalay for ordinations and confirmations, he noted that the "barbaric splendor" of the great Buddhist palace was being allowed to decay

"FELLOW-SUBJECTS OF OUR GRACIOUS EMPRESS"

fast, and the colonial government would never allocate funds for vermilion and gold-leaf decoration.[55] On the other hand, multicultural and multiethnic confirmation services held in Mandalay were a positive reflection of the rich tapestry of society; confirmation candidates there belonged, respectively (largest group first), to the Burman, Shan, Manipuri, Chinese, Tamil, Malayali, Eurasian, Indo-Burmese, and Armenio-Burmese ethnic groups.[56] Mixed congregations of four, five, six, or more ethnicities became fairly normal, especially in the cities and more important towns, such as the popular hill station of Maymyo (Pyin Oo Lwin). To a surprising extent, this remains true today. As time went on, the Church would include members of ever more remote and exotic groups. Bishop Rollestone Sterritt Fyffe proudly reported forging new contact with the Palaungs, a hill people living near Mandalay, in 1914. Mr. Francis Robert Edmonds, renowned for his work seeking out remote communities, had been up there and found people interested in learning about Christianity.[57] They were Buddhist but apparently unusually open-minded, in Fyffe's assessment.[58] Edmonds, who was later to be ordained and was also a gifted musician and composer, served with the Winchester Brotherhood from 1906 to 1924, eventually leading the mission.[59]

Challenges of Leadership in a Missionary Diocese

Providence dictated that by the beginning of the twentieth century, the Church in Burma was at last fulfilling its ambition of being a real missionary church. Numbers of native clergy and catechists were increasing, but an enduring and persistent challenge existed in trying to cater to the incredible variety of ethnicities and languages that made up Burma. To be an effective missionary was to be, at a minimum, an exceptionally good linguist and a highly skilled diplomat.[60] Language and diplomacy provided just two examples of the many difficult and perplexing questions, but the source of the difficulty was not always easy to ascertain. Strachan recalled how one native clergyman, known as a good and earnest man, had been "foolishly led astray" by some of his people and refused to follow the directions of the missionary in charge and of the bishop, the latter feeling compelled to withdraw the man's license. Strachan did not recall the specific nature of the disagreement that sparked this mini-schism.[61]

This case of the "good and earnest" priest does not appear to have been an isolated one. Such cases were exacerbated by the fact that, for Christian development, the Anglicans were not the only option on the market, and there was constant worry that such individuals and even their congregations might join the Baptists or Roman Catholics. The memory, and the danger, of converts abandoning the Church or defecting to other faiths was always lurking nearby, it seemed. Though there were no large-scale schisms from Christianity altogether, there was always a small amount of movement between the Christian denominations. It could not be ignored that many of the Anglican Church's adherents had come into the fold as a result of a schism from another denomination. Strachan considered such movement between denominations to be a sign of a very loose attachment to Church principles. His attitude sometimes seems distinctly pejorative and dismissive, writing as he did that not much could be expected of these ignorant people, but his attitude was not exactly cruel and probably only typical of the limitations in worldview of that time. Strachan considered the local people childlike in their thinking, vulnerable to specious promises, unappreciative of their sacred bond to the Church, and easily swayed by temporal charms when these were offered.[62]

Native Anglican converts were not the only concern, however, especially when it came to temporal charms on offer. Since the complete annexation of Upper Burma in 1887, the Church had acquired responsibility for a vast and unmanageable territory, with British and European personnel thinly spread out across it. The Church's official target audience of Anglicans was made up of tiny pockets of such people deployed in dozens of remote locations. Logistically, travel in Burma presented every kind of obstacle and hazard. Even the trip to Kemmendine, today only a short drive from downtown Rangoon, was described as an "expedition" in the 1880s.[63] Regular pastoral visits to all of the outposts would have been impossible and appointing a resident minister for each place even less realistic. The result, logically, was that many of the people under the Church's explicit pastoral responsibility had little or no contact with the Church during their time in Burma. This was a cause of deep anxiety for Bishop Strachan. It meant that when a visit *was* finally made to some remote outpost, the clergy, or Bishop Strachan himself, would find a distinct deterioration in Christian habits, behavior, and moral standards. Some of these issues would appear rather trivial today, such as cards and billiards being played on Sundays.[64] This was the natural consequence, it was thought, of the Church failing to provide pastoral care and allowing human foibles to take over. These were the children of the Church, Strachan pointed out, "left to wander in the wilderness without the care and guidance of a shepherd."[65]

"FELLOW-SUBJECTS OF OUR GRACIOUS EMPRESS"

Strachan was committed to visiting parts of his remote flock as often as possible, and he was by all accounts heartily welcomed everywhere. He would go on a tour of as many as twelve different villages, all at considerable distances from one another. In each of these, candidates for confirmation would be assembled for his arrival. Everywhere, the bishop saw a need for more missionaries, especially those with some medical knowledge. Strachan himself, being a medical doctor, treated a very large number of cases on these tours, and many more had to be left for want of time and the proper supplies.[66] The bishop's tours were neither comfortable nor easy, and it was all too well remembered that an accident on just such a trip had eventually put an end to Bishop Titcomb's career and shortened his life. Visits to the Karen mission outposts around Taungoo consisted of a very hard and rough journey lasting more than three weeks, during which the people did their best to take the utmost care of Bishop Strachan. They would arrange to carry him all the way, sometimes in an upright chair fastened to two poles, similar to a sedan chair or a litter, and when that was impossible due to the terrain they carried him in a sort of hammock made of bamboo and cane slung on a long single bamboo pole. It was apparently decided that the latter was the safer mode of transporting the bishop, though it was somewhat uncomfortable. Sometimes as many as sixteen men were employed in carrying him at a time, while at other times just eight could manage.[67]

Even the younger and more athletic missionaries needed every reserve of strength, health, and patience for such expeditions. Rev. Alexander Salmon wrote that missionaries in Karen country must either ride a pony or walk from village to village, and he described the whole experience in detail.[68] Once in the mountains, walking was said to be very pleasant unless there was some exceptionally steep climbing to be done. If the missionary could manage it, he would always have a pony at hand, in case of exhaustion from walking. For food and daily necessities, the traveling missionary relied on the kindness of the people he visited along the way; if he was lucky enough to encounter Christians en route, they would willingly supply him with rice, eggs, fowls, and yams. But he was also wise to carry a supply of emergency rations, a few cooking utensils, some tins of compressed meat, soups, bread, tea, coffee, and so on, to make life bearable. It was also advisable to take blankets or a rug, as it was sometimes very cold at night in the mountains. The missionary would eventually arrive at a village, travel-stained, tired, and hungry, but with immediate duties to perform: he had to shake hands with the entire population, from the oldest to the youngest. "Some of the hands thrust out—Salmon wrote—or in the case of babies

THE ANGLICAN CHURCH IN BURMA

pulled out by their parents or guardians, appeared anything but clean, but, *nolens volens*, it had to be gone through."[69] The passing of several decades would see these aspects of the missionary's job change very little, and even when mission centers and parishes became well established, there was nearly always a "round" of outlying stations to be done regularly. From a civilized base in Maymyo, for example, the cycle of Sunday visitations would be Kalaw on the first Sunday of the month, Taunggyi on the second, Kalaw again on the third Sunday, Meiktila on the fourth, and either Myingyan or Thazi if there was a fifth Sunday; otherwise, they would receive a weekday visit.[70] This itinerary would actually be a serious logistical and physical challenge under today's conditions, so one hundred years ago it was an astonishing feat.

Wherever they went, in addition to all the other difficulties, missionaries faced many challenges inherent to being a Church largely made up of recent converts, not least the hangovers from previously held beliefs and superstitions, which could be extremely stubborn and resilient. The spiritual landscape of Burma was by then made up of a full range of indigenous, pre-Buddhist, Buddhist, and some post-Buddhist elements, but the largely unchanging way of life—rural, pastoral, agricultural—meant that recourse to the supernatural for protection and blessing was normal. *Nat* (spirit) worship, animism, or combinations of ancestor worship and animism were very widespread, as was the custom of consulting astrologers.[71] These beliefs and belief systems were not usually regarded as mutually exclusive or incompatible with other beliefs (in the sense that a Christian might regard it as untenable to profess elements of Wicca or Hinduism alongside Christianity), and elements of one belief system were broadly regarded as transferable to others, in principle.

Rev. George Whitehead described an incident of dealing with a sincere inquirer who had long had doubts about Buddhism and was leaning toward Christianity; his occupation, however, was given as "image maker."[72] This man approached Whitehead to inquire whether, if he decided to convert to Christianity, he could continue to exercise this craft—tied to spirit worship and ancestor worship—as his source of income. Whitehead was torn: he could not in good conscience tell the man that this would be acceptable, but he did not want the man to be completely discouraged; "we hope and pray ... that he may become a worthy convert."[73] This type of situation illustrated a struggle that would never completely go away. There were plenty of failures as converts lapsed, the Church admitted, but they heartily celebrated every occasion when the old superstitions were defeated: "For example—a missionary reported—the other day I asked a young man who wants to join us if he were afraid of the thuyes, the things which sit in trees at night and kill by stones or by fright. 'No, I never see them now. They're afraid of me,'" the youngster replied, clearly boosted in confidence even though he had not yet fully memorized the Lord's Prayer.[74] After decades of work, there were clear signs that the old fears, of the Burmese people being capable of only a very loose attachment to Christianity, were no longer so well founded.[75] The mood in the twentieth-century Church switched to one of faithful optimism.[76]

Summary

Anglican missionaries went into the Burma adventure almost completely unprepared for the vast range of obstacles that awaited them, but it remains difficult to see how they could have done otherwise; Burma, its peoples, and their habitats, beliefs, values, customs, and languages were all either literally or metaphorically uncharted territory. Even before their arrival in country, the missionaries suffered from a serious handicap: they were few. Tied as they were to the model of a strictly hierarchical, sacramental, and clergy-led Church Catholic, effective missionary work was dependent on the need to train and ordain willing missionaries from Britain, and wild Burma was too daunting a prospect for most. Furthermore, it was not enough to be willing; the ideal missionary needed to be equipped with inexhaustible diplomacy, boundless energy, linguistic talent, considerable athleticism, and exceptionally robust health, though even possession of these qualities could not rule out injury or death from an accident or tropical disease. Though the need for foreign missionaries could never be fully satisfied, the Church in Burma was slow to channel resources into training native catechists, evangelists, and teachers, as the Baptists were already doing.[77] As a result, the Anglicans had no plentiful supply of personnel at all, neither native nor expatriate. Missionaries who were successfully convinced to venture out to Burma faced enormous physical demands, not least of which was the need to cover vast distances while trying to stay fit and remain self-sufficient. And yet, an exceptional few did manage to rise to this complex challenge, and a number of circumstances combined to boost the Church's membership considerably, especially among marginalized economic and ethnic groups.

Once the main missionary objective of winning a soul for Christ had been achieved, the problems were far from over. It was often difficult to

THE ANGLICAN CHURCH IN BURMA

retain converts once they had converted, and working to maintain allegiance and trying to sustain commitment were ongoing tasks. One persistent question was how to encourage the convert to definitively break ties to old customs (spirit worship, astrology, and various other superstitions) and hold fast to the Anglican identity (avoiding schisms and defections to other denominations, and not reverting to animism or Buddhism). On reflection, the challenges and dilemmas of doing mission among the various far-flung ethnic groups of Burma constituted a veritable compendium of every possible missionary challenge that a colonial church *could* face. In addition to the many recent and not-so-recent converts from an extraordinary range of ethnic and national groups, the Anglican population also consisted of small pockets of mostly British colonial functionaries dotted around the large country. Among these expatriates, as with the new converts, lapsing from the faith was a constant danger. In their case, the main temptation was not the lure of other religions but the appeal of simple pleasures frowned upon by the Church and the sheer remoteness of many colonial outposts. The fact that both native and colonial populations were so widely spread out is something that limited the missionary considerably. It could take several years to really master a local language and the regional geography, and yet these skills were not the slightest bit transferable, not even useful for communicating with the people of the neighboring state, city, or town in many cases. Huge amounts of work went into not only learning languages but teaching languages, teaching basic literacy, and translating. And yet again, it remains debatable whether they could have accomplished this differently, or better.

Anglicans brought with them some quite inflexible ideas about what the Church should look like institutionally and about how Christians should behave, but they were not immune to harboring prejudices of a far less dignified kind as well. With the Church headquartered relatively comfortably in the more cosmopolitan areas, the surrounding hills and countryside of Burma seemed to them to be crawling with "swarthy," "ignorant," "wild," "bloodthirsty," and "warlike" "heathens" who indulged in drinking, gambling, fighting, robbery, extortion, witchcraft, and murder. On the one hand, the Church embraced all of Burma's peoples as "fellow-subjects of our gracious Empress,"[78] but the reputation of being "treacherous savages who would murder any European at the slightest provocation,"[79] as Dr. Marks had once been warned, still persisted. Fortunately, the Church's more enlightened leaders worked to overcome these prejudices and invariably found good in all of Burma's peoples: "let every man speak as he finds," Dr.

Marks recalled. "I have trusted my Burmese friends, and no people on earth could have repaid my confidence with greater hospitality and kindness."[80]

There is much to discuss regarding the missionaries' successes and failures in overcoming prejudices. Perhaps, also, the missionaries have been victims of prejudice too, given the enormous expectations placed on them during their lifetimes, the general assumption of their complicity in the worst excesses of colonialism, and history's condemnation of their presumed practice of class and racial discrimination. As the twentieth century got underway, it would become increasingly clear that the Anglican Church in Burma would not actually be a culturally dominant colonial church for very much longer. The more enlightened Church leaders would have to become adept at training the local natives and handing over responsibility to them, something that the Church had so far not been very good at. A few pioneers did break ranks and seek to address the need to enable the local members, but on the whole this is an area in which the Church could and should have done better. Increasingly, the Anglicans in Burma would need to have one eye on the future and begin preparing themselves for the foreseeable and unforeseeable challenges of the new age.

Chapter 4

"WHERE THERE AIN'T NO TEN COMMANDMENTS"

The Church in the Early Twentieth Century

As the sun began to set on the Victorian era, there was an atmosphere of quiet optimism in the Church in Burma. The Diocese of Rangoon, when first founded in 1877, had included Lower Burma and the Andaman and Nicobar Islands; in 1887, after the third war of annexation and the ignominious expulsion of King Thibaw, Upper Burma had been formally added to the by-now-enormous diocese. According to the census conducted at the end of the nineteenth century, there were, in the diocese, excluding the islands, 11,854 members of the Church of England, of whom 3,177 were natives.[1] Bishop Strachan boasted that 1,200 of these people were Burmans.[2] These census numbers are not very reliable, it must be said, and they do not correspond at all with the estimates of 6,000 Karen Anglicans alone. It is not clear whether the census took proper account of the actual existence of women, youths, and children, rather than just relying on the word of village patriarchs, who may have responded to the census taker on behalf of a whole household or even an entire village.[3] It is also unclear how children staying elsewhere in residential schools or orphanages, or youths working away at government or other institutions, for example, would have been counted, if at all.

Rangoon city was dotted with churches by the turn of the century, including the red-brick St. Philip's with its easily identifiable dome (in east downtown Rangoon, the building is now used by the Siyin Baptists) and the handsome St. Andrew's, one of several long-lost churches. Christ Church in the middle of the British Military Cantonment (the old cantonment area is still a military zone today, now home to the central military hospital), an important landmark for the Anglican community, may be added to this latter category. Dr. Marks described the first incarnation of Christ Church as "a large iron structure which might have served equally well if not better as a railway station, or, if you closed the doors and windows, for baking bread during the middle of the day."[4] Bishop Strachan's pet project was Holy Trinity Cathedral, in full use (though spireless) by the end of the nineteenth century, standing just within view of its grander Roman Catholic rival. November 1898 had seen the dedication of the mighty new red-brick St. Michael's Church, still in use today in Kemmendine, and in the same month came the dedication of Holy Trinity Church in Pegu (Bago).[5] As Rangoon continued to grow, the outlying district of Kemmendine had become a suburb of Rangoon. Kemmendine continued to be a hub for ambitious missionary expeditions all along the river and as far away as Katha, a remote northern station located between Mandalay and Myitkyina; at nearly 620 miles (one thousand kilometers) from Rangoon, a missionary managed to make a pastoral visit to Katha once a quarter.

Despite this feeling of optimism in the run-up to the turn of the century, a series of adverse circumstances saw the Anglican Church in Burma reach a very low ebb once again. The number of SPG missionaries working in the diocese had dropped to eight, from eleven just a few years previously. Among these eight, only four were familiar with the Burmese language and the other four knew some Karen language. The Karen Anglican community of more than six thousand lived in 110 villages in the vast hilly region east of Taungoo and the Sittaung River, but transportation was so difficult that the missionaries could not reach them all. Most of these Anglicans were once again like a flock without a shepherd. To make matters much worse, the Church's flagship mission at Taungoo was unexpectedly deprived of its enigmatic leader. In 1899, after more than fifteen years in Burma leading the Karen mission, Rev. Alexander Salmon died almost immediately after arriving in England on sick leave. Bishop Strachan considered Salmon's loss to be the heaviest blow that had befallen his diocese for many years.[6] Salmon had actually mastered the Karen language, critically as well as colloquially, which had allowed him to get to know the people extremely well, Strachan recalled, praising Salmon's powers of administration, scholarship, and leadership. At the time of his death, Salmon seemed to have reached that yearned-for maturity as a missionary—awareness, tact, deepened spirituality—that had driven the mission to success and suggested greater things to come.[7] Salmon's elder two children, aged eleven and nine, would be sent home and educated at Denstone College in Staffordshire; the youngest, Cecil Gordon, then aged only five (of whom we shall learn more), would join them at Denstone a little later. Mrs. Salmon would become matron at the school.[8]

Bishop Strachan's lengthy stewardship of the diocese was therefore to end on a somber note. He was clearly deeply saddened by Salmon's untimely death, which seemed to sum up the hardships and sacrifices demanded by this whole project, and arguably for only modest gains: "Taking a wide vision of the people of this country, all seems to be much the same as before," Strachan wrote. "For the millions remain as they were. Pagodas are being built, Buddhism, Hinduism, and Mahomedanism [sic] are still indifferent, or contemptuous, or hostile towards the claims of Christ."[9] Strachan did acknowledge a degree of success in preaching to Buddhists and "heathens," and he recognized that the Church counted many loyal and spiritual members, but he admitted feelings of frustration with the apparently slow maturation of God's plans, such as he had experienced during his time in Burma.[10] He had spent nearly thirty-nine of his sixty-seven years in India and Burma, and he was far from triumphant: "one feels that the shadows are deepening, and that the evening of age, of sickness, of death is approaching when no man can work. In looking into the past one feels how little has been achieved and how necessary it is to redouble effort before the last sleep comes."[11] After twenty years at the helm of the diocese, Bishop John Miller Strachan, MD, DD, began a short retirement in 1903, and the doctor-bishop went to his eternal reward just three years later.

The New Bishops

In 1903, Rev. Arthur Mesac Knight, dean of Caius College, Cambridge, was consecrated as the third bishop of Rangoon. Finding a resurgent atmosphere of uncertainty in diocesan affairs, and aware that there had been no diocesan conference for ten years, the new bishop announced a conference to take place at Epiphany 1904. At the conference, it was reported that there were now nine SPG missionaries, sixteen native clergy, and sixteen government chaplains in the diocese. During the six comparatively short years of his episcopacy, Knight would reorganize the diocese with great zeal, recruiting valuable new missionaries from England. In 1904, the Delta mission was extended from Kyaiklatt (or Kyaiklat) to the Kyaungdawlay area, Pantanaw township, in the large area to the west of Rangoon, reaching out toward the coast. The missionary work in these areas was quite successful, and after 1906 the mission was extended further to take in some of the other villages in the Delta area, such as Bawoi, Wetchaung, and Daw-wah.[12] At St. Michael's mission base in Kemmendine, a welcome new addition to the team was Charles Randolph Puner, known as "Rand" to his friends. Rand arrived in Burma as a layman in 1906, and, having already worked as a teacher in England, he at once set about developing the educational side of the mission at St. Michael's. He was said to be equipped with a magnetic personality that immediately infected fellow school staff with enthusiasm and optimism. The number of pupils soon doubled, and Christian parents from the jungle villages came begging for their children to be admitted to the school as boarders.[13]

Bishop Knight also turned his attention to the cathedral, which had been finished, but in a somewhat rudimentary fashion. By contrast, the Roman Catholic Cathedral, Rev. W. C. B. Purser wrote, was perhaps the finest Christian building in the British Empire. The architect of this latter building was a Dutch priest who, though severely disabled, oversaw the laying of every brick during the ten years that the cathedral was under construction by wheeling himself around the place in a wheelchair and having himself hoisted to the top of the roof by crane.[14] For the embellishment of the Anglican cathedral, Bishop Knight was fortunate enough to receive a very generous offer from a wealthy Indian Christian to provide stained glass for the windows above the altar in the cathedral's apse. The Gothic-influenced architecture, with east windows, came to be regarded as misconceived in the tropical climate, but the windows could not be moved. Knight stripped away some apparently meaningless stone ornamentation in the windows and opted for darker glass to moderate the sun's fierce rays as much as possible. The windows of King's College, Cambridge, with their heavy blue background, had inspired him. The cathedral was transformed and now conveyed, it was said, an invitation to reverent worship that appeals powerfully to all who enter. People praised Bishop Knight's careful planning and cultivated taste. It was also considered to be an encouraging indication of Knight's attitude to missionary work that the prominent legend in each window was in Burmese rather than English. As was customary, the original construction of the cathedral had left the tower as a "stub" with "battlements" and not the bell tower and spire that were part of the original design. Knight seized the opportunity of the recent death of Queen Victoria to raise funds in her memory to complete the construction according to the original design. The money raised was enough to add an arched porch through which carriages could pass, regarded as an indispensable addition to any public building with an annual rainfall like Rangoon's. Knight was also credited with overseeing the design and layout of the cathedral grounds.[15]

Bishop Knight would need all his powers of industry, discernment, and sensitivity to face the challenges of the new era. During the first decade of the century, the official perception of religion's role in colonial society began to change. The Church, for its part, still accepted and respected the government's policy of religious neutrality, but colonial officials themselves began to question the benefits of holding religion down. As Burma became increasingly urbanized, cases of unrest and lawlessness were blamed on moral decline, to which religious education (of Buddhism, for the majority were Buddhist) was seen as a possible antidote. Critics rejected this notion, pointing out that the rising crime and social degeneration had more to do with the decay of old traditions and the loss of old ways of life, as people increasingly abandoned the villages and moved to the cities.[16] The bishop of Rangoon ruefully but lucidly commented that these developments were part of a much bigger wave of changes taking place, with increased interaction between East and West and the imposition of Western ways of life onto the East.[17] Whatever the truth may have been, British policy was about to change, and from 1910 religious instruction was permitted in government schools, as long as it was done outside of normal school hours. This did not directly impact Christian schools, which were still consistently successful, and many Buddhist parents were happy to send their children to them. These parents accepted the proviso that the Christian faith would be preached to their children, but in reality there were very few conversions from Buddhism resulting from this arrangement.[18] As for Buddhist monastic education, now more openly permitted by the British, it would ironically be within this environment that nationalism, anti-colonialism, and anti-Christianism would be most successfully nurtured.

In theory, the government itself maintained its official stance of religious impartiality, though it was not without sympathy for the Anglican Church. In mission schools, of course, the Bible and Christian doctrine were already taught, and over time they too would benefit from the new atmosphere of religious laissez-faire. There had always been cases of favoritism and preferential treatment, but the new rules allowed for the more open and

"WHERE THERE AIN'T NO TEN COMMANDMENTS"

systematic granting of privileges for the mission schools, who now received not only considerable freedom but also grants.[19] Official neutrality had never really deterred the Church from interpreting its role as being, at least in part, to evangelize the peoples of Burma, as Bishop Knight admitted.[20] In his opinion, members of the general British population of Burma were also to be seen as ambassadors for Christian civilization, and they had a solemn responsibility to accurately represent, by their lives, the faith of the Church of Christ.[21] Witness needed to be stepped up, Knight believed, and he facilitated the arrival of new missionary societies such as the Mission to Seamen and the Winchester Brotherhood. The latter was the brainchild of Rangoon's first bishop, Titcomb, who after retiring due to ill-health had persuaded his home diocese of Winchester to create a way of maintaining active ties to Burma.[22] By 1911, following Knight's tenure, the SPG's numbers had rocketed to thirty-seven missionaries, including fifteen clergy, and Knight had considered even these to be pitifully few. Whole tracts of the country were still never reached by Christian missionaries, and the recent changes in the rules of religious practice were seeing an increase in the profile, visibility, and influence of Buddhist identity in Burma.

The new century had seen an increased yearning for national independence in Burma. This movement took inspiration from Burman Buddhist identity, and in turn it also promoted and nourished that same identity, channeling powerful motivations into a political quest. This was the beginning of the process that would ultimately turn yesterday's Burma into the Myanmar of today. In 1906, the Young Men's Buddhist Association (YMBA), modeled on the YMCA, was created. The YMBA took advantage of the fact that colonial law now permitted strictly religious associations as being one application of the new freedom of religious instruction. In reality, the YMBA constituted Burma's first modern political organization, and it would become the foundation stone of the nationalist and independence movement.[23] In 1909, Bishop Knight retired, and Rev. Rollestone Sterritt Fyffe took his place. Fyffe had arrived in Burma in 1905 as the leader of the Winchester Brotherhood in Mandalay. He had been working in Mandalay for just four years before becoming the fourth bishop of Rangoon. His tenure would see the continued expansion of missionary activity in the diocese. The years 1910–11 saw a new mission to the area around Hmawbi village, about thirty miles (forty-eight kilometers) north of Rangoon, and also to the other Delta areas headed by Purser of St. Michael's and the mission center in Kemmendine. Most of this work would be funded by the SPG.

The First World War

68 In comparison with all the wars Burma had experienced up to that time and would experience still later, the so-called Great War did not substantially affect Burma. The Rangoon Diocesan Association (RDA) bulletins of 1914 and 1915 make only passing mention of the war in the West, which was not even having a significant impact on postal services to the East.[24] As the war progressed, however, sources of finance normally earmarked for the missions became strained, and many charitable endeavors in Britain were diverted to supporting war-related causes.[25] But the effect on day-to-day life was still mild, and if Burma suffered from anything it was a feeling of being lonely and forgotten by world events; the danger of war was remote, "like a storm beyond the horizon."[26] For the well-living British civilian residents, avoiding any direct involvement in the war was easy to do and seemed natural at the time. They had a comforting theory that "sticking by one's job" was the truest patriotism, as George Orwell later wrote, and there was even covert hostility toward those who gave up their jobs in order to join the army.[27] Significant numbers of Burmese men from different ethnic groups did volunteer for the British Army, though for various practical, political, and prejudicial reasons not many were accepted.[28] In terms of human contribution, the Church would eventually be disproportionately impacted by the war compared to other sectors of colonial society. This may be because the Church tended to include people with a deeper sense of commitment to the higher ideals of the empire, who were more able to interpret the war in terms of an ideological and existential struggle. The clergy and missionaries in particular tended to subscribe to the ideal of the empire as a vehicle for spiritual enlightenment, for all its possible faults, and were more likely to find a way to construe the war effort in similar terms. As a result, many of them would willingly serve in the war, and the Church's share of tragedy would not be long in coming.

A sad footnote to an earlier tragedy was written in 1915, when news arrived that a son of the Church in Burma had been killed in combat. Lieutenant Cecil Gordon Salmon, of the Third Battalion (attached to the Second Battalion), the Sherwood Foresters, was the youngest son of the late Rev. Alexander Salmon, for many years head of the Karen mission at Taungoo. Lieutenant Salmon, born 4 December 1894, had planned to go from Denstone School to Cambridge and follow his late father into Holy Orders. He volunteered for the army in August 1914 and was killed at Ypres on 13 June 1915.[29] His widowed mother, heartbroken, passed away in February 1918, aged fifty-seven. By the middle year of the war, with the massive expansion of the British Army, several of the clergy in Burma had been called upon to serve as chaplains. For the most part, the clergy of Burma would serve locally or in India, thereby allowing more experienced chaplains to be deployed to the Western Front. Rev. William Rolfe Garrad of the Winchester Brotherhood found himself stationed in Poona and Bombay, India, while Rev. William Robert Park served as a chaplain with Indian units in Mesopotamia (Iraq). Rev. Ernest Hale Dunkley also served in Mesopotamia and India, first as an infantry officer and later as a chaplain, and he was decorated with the MBE (Member of the Order of the British Empire) for service on the North West Frontier.

A number of other missionaries and ordinands volunteered as infantry officers rather than chaplains; Lieutenant G. H. Bruce Kerr served with Indian forces in Mesopotamia, and Lieutenant C. R. Bathurst served in France. Bathurst was badly wounded during the early phase of the Battle of the Somme and lay unconscious for six hours out in no-man's-land, a mere hundred yards from the German trenches, before being helped by another wounded man to crawl back to their trench.[30] Rev. C. V. Burder, a former missionary, was commissioned in the Artists Rifles, was wounded, and was decorated with the Military Cross. Over seventy old boys and former masters of the Rangoon Diocesan High School were in uniform by 1917, and one teacher and three old boys had already given their lives.[31] A second teacher to perish was Lieutenant Bernard Moore Blakeston. He had graduated from Cambridge in 1913 and almost immediately set sail for Burma to teach, first in Mandalay and then in Rangoon. He had intended to prepare for ordination. In August 1915, he was commissioned as a second lieutenant in the Indian Army and sent to India for training before going on active service in Mesopotamia, where he was killed in action on 25 March 1917, aged twenty-five. His death was considered a great loss to the teaching strength of the diocese.[32]

As 1918 began, the Church reported urgent vacancies in many areas and made an impassioned plea to Britain for any available ordained men.[33] But for some members of the clergy in Burma, serving in the army was seen not just as a patriotic duty but as an extension of their missionary work. One such case was Rev. Charles Randolph "Rand" Puner, the popular teacher at St. Michael's, Kemmendine. After about two years at Kemmendine, Rand had returned to England to train for ordination at Westcott House, Cambridge, where he was known as "Burma" among his fellow ordinands, and he then returned to Burma. During the war, many of the most devoted Karen Christians, true to their own military tradition, joined the Burma Rifles and were sent to India. Rand considered it his duty to follow them and was given a commission in the army, which took him away from the mission from 1917 to 1919. After the war, he would once more take up the work he had left, living the hard life of a Karen peasant and sharing all the hazards and hardships of jungle life in peacetime, before taking over the Chin mission at Prome (Pyay).[34] Rand married Margaret Hackney, herself a missionary and the daughter of Rev. John Hackney of the Karen mission. As for the Church's manpower predicament, it would only really be remedied by the signing of the peace treaty in 1919 and the hastened return of Burma's uniformed clergy.

The Church in the Life of the Nation

After one hundred years of official presence, it was felt that Christianity had made some notable progress among many of the peoples of Burma.[35] By that time, a wide variety of American as well as British and European missionaries were actively working in the country. It was always difficult to assess the real influence of the Christian religion during the colonial period, and there is an enduring risk of oversimplification. It would be a mistake to imagine a clearly delineated society composed of white European Christians on one side and dark native Buddhists on the other, and it would be equally misleading to imagine a steady organic spread of Christianity or a gradual increase in mobility between religions. Both a general demographic and a specifically religious census were being regularly taken by the 1920s, but Alexander McLeish, the survey official of the National Christian Council of India, Burma and Ceylon, warned in 1929 that the complexity and fluidity of the situation defied mere statistics.[36] There were 257,106 Christians in Burma at that time, no less than two-thirds of whom lived in urban areas. Rangoon, in those days, was much more multicultural than it is today; Burmans were actually in the minority there, and McLeish struggled to find opportunities to savor some authentic Buddhist atmosphere.[37] Rev. W. C. B. Purser had also previously testified to this, writing of bewildered travelers arriving in Burma and wondering "Where are the Burmans?"[38] But the multicultural mayhem of Burma somehow worked well, according to Bishop George A. West's recollections: "The British had their offices and their club; the Burmese their monasteries and pagodas; the Indians their stores and temples; and all played football."[39]

"WHERE THERE AIN'T NO TEN COMMANDMENTS"

As both Purser and McLeish noted, the complexity of the demographics was reflected in the complexity of the religious situation. McLeish warned that no statistics could adequately represent the real impact of Christianity upon the religions and people of Burma, but a limited overview of the general situation was achievable.[40] Of the 257,106 Christians in Burma in 1921, 71,941 were Roman Catholics, and of the remaining 185,165 Protestant or non-Catholic denomination members, all but 24,509 of them were Baptists, thanks to the extraordinary achievements of American missionaries following in the footsteps of the great Judson. Out of that remaining 24,509, there were a reported 20,410 Anglicans. The remaining 4,099 were composed of fairly equal numbers of Presbyterians, Methodists, and others, including the Salvation Army. Of the grand total of 257,106 Christians, 231,818 were non-Europeans or locals, with by far the biggest group of them (178,225) being Karens. The next biggest group, a distant second with 19,861, were the Tamils and Telugus from south-central and southeast India, and they were mostly Roman Catholics. Shan, Chin, Kachin, Mon, and Burman people were already represented among the remaining number of Christians by 1921.[41] Ten years later, in 1931, there would be just more than 331,000 Christians in Burma, with Baptists accounting for 64 percent, Roman Catholics 27 percent, and Anglicans 7 percent.[42] The constancy of these proportions is one of the notable features of Christianity in Burma.

From the earliest surveys and throughout all the upheavals of the twentieth century, the respective proportions and ranking of Christian groups in Burma would not change significantly. Roman Catholicism, the first denomination to arrive in Southeast Asia, has always been in a respectable but not very close second place to the Baptists, with the Anglicans always in a stable third place, numerically. The early and successful introduction of the Baptist Church seems to have been decisive in setting the balance. The Baptists' superiority is not entirely surprising in that they enjoyed several advantages, including having been in Burma early, having had exceptionally gifted early leaders, and in not having the wide range of political, institutional, and hierarchical concerns that hindered the Anglicans. Whether the Baptists were more zealous or hungrier for converts is debatable; had the Anglicans enjoyed the resources, flexibility, and freedom to operate as the Baptists did, who knows what they could have achieved? The Church of England entered the field late, and the supply of men and means was always limited.[43] Roman Catholic missionary societies, like the Baptists, were able to operate quite freely (with British colonial approval and protection, of course) while also having several centuries of experience in

Southeast Asia to draw upon. So although it is not surprising that first and second place went to the Baptists and Roman Catholics, with the Anglicans third, it is perhaps surprising that once this three-way balance was reached it remained substantially the same.

Like the Anglicans, the Roman Catholics had little success in converting the Burmans, and they virtually abandoned this mission, focusing on their main adherents: Tamils, Pwo Karens, Eurasians, and a very successful mission among the Chinese.[44] Some Anglicans admired the Roman Catholic priests' devotion, as few of them ever returned to Europe after going out to Asia, and their missionaries lived right among the natives. The nuns won great respect for their work among lepers and the elderly, which also earned the full endorsement and active assistance of the British government.[45] Perhaps most famous of all were the Roman Catholics' educational establishments, especially St. Paul's School, Rangoon, one of the largest and best-equipped boys' schools in Asia.[46] Purser lamented that many Anglican and other Protestant children were receiving an education from the Roman Catholics, and Bishop Fyffe also noted with regret that "hundreds of our Anglican boys" were being educated in Roman Catholic schools.[47]

Education would continue to be a source of pride as well as rivalry, and it would forever be a top priority for the Anglicans, ever since Dr. Marks had described it as the glue that held the Church together.[48] Marks, the great education pioneer, had retired at the turn of the century and died in October 1915. By 1926, there would be 105 Anglican mission schools up and down the country, often with clinics or hospitals attached to them. But success was often tinged with the ongoing animosity between the Anglicans and the Roman Catholics. Bishop Fyffe wrote that he admired many individual Roman Catholics, but he believed their organizational setup, with its centralized foreign control, to be bad and dangerous. Fyffe believed that a significant part of the Church's role was to bear witness to Anglican ideals in the face of the increasing influence of Roman Catholicism.[49] This view contrasted with what some saw as the only way forward for the spread of Christianity: cooperation. It was an opinion exemplified by the influential writer Rev. Dr. Percival Dearmer, who proposed that when faced with millions of people for whom Christianity was totally alien, missionaries of the empire must highlight the essential unity of Christianity.[50] They must learn that the business of Christians is not to quarrel with other Christians but to demonstrate their reasonableness, Dearmer wrote in *The Guardian*, thus helping to popularize the idea that those things that hold Christians together are far greater than those that divide them.[51] Certainly, all of the

"WHERE THERE AIN'T NO TEN COMMANDMENTS"

Christian denominations faced similar challenges and problems in Burma, and indeed it was often through some form of cooperation—sharing translations, literature, surveys, maps, contacts—that difficulties were overcome and achievements were made.

Despite the well-documented difficulty in persuading Buddhist Burmans to convert, the Anglican Church was not without its high-profile successes. One such case was Maung Tha Dun, known as the Hermit, who came into contact with St. Michael's Church in Kemmendine around 1910 and became a Christian, taking the baptismal name John Baptist. The Anglicans called him the Hermit as a translation of the Burmese word "Yathé," which was what his followers called him. As a youth, the Hermit had tested his vocation in a Buddhist monastery and found it lackluster. Since then, he had opted to live a life of extreme asceticism, devoted to itinerant preaching along with his followers, and he apparently channeled this unusual vocation into his new life as an Anglican.[52] His lifestyle was perhaps more comparable to that of a friar than a hermit, strictly speaking, but before becoming a Christian he had been a recluse of the strictest kind, even spending several years in a cave, thus fully earning the title "hermit." After his baptism, with the exception of certain periods set aside for retreat and meditation, he spent all his time tirelessly traveling and preaching. With an ethereal appearance and a gentle manner, the Hermit was a rigorous ascetic, allowing himself just one meager meal a day, which he ate before sunrise. His austere existence apparently reduced him to skin and bone, and yet in that state he could walk for a whole day without food or drink. At the end of a day's journey, he would cheerfully begin preaching to the villagers, just when his most robust European counterparts would consider it necessary to indulge in a prolonged rest.

The number of the Hermit's supporters who followed him into the Church ran into three figures, most of them characterized by the same gentleness and self-denial that were so conspicuous in their beloved teacher. The Hermit's converts were highly regarded in the Church, in part because of their exemplary devotion and also because of their ability to reconcile the differences between Christianity and Buddhism that had always proven so divisive. The RDA opined that with this harmonizing influence the Hermit's converts brought into the Church the most attractive virtue of Buddhism, and that this virtue had been consecrated and deepened through the blessing of the Christian Sacraments. The Church did not want to tempt fate by predicting a revolution in Christian–Buddhist relations thanks to the conversion and life of the Hermit, but there was little doubt that the Burman communities around St. Michael's Kemmendine were deeply marked by him. It is impossible to say how many conversions resulted directly or indirectly from the legend and memory of the Hermit, but hopes ran high that Burmese Christians would be inspired toward a new and dynamic spirituality, which could become the distinctive Burmese contribution to the worldwide Church.[53]

Another extraordinary individual of this period who cannot go without mention is Rev. William Henry Jackson (1889–1931), known to many as Father Willie, who was totally blind from early infancy and became the champion and teacher of blind students in Burma. Jackson had sailed to Burma in 1917, when the First World War was still in progress, and two of the ships in his convoy were sunk by enemy action. Unflustered, Jackson had begun learning Burmese during the voyage and mastered the language within six months. He used his existing knowledge of Braille to create Burmese Braille, later using a converted mangle as a printing press. Burma's present-day schools for the blind, notably the one founded by Jackson at the mission in Kemmendine, owe their development, and the existence of Burmese Braille, to Father Willie, who became affectionately known locally as "apegyi," or "great father," to the blind.[54]

The Church in the Life of the Empire

A practice began of sending local native ordination candidates to Bishop's College in Calcutta for training, the first such candidate being sent in 1916, though it appears he did not complete his studies. The second to be sent was Peter Khin Maung, a Burman, in 1920. He achieved his bachelor of divinity (BD) degree and was then ordained to the priesthood. As the first Burman to receive a full theological education, Rev. Peter Khin Maung went on to lead the clergy training center in Kemmendine.[55] In 1928, Bishop Fyffe retired and Bishop Norman Henry Tubbs became the fifth bishop of Rangoon. He was apparently a talented administrator who would set out to streamline the diocese and make it more efficient, but it would perhaps be a mistake to imagine Bishop Tubbs only trying to run the Church from behind his desk. Tubbs was clearly a practical and pragmatic leader, a former CMS missionary who had gained precious experience serving as principal of Bishop's College. He saw that with Burma's growing nationalism, burgeoning independence movement, and increasing incidents of civil unrest, it was going to be even more difficult to recruit British clergy who would come out into this fairly volatile environment. As a result, at the diocesan council of 1929,

Bishop Tubbs decided to increase the provision of, and raise the standard of, theological education in the diocese. The aim was twofold: to reduce the dependence on clergy sent out from Britain and to reduce the dependence on Bishop's College in Calcutta for training clergy. Tubbs also took one of the first major steps in the promotion of local clergy to senior leadership roles, appointing Rev. John Hla Gyaw to lead the Taungoo mission.[56]

At around the same time, in 1929, the Indian Church Act was passed, which announced that the following year would see the creation of a new Church of India, Burma and Ceylon (CIBC), of which the Diocese of Rangoon and all Anglican activities in Burma would become part. Thus, in March 1930, the self-governing CIBC was inaugurated as a full-fledged new province of the Anglican Communion. This was a clear indication of a shift in the government's worldview as well, and a move toward independence in the broad sense of the word; the political undertones were not lost on the people of Burma. The Anglican Church in Burma was no longer an incongruous extension of the Church of England—the Established Church—and therefore no longer a directly Westminster-driven vehicle; it was a Burmese affair now. These developments added to the general feeling of uncertainty of those years, in which Burma was shaken by severe earthquakes, social unrest, economic woes, and political clashes.[57]

For the stewards of the Church in Burma, changing times would present both new opportunities and new responsibilities, and in 1932 a clergy conference was held in Rangoon to discuss the future. The shape, strategy, and visibility of the Anglican Church in Burma were in flux, but the usual ratio between the Christian denominations still asserted itself: one in ten Christians in Burma was an Anglican, compared to six in ten Baptists and three Roman Catholics.[58] Buddhists constituted, then as now, around 90 percent of the population (compared with around 7 percent Christians), and nationalist militancy tied to the dominant religion was increasing. Central to this nationalist activism, as always, was the Young Men's Buddhist Association (YMBA), which had developed into a powerful body campaigning for independence from Britain and for the establishment of Buddhist majority rule.[59] The YMBA also laid the foundations of the even more militant General Council of Burmese Associations (GCBA), whose activists included the most fervent monarchists and nationalists.

One such GCBA activist was Saya San, who organized a revolt against the British and declared himself a pretender to the Burmese throne. When earthquakes hit the Pegu area in October 1930, these were interpreted as positive omens by Saya San's fanatical supporters, who crowned him king

THE ANGLICAN CHURCH IN BURMA

at a pagoda near Rangoon. Plans were drawn up for a royal city for the new king and his retinue of five queens, four ministers, and four regiments of troops. His followers were promised the restoration of Burmese authority, the elevation of the Buddhist religion, and the expulsion of the British, as well as being assured of protection by Saya San's magical charms and tattoos.[60] The Saya San Rebellion exploded, and it was to last nearly two years, until late 1932. By then more than 1,000 rebels would have been killed (some estimates go much higher) and 9,000 more would have surrendered or been taken prisoner. Saya San himself and 125 others were hanged, and almost 1,400 were sentenced to terms of imprisonment or transportation to penal colonies. Karen Christians, who had always served loyally alongside the British, played their part in suppressing the rebellion of 1930–32, a fact that would contribute to the continuing buildup of tensions between the ethnic groups.[61] There would be no easing of tensions after the bloodletting of the Saya San revolt, but it was also clear that the nationalists would achieve nothing by claiming thrones and waiting for omens. The Burman nationalist movement found new impetus and new direction under the level-headed Aung San (father of Aung San Suu Kyi) and a group of activists who each took the title "thakin" (master). These thakins formed the basis of the "Thirty Comrades" who secretly went for training by the Japanese and later formed the pro-Axis Burma Independence Army (BIA).[62] The British, for their part, did not exactly change course after the Saya San Rebellion. They were already preparing to move in the direction of granting autonomy to Burma, but more slowly than the nationalists would have liked.

The year 1934 saw the start, at last, of the construction of a new college to train clergy in Rangoon, in order to increase the educational and general self-sufficiency of the Church. This institution would become known as Holy Cross, taking its name from the church next door, which had been built as a simple university chapel in 1930. It would be known as the College of the Holy Cross upon opening in 1935 and is today called Holy Cross Theological College (HCTC). The site chosen was near Victoria Lake (now called Inya Lake), a large man-made reservoir created by the British in 1882–83. It is the university district, which in the 1930s was considered to be toward the north of the city and is nowadays defined as midtown in relation to the downtown and uptown areas. The university district, and Rangoon University itself, were hotbeds of nationalist activism at that time. The SPG's Rev. George Appleton (later archdeacon) was appointed principal of Holy Cross, which opened with a student body of twenty-three representing several regions of Burma, including Car Nicobar Island. There were two plains (Pwo) Karens and six hills (Sgaw) Karens, five Burmans, four Chinese, two Chins, two Indians, and two Anglo-Indians, as well as guest students from Singapore. At the time of opening, Appleton was joined by Rev. Claude Sauerbrei as vice principal.[63] They were then joined by Rev. R. Pereira (a graduate of Bishop's College, Calcutta) and part-time teachers Rev. A. Dilworth, Burmese teacher David Po San, and English teacher Mrs. Appleton. Twenty-one local native ordinands would successfully pass through the three-year program of study before the Japanese invasion in 1942.

In 1935, Bishop Tubbs retired, and his proposed replacement was Rev. George A. West, MM (Military Medal), of the SPG, a decorated veteran of the First World War. West had been doing remote rural work, living very simply among the Karen villagers, since 1921. He was initially unwilling to give up the relatively free and self-sufficient life he led in the village, but after an election confirmed the proposal, he accepted the job of bishop.[64] In 1937, Burma was separated from India and came under direct rule from London. The governor was still British, but the premier and his cabinet were now Burmese. Bishop West envisaged a role for the Church in helping to pave the way for a harmonious future Burmese state, leading by example. West wanted the "ever-open doors" of Bishopscourt, the bishop's official residence in Rangoon, to become a symbol of peaceful cohabitation, "a heart-beat for the whole nation, a place for British and Burmese, Indians and Karens to meet and find a common mind on an entirely new level of unselfish statesmanship, a place where the spirit of God might touch and heal the bleeding wounds of Burma."[65]

Empire Values in the Life of the Church

Growth among the Anglican Church's traditional core audience had apparently reached a plateau by the 1930s. The main urban centers of Rangoon, Mandalay, and Moulmein continued to be the foci of British expatriates, whether public servants, teachers, merchants, traders, clerks, soldiers, or what George Orwell described as nondescripts. The empire always attracted more than its fair share of adventurers and eccentrics, and by no means every obscure colonial functionary would have been receptive to the Church's teaching. Rudyard Kipling captured the attitude of the apathetic nondescripts of the empire when he wrote: "Ship me somewheres east of Suez where the best is like the worst / Where there ain't no Ten Commandments an' a man can raise a thirst."[66] This unflattering glimpse of the Englishman heading out to the colonies shows him longing to abandon not only conventional morality but also the oppressive British class system, so that society's supposed best and worst may be on the same level. As soon as he passes through the Suez Canal, social niceties, class distinctions, moderation in drink, and his Christian upbringing can be hurled over the side; it is a story that has been borne out countless times. Bishop Strachan had been acutely aware of the moral problem at the turn of the century, especially when his largely youthful flock was scattered far and wide in remote outposts: "We know how hard it is to lead a Christian life, even with all the blessed surroundings and restraints which are so helpful in England," Strachan wrote. "Now these [restraints] are entirely absent in Burma, and we need not wonder if young men forget their religious duties when week after week there is nothing to remind them of them."[67] The prevailing view was that Christian conduct relied on regular intervention by the Church's ministers, rather than on developing an inner moral compass: "It cannot be a matter of surprise if the ardor of religious life cools, or if the lessons of early life are forgotten, or if people lapse into indifference—nay, even into immorality—when there is a visit from the clergyman only once in three or in six months, or perhaps when there is no such visit at all."[68]

George Orwell made his observations on the behavior of the British in Burma from the point of view of a young police officer who had been born in India into an established Anglo-Burmese and Anglo-Indian family. As a devotee of Kipling, Orwell confirmed the truth of the line "the best is like the worst," pointing out that the class distinctions dividing and stratifying British society seemed to disappear in the East, where there was "no obvious class-friction"[69] among the British, he wrote. But instead of ushering in social justice, this lack of a class system merely gave way to even more base forms of discrimination; "the all important thing," Orwell recalled, "was not whether you had been to one of the right schools but whether your skin was technically white."[70] True social class-based snobbery would not even have worked in Burma, where, Orwell wrote, "most of the white men . . . were not of the type who in England would be called 'gentlemen,' but except for the common soldiers and a few nondescripts they lived lives appropriate to 'gentlemen'—had servants, that is, and called their evening meal 'dinner'— and officially they were regarded as being all of the same class. They were 'white men,' in contradistinction to the other and inferior class, the 'natives.'"[71] Anthony Burgess, following a familiar path "east of Suez" in the 1950s— not to Burma but to Malaya—echoed Orwell's observations of thirty years earlier, writing that the colonial officers' positions may have implied a degree of education and refinement, but most of them were rascals given to delusions of color supremacy.[72] The culture of casual color prejudice was no mere trivial point of curiosity for Orwell, whose family was from Burma and who had a first cousin, around his own age, who was "mixed race" Anglo-Burmese. A variety of factors contributed to making the East a playground for British expatriates, and Burma was no exception. Archdeacon Chard had actually blamed this on the old enemy, that "clinging atmosphere of heathenism" that caused Englishmen to "fall below their own level, not to mention the ever-rising standard which Holy Scripture intends us to aim at."[73]

The Anglican Church had its work cut out to reach such carefree people. The substantial and on the surface fairly respectable British community was made up of technically "churched" individuals, so, in theory, the task of ministering to them should have been straightforward, which could have allowed the more outgoing ministers to focus on disadvantaged and marginalized communities. However, even though most of the British expatriates had been at least partly educated and nominally inducted into the Church, the absence of the codes and expectations of home society had a notoriously liberating effect on the largely young and male colonial cohort. In the eyes of the Church, they were fairly innocent young Christian men, many of them the sons of clergymen, placed far from good Christian influences and surrounded by temptations.[74] The moral dangers facing young women, too, aroused concern, and for this reason in about 1900 the "leading ladies of Rangoon" had petitioned for a proper branch of the Young Women's Christian Association (YWCA) to carry out social work among the young women of the city.[75] Within a few months, the good ladies' prayers for a branch were answered, along with the arrival of an anonymous donation of £4,000 (equivalent to £495,000 or $640,000 today). The branch was inaugurated in 1902.[76] The Church in the early twentieth century took great pride in its wide range of activities aimed toward women.[77] Large numbers of girls from many ethnic groups received schooling, a Girls' Friendly Society and Mothers' Union operated within the country, and there was considerable support for orphans and destitute or abandoned women, lamentable by-products of the not-so-innocent temptations of the empire.[78]

Christian Morality in the Life of the Empire

As ineffectual as the Church's moral insistence may have seemed, it was no symbolic puritanical stance. The problems were very real, and the human price to be paid for the sexual laxity of the British Empire, not least in the constant threat of the spread of venereal disease, was considerable. Anglican clergy did not relish addressing this topic head-on, referring somewhat cryptically to "circumstances well known to all acquainted with Eastern countries under European government" resulting in "large numbers of boys and girls of mixed parentage in Burma, most of them being the offspring of European fathers and Burmese mothers."[79] The Burmese considered such unions to be no particular stigma as long as the marriage of sorts was correctly, if very cursorily, solemnized, and even then such unions were easily dissolvable.[80] But the institutions of society, the schools and the professions, were controlled by the British, and so-called mixed-race offspring would face discrimination, hardship, and difficulties in integrating. Relations between locals and the British were frequently soured by scandals involving married men and local women, which could lead to disgrace, destitution, ostracization, and sometimes suicide.

The carefree and unmarried "east of Suez" British men tended to take the whole matter of mixed relationships extremely lightly, knowing that as long as they could bypass their consciences the loose local marriage bond itself was easily undone. The presumptive wife and her children would be deserted and the man was free to return to England and marry, no doubt keeping his abandoned "empire family" a secret forevermore.[81] The inevitable by-product was a pressing need for orphanages to house a huge number of children. "These are *our* orphans," Dr. Marks had controversially written, insisting that the Church accept the burden and perhaps in part the responsibility, considering the situation to be a failure of Christian moral teaching.[82] As far back as 1850, there had already been at least three orphanages running in Moulmein alone—one Anglican, one Roman Catholic, and at least one Baptist.[83] The first orphanage in Rangoon was begun on the grounds of St. John's College, though Dr. Marks, fearing a scandal, had not dared to ask for financial assistance from sources in Britain, and the economic maintenance of the orphans would cause Marks "many an anxious thought and sleepless night."[84]

Anglican Church leaders one hundred years ago were hardly trained to deal with such matters, yet this was the reality they faced, and they tried hard to be effective and just. It is fair to conclude that they were usually driven by sincere Christian values and a belief in a better society, not just motivated by outdated and prudish attitudes. On a range of sensitive issues in a rapidly changing world, and working in a challenging multifaith context, senior clergy often showed vision that was well ahead of their time. In highlighting the increasing interplay between East and West, the intrusion of Western ways of life into Asia, the impact of rapid urbanization, the need to become acquainted with local religions and customs, and the need to take responsibility for society's unplanned orphans—"*our* orphans"—Church leaders identified some of the thorniest questions for all Christian missions in the twentieth century. Visitors from supposedly advanced Britain had sometimes been struck by the respect and consideration for local culture that was part of the Church's work in Burma.[85] The Anglicans at least tried to balance their dual concern for the native communities and the expatriate personnel, while seeking to focus on the positives. It was a kind of faked optimism, Bishop West would come close to admitting: "All you saw was the dignity and friendliness and the mingling of races and the sense that this was the world that would last for ever."[86]

Some missionaries of different denominations no doubt went beyond "friendliness and mingling" to embrace temptation. George Orwell observed this, making two of his characters in *Burmese Days* the unwanted offspring of missionaries, one Baptist and one Roman Catholic (it is possibly a sign of Orwell's residual loyalty to the Church that he excluded Anglicans from this critique). Orwell had already reflected on the temptations, contradictions, and hypocrisies of colonial Burma, as he saw them, in the first piece of writing he did there. It is a poem, set during two successive Holy Weeks, about a British expatriate, a somewhat conflicted churchgoer like Orwell himself, torn between entering the "house of God" and the "house of sin." As in Orwell's much later, final, and most famous work, *Nineteen Eighty-Four*, sounds of church bells and women singing punctuate this early writing. The "house of God" of the poem is presented as an uninspiring prospect, with "old maids caterwauling a dismal tale of thorns and blood" and "devout old maids . . . bawling their ugly rhymes of death and pain." Orwell's narrator turns into the "house of sin," with dying flowers around the doors and betel juice spittle lodged between the rotting bamboo of the floors. The narrator is seemingly revolted by his experience in the brothel, though it is clearly not his first visit. The following Holy Week, the narrator shuns the prostitute, and, still "musing on her oily hair," he halfheartedly turns into "the house of God." Orwell called the poem "The Lesser Evil," a title that gives a strong clue about Orwell's thinking with regard to two of his lifelong preoccupations, both of them rapidly losing popularity by the 1930s: colonialism and the Christian faith.

Summary

Both Burma and its Anglican Church had grown significantly by the end of the Victorian age and up to the First World War. The flagships of this growth for the Church were, as ever, great success in the sphere of education and effective outreach to some of the minority ethnic groups. The downsides were that the demands of missionary life regularly claimed the physical health of some of the Church's best people, while others were left disillusioned or with an enduring sense of frustration that the Church's impact nationally was still minor. The religious and social fabric of Burmese life continued to become ever more complex, with the arrival of more denominations, charitable societies, and missionaries from both Europe and America, increasing multiculturalism, increasing plurality of religions, and the advent of political movements with strong religious inspiration. As fluid as the situation may have seemed, the basic breakdown of religious affiliation remained proportionally the same, with Anglicans in clear third place among the Christian minority, always behind the Baptists and Roman Catholics.

The balance may have remained frustratingly unchanged for the Christians of Burma, but at the global level the early decades of the twentieth century were a time of social transformation, and this affected Burma too. One of the effects of this was that colonial administrators began to reassess elements of imperial rule, and it was acknowledged that a degree of religious instruction and religious organization could be beneficial for maintaining social order and morality if it were allowed, at last, into the public domain and institutions. It was arguably a nominal development for the Anglicans, who had secured a number of formal and informal concessions in order to operate freely and who also counted on the personal loyalty of some colonial officials. Could it perhaps be argued that the Church was already the official—that is, government-endorsed—religion of Burma, in all but name? The community that would really benefit from and take full advantage of the relaxation in the rules prohibiting religious activity would be the majority Buddhists. Buddhist groups benefited both in terms of more allowance for Buddhist education and also for the toleration of Buddhist social and community organizations. This development would pave the way for movements focused on Buddhist nationalism fused with Burmese independence, leading to a dynamic reimagining of national identity and the forging of a strong opposition to British colonial rule. An ill-conceived nationalist revolt from 1930 to 1932 claimed many lives, and its failure prompted a rethink of

"WHERE THERE AIN'T NO TEN COMMANDMENTS"

strategy and a change of nationalist leadership. After that, Burma seemed to be on an inevitable path to independence, peacefully or otherwise, and militant anti-British activists started to look to another empire, Japan, for encouragement.

For the Church, significant structural change came in this period, with the creation of the CIBC in 1930. With this granting of full status as a province of the Anglican Communion, the launch of the CIBC was seen as a step toward a postcolonial Church. Internally, this period saw a plateau in terms of Church membership. Social transformation, worldwide political recalibration, and the coming of age that was the First World War had all contributed to a revolution in religious adherence among the kind of young white males who had always staffed the British Empire. This revolution was not always to the detriment of religion, though; Roman Catholicism, for example, experienced a revival among intellectuals and literary figures across the English-speaking world during the interwar years, and some Westerners showed an interest in Eastern religions for the first time. But there had always been something about the empire life, as authors from Kipling to Orwell observed, that drove certain categories of people to an abandonment of high ideals and an embracing of various everyday forms of cruelty and abuse. The Church in Burma had always been aware that mundane temptations like billiards and cards drew young colonial functionaries away from the faith, but these simple pleasures either masked or had given way to new depths of decadence and amorality. Were the Church's own critics right to conclude that this was a failure of the Church to impart basic morality?

A profound color prejudice had also set in among the ruling white colonial population, even more powerful than class prejudice, which largely became irrelevant in the reduced social circles and simplified pecking order of the empire. In British society, class distinctions had been eroded by the experience of solidarity found in the wartime trenches, but a different kind of solidarity survived in the colonies. It no longer mattered much whether an English officer had been to the right school, or came from the right family, as long as he was white. In what were widely regarded as relatively enlightened times, with so many people looking positively toward the postcolonial world, how can we interpret this racist backlash? Certainly, some Anglican leaders were prominent in combatting prejudice, and the Church was actually mature enough to take stock of moral failings on behalf of all of the (mainly male) colonial community. The abuse of local women and girls, resulting in large numbers of abandoned mixed children, had disastrous consequences for victims who already lived on the cusp of extreme poverty. Despite these colossal systemic failings, many Anglicans continued to see the good in the colonial endeavor in the first four decades of the twentieth century. The Church could proudly point to examples of harmony and respect between very different peoples and between people of different cultures, languages, colors, ages, and genders. Would it be unfair to say that the Church's prevailing optimism shone like a blinding light, which made it possible to not see (or to ignore) the negatives? This shining optimism even made it difficult to read the signs of an approaching global war, after all. In an age when atheist ideologies and anti-colonialism were at their peak, some stalwarts concluded (as George Orwell seems to have done) that religion and empire were still the lesser evils.

Chapter 5

"PATIENT IN TRIBULATION BUT RESOLUTE IN FAITH"

The Church and the Second World War

The world was still living in the shadow of the Great War of 1914–18 when some shrewd observers already began to see a troubling future for Southeast Asia. Japanese military and economic ambitions were no secret, and these ambitions became consolidated in the policy of expansionism. With the invasion and annexation of Manchuria in 1931, fears of regional conflict became a reality, and when the situation deteriorated into all-out war with China on 7 July 1937, the eight-year-long Pacific War had already begun. Less than twenty years had passed since the 1918 armistice, but for Southeast Asia, references to the war began to mean the new one already in progress, rather than the Great War. Southeast Asia had been left substantially unaffected by the 1914–18 war, which had seemed like a storm rumbling in the distance, and colonial residents had carried on with their lives largely as normal, which was regarded as the patriotic thing to do.[1] It was all going to be very different after 1939, and even before the outbreak of hostilities in Europe the war was less a storm in the distance and more like a tornado in the backyard, or, in fact, just over the border in China. The newsletter of the Rangoon Diocesan Association (RDA) in the immediate prewar months struggled to hide the foreboding atmosphere.[2] The RDA was affiliated with the SPG (Society for the Propagation of the Gospel in Foreign Parts) missionary society, but its target audience was the whole of the Church in Burma. The RDA maintained contact with schools and chaplaincies throughout the country, whether these were affiliated with the SPG or not, because the whole country constituted the Diocese of Rangoon. The Bible Churchmen's Missionary Society (BCMS), meanwhile, was working independently of both organizations in Upper Burma, centered on Mohnyin, Kachin state.[3]

The RDA's other main readership consisted of people back home in England who had some personal or pastoral connection to the Church in Burma. Well-informed RDA supporters were gradually becoming aware of Burma's significance in the changing regional scenario and what its role might be in the coming conflict. A major new road linking China to Burma, as one missionary explained in the RDA's *Burma News* in 1939, had huge strategic and logistical implications for the region. It provided a chance to aid China—already embroiled in war—and to found a new mission hospital right on the border, with the combined support of the CMS, SPG, Rangoon diocese, and, they hoped, a rich donor.[4] It had long been known that only one hidden corner in the often frozen and wet northeast, where Burma joins the Chinese province of Yunnan, provided a safe year-round point of access.[5] The Church appears to have grasped the significance of this road long before the Japanese or Allied military did, and this vital Burma Road, first hailed as an opportunity for relief work to the beleaguered Chinese, would become one of the key battlegrounds of the war.

In 1939, the Burma Road was part of the extensive Riverine chaplaincy under Rev. Canon Joseph George Caldicott, known as "Caldie," a long-serving missionary who was coming up to twenty-five years of service in Burma.[6] Caldie still toured his vast "parish" regularly and also did work on the war-torn Chinese side of the border, because although that was officially part of the Diocese of Hong Kong, Caldie was the only person who could reach Yunnan. Over this border there was, remarkably, a huge airplane factory employing American and Chinese Anglicans, about a hundred miles east of Bhamo.[7] Caldie said that the road was good in dry weather but a death trap in the rain. Along with such hazards, the war over the border began to cause major supply problems for the missions of Upper Burma.[8] Of more immediate concern for most Church members, however, was the now more or less constant state of nationalist and anti-colonial unrest in the urban centers of Burma, which was adversely affecting trade.[9] This was a volatile situation that the Japanese aimed to take full advantage of. Fleeting consolation came with news of an exceptional rice harvest, potentially meaning big export revenues. Sir Charles Innes, former governor of Burma and then chairman of the Mercantile Bank of India, predicted on 28 March 1939 that Burma could look forward to better times, if only law and order could be restored.[10]

The Approach of War

Clearly, the nature and extent of the disruption to come were not foreseen. The new conflict arrived on Southeast Asian soil on 22 September 1940, when the Japanese initiated an undeclared four-day war with the purpose of annexing Vietnam. The Japanese found a compliant local administration in the Vichy French. As allies of the Nazis, the Vichy government had maintained French hold over Indochina, making the invasion a walk-in for the Japanese. In their plan to control Asia and the Pacific, Vietnam did not have quite the same long-term importance as other parts of Southeast Asia. It did not have the strategic location or natural resources of Singapore, Malaya, and Burma, but Vietnam was full of essential rice to feed the Japanese Army. Most crucially, perhaps, it was considered vital to blockade China from using Vietnam's ports, especially Haiphong in the north. This port blockade further highlighted the strategic importance of the Burma Road as China's only land supply route in the west, and as a result more eyes turned to Burma. This increasing pressure moving westward would both psychologically and militarily demolish Siam's (Thailand's) hopes of resistance, and this country, too, was quickly annexed by the Japanese. This gave them a wide range of options for future attacks on Burma and Malaya.

The objective of this campaign was uncompromising—complete control of Southeast Asia, from which to then attack and conquer British India. For the moment, however, day-to-day life in Burma was still, incredibly, unaffected: "Everything goes on out here much as usual," *Burma News* reported, as 1940 turned into 1941. "Letters and papers take much longer to come from England, but, apart from that, there is little except the local Press and the radio to remind us that there is a war going on! We wish you [in England] could say likewise."[11] The Japanese threat was not considered particularly imminent, and Burma seemed far removed from potential combat zones anyway, with the possible exception of that remote northeast corner.[12] In terms of the war effort, the focus was on collecting comforts, clothing, and medical supplies to send to British soldiers on other fronts, such as the Libyan desert.[13] News from the Burma Road, with its Allied factories now at the center of the intensifying war with Japan, soon brought the conflict closer to home. Canon Caldicott, visiting his mission stations along the road and across the border into China, arrived in the aftermath of extensive bombing and found a large number of casualties.[14] The Church had suddenly begun to count its own victims of the war.

THE ANGLICAN CHURCH IN BURMA

Rev. Albert Victor Woodcock of Birkenhead, England, was on his way to Burma as a missionary in February 1941 when his ship, the SS *Empire Citizen*, was sunk by the Germans. His bishop was Norman Henry Tubbs of Chester, the former bishop of Rangoon, who described Woodcock as a devoted parish priest with a gift for relating to all classes of society. Woodcock had long dreamed of serving as a missionary overseas, but it was ironically only at this most challenging historical moment that the opportunity came about, Bishop Tubbs wrote. This tragedy, he said, brought home the futility of war.[15] Then, news arrived that Miss Lilian Mary Seavell, who was returning to duty as a nurse in Burma, was on the same ship as Woodcock, and she had also been lost. She was a cherished member of the Church who had worked in Burma at the Queen Alexandra Children's Hospital in Mandalay since 1931. With a growing sense of apprehension for the situation, Bishop West of Rangoon designated the Rev. A. T. "Tim" Houghton, founder of the BCMS mission in Kachin state, to become his assistant bishop with special responsibility for northern Burma. Houghton, who had been on leave in Britain, set sail for Burma only for his ship to be badly damaged by enemy action. He was comparatively lucky to make it to shore in an overcrowded lifeboat, but his plans for returning to Burma ended there.[16] Bishop West was therefore deprived of excellent clergy, including a talented would-be assistant bishop, and the bad fortune was nowhere near at an end; West himself was very seriously injured in a road accident in Rangoon on 9 June 1941, the exact details of which would never become clear. West, unusually for a bishop, had served as an ordinary artillery soldier in the First World War—a bombardier in the first war and a bishop in the second, as he put it—and the bravery that won him the Military Medal no doubt served him well on this occasion too.[17] He spent six weeks in the care of Rangoon Hospital, where, *Burma News* reported, he was comforted by English, Chinese, Indian, and Anglo-Indian visitors, and even Buddhist monks. His initial recovery was successful, and he was able to go for convalescence, first in India and then in the United States. Shortly after this, the Andaman and Nicobar Islands, part of the Diocese of Rangoon, were invaded.

The Japanese Invasion

Rev. Vickerman Nicholson "Vick" Kemp, then in his early sixties, was stationed on South Andaman when the capital, Port Blair, fell to the Japanese on 22 September 1941 and he and his staff were taken prisoner. The first thing the Japanese did was confiscate any writing materials. "It was death even to have a pencil!" Kemp recalled,[18] as a pencil could have been used to make a record of the barbaric and destructive occupation of the Andaman and Nicobar Islands. Bishop West was at sea and en route to the United States at the time, so he was utterly powerless to do anything for his invaded diocese. He arrived in New York five days before the attack on Pearl Harbor. Various routes by which to return the bishop to Burma were mooted, but ultimately West faced a wartime exile, and Rangoon was to be deprived of its bishop for almost the entire war.[19] Before communications were completely cut off, however, *Burma News* reported that many British children had arrived in Burma as evacuees and were set to attend the diocesan schools.[20] How tragically ironic, in retrospect, that British children were being evacuated *to* Burma for safety. Some people, including Bishop West, finally realized that colonial society in Burma had been in denial for two years: "We worked hard, played tennis, had dinner parties, listened to the radio, thought and prayed for our folks in blitzed England, sent parcels to the Libyan desert and speculated as to the length of the war. But we had the complacency of the selfish, the mentality of 'it can't happen here.'"[21]

A week after the attack on Pearl Harbor, alongside the invasions of Hong Kong, Malaya, the Burmese islands, and the Dutch East Indies, on 14 December 1941, the Japanese captured Victoria Point on the southern tip of mainland Burma. So began the largest land campaign fought by the Allies against the Japanese, and the longest campaign ever fought on land by the British. Top priority for the Japanese in Burma was to protect their flank during the invasion of Malaya, but this strategic precaution would soon give way to a vision of Burma as the western edge of Japan's new empire. Conquering Burma would allow them to cut off the only Allied land supply route to China, the famous Burma Road. Burma's many natural resources, especially oil, were a very significant bonus. The time of anticipation was therefore over, and Burma felt the full force of war. Two days before Christmas, Rangoon was bombed from the air. Until very recently, Church members had still been raising funds to repair their friends' bomb-damaged churches back in England. Students of St. John's College, Rangoon, had raised money to help repair the RDA honorary secretary's church at Teynham, which had been damaged by enemy action. By the time their donations arrived in England, *Burma News* reported, some of their own churches in Burma had been bombed by the Japanese.[22] St. John's, the most prestigious Anglican school in Rangoon, had begun the school year with

THE ANGLICAN CHURCH IN BURMA

more Christian students than ever before, and nearly all of its two hundred boarders were Christians. Many of the boys were now leaving to urgently fill the ranks of the army, and their good education made them candidates for commissions as officers. Nearly all of the college staff were in the Civil Defense, including Po Kah, the divisional ARP (Air Raid Precautions) warden, and Mg San, his deputy.[23]

The Evacuation

As Burmese youths joined the forces, civilians endured the intensifying aerial bombardment of cities and towns, with some locals seeking the relative safety of the surrounding countryside. Members of the expatriate community also began hurriedly making preparations to flee to India, with particular concern for the children, many of whom were boarding at schools. The diocese learned by cable from Calcutta on 6 March 1942 that Miss Ada Tilly, principal of St. Matthew's High School, Moulmein, had been killed by enemy action at Pyinmana railway station while evacuating her two hundred schoolchildren to Upper Burma.[24] The evacuees' train had been bombed by the Japanese; the children escaped unharmed, but Miss Tilly, a devoted young teacher, was severely wounded and died on the platform.[25] Her colleague Miss Lilian Bald took charge of the group and got them to Mandalay, where most of the children were housed in a convent until they could be evacuated to India. Miss Bald continued the journey north with a smaller group of forty children, but they tragically finished up stranded in the mountains amid storms, floods, and landslides, and only five children survived.[26] Miss Bald managed to pen a final letter relaying the tragedy, which was carried to India by Staff Sergeant Harry Shaw, who had risked his life trying to help the children:[27] "We have trekked 256 miles and are still 100 miles from the railhead in India," wrote Miss Bald. "On an average we do six miles a day. We have slept in the jungle without shelter, and with highly decayed corpses around us. . . . Trusting you will remember us in your prayers."[28] As news of such horrors poured in, the government finally ordered the complete evacuation of the Church's British and Irish missionaries. This order was obeyed, reluctantly, when it was explained that the continued presence of the British would further jeopardize the safety of the locals, especially the native Christians. The bombing was unlikely to cease with the departure of the British, but it was presumed that on arrival in Rangoon the Japanese occupiers would not single out Asian Christians just for being Christian, as long as the British were gone.[29]

For the European missionaries, it was to be the "Valley of Humiliation," but the Church's work was set to continue in the hands of the local clergy, even though in many cases their schools and churches had already been damaged or destroyed.[30] The local Anglican community found it difficult to accept that the British missionaries would not be coming back anytime soon. One British airman who was forced to parachute into a Burmese village was surprised when the villagers rushed up to welcome him and their leader addressed him in English. He was even more surprised when they tried to convey him at once to the village church in order to preach the sermon. It was assumed that every Englishman was a Christian missionary.[31] As the grueling evacuation northward into India continued, evacuees faced an incredibly hard journey of steep mountain climbing in pouring rain, through dense tropical jungle inhabited by wild animals, struggling across dangerous rapids, walking through paddy fields and ditches waist-deep in water, and pushing through jungle paths often thigh-deep.[32] Tragedy followed them all the way.

Some of the most painfully ironic tragedies would still be recalled in detail decades later, such as the story of "Higgie." Before going out to Burma as a missionary, Archdeacon William Harold Spencer Higginbotham, known as Higgie, had served on the staff of the parish of St. Mark's, Camberwell, South London. His former vicar, Rev. Canon H. G. Veazey, remembered him as a jolly Irishman who had taken double honors at Dublin University, and as the most fearless man he had ever met.[33] Higgie showed his courage during the final frantic departure from Rangoon, when he loaded up his car with the diocesan archives and drove straight through territory already patrolled by the Japanese, simply putting his foot down and praying for the best.[34] He somehow made it to Mandalay, and from there he continued the evacuation to India, trekking through torrential rain with a distinguished academic, Professor D. Rhind of the Agricultural College, Mandalay, and a party of Anglo-Indian refugees. When they reached shelter at a sugar factory at Sahmaw, the archdeacon decided to stay behind with a group of the Anglo-Indians while the main party pushed ahead. Unfortunately, the Japanese were now catching up quickly. They overran the factory and began looting and robbing the refugees. When Higgie stepped in to defend the refugees, an officer drew his sword and attacked him, inflicting a fatal wound. Higgie died two days later, on 23 May 1942, aged forty-two.[35]

THE ANGLICAN CHURCH IN BURMA

Similar tales of heroism and selflessness abounded. Rev. David Alexander Patterson was a thirty-one-year-old SPG missionary and Cambridge scholar who had taught at St. John's College in Rangoon before the war. Later he was made vice principal of St. John's and then headmaster of a remote and isolated school in Shwebo. He earned respect and friendship for his combination of dry, intellectual humor and natural gift of quiet leadership. This made him popular with the locals, to whose cheerful, carefree ways he became very attached, living among them, adopting their lifestyle, and speaking their language.[36] The Shwebo school flourished greatly under him until the invasion. Patterson oversaw the safe evacuation of the school, staying on at Shwebo until the last moment, and then began the three-hundred-mile march to India himself.[37] On arrival in India, he immediately volunteered as a military chaplain with front-line units, in order to be among the first to liberate Burma. He was speedily commissioned as a chaplain captain in the Indian Army Ecclesiastical Establishment. Also heading to India were two Tamil clergy based in Mandalay, whose names are recorded simply as Joseph and Swamidass. They too had selflessly stayed behind until the last of their flock had made it out to safety, but on the long trek to India they both died from exhaustion.[38]

The Japanese Occupation

"Looking back," Rev. George Appleton later recalled, "I feel that it was a mistake for all of us missionaries to come out as we did. . . . We never thought that we should have to leave Burma altogether, but gradually we were pushed further and further north until we were completely separated from our people . . . it was a mistake made in all sincerity."[39] The relationship between the British clergy and the people of Burma would never quite be the same after the unavoidably divisive evacuation experience. The few who did stay behind in Burma, willingly or not, would receive no special treatment from the Japanese just for being clergy or missionaries. This was even the case with those from neutral Ireland or, in the case of some Roman Catholics, Axis Italy and Vichy France; they were all considered part of the conquered peoples with little discrimination. Prison camps awaited the "stay-behinds." Rev. Vick Kemp, who had chosen to stay with the rearguard until the arrival of the Japanese, recalled that they were kept prisoner at Port Blair, where they had been captured, until November 1942 and then transferred to Rangoon jail until April 1943. Finally, they were dumped in a squalid camp in Tavoy and held in a state of semi-starvation for two and a half years.[40] A few other missionaries remained at large and incognito for a while in remote parts of Arakan (Rev. E. Francis and Rev. G. Molyneaux) and in the Hukawng Valley in Kachin state (Mr. and Mrs. Darlington and their newborn baby), who later all escaped to Assam. All the other surviving British missionaries had made it into exile in India.[41] The campaign of the British and Empire Army in Burma had begun with a chaotic retreat. Bad timing and poor coordination by the British commanders aided and accelerated the advance of the Japanese, even though they did not yet have their later experience or fame as tenacious jungle warriors. While the military commanders began to busy themselves expanding and reorganizing the armies in India, there was little for the exiled Church to do except face the reality of being divided into two parts: one part in exile overseas and the other just trying to survive at home in Burma.

Bishop West was marooned in the United States, and his assistant bishop designate, having been shipwrecked on his way to Burma, was stuck in England.[42] There was scant news getting out of Rangoon, and only a vague picture of the Church under the Japanese occupation could be gleaned. Compiling parting messages and last-minute recollections from evacuated missionaries, the RDA described the Church's native clergy and people as "patient in tribulation but resolute in faith, awaiting the opportunity of reconstruction."[43] The RDA's Annual Report for 1943 announced the near total loss of printing presses and materials.[44] Bereft of resources, support, and foreign clergy, a couple dozen local clergy had bravely resolved to carry on the work of the Church under Japanese oppression, quite openly risking their lives because of their association with the British enemy. They would face great material hardship as well, because they would, of course, cease to receive any salary, and many of the clergy were forced to become part-time traders or subsistence farmers.[45] Many local Anglican teachers bravely and selflessly vowed to remain at their mission schools during the invasion, managing to keep some of them partially open and eventually reopening others.[46] The degree of risk involved in this must not be underestimated: numerous teachers and church workers, and their families, were summarily executed, sometimes upon exiting chapels or mission buildings that were then burned to the ground.[47] Whenever possible, Christians would relocate to rural areas where they would be less visible, as Anglicans' guilt by association with the British applied to laypeople as well as clergy and teachers. Worship would be strictly confined to people's homes in what was now

THE ANGLICAN CHURCH IN BURMA

an underground church.[48] Bishop West eventually managed to broadcast his moral support to the Church via radio from San Francisco.[49]

The onslaught of Japanese expansionism was total and overwhelming, marking the beginning of the end for the old European rulers of the region. All the nations of Southeast Asia, with the single exception of Siam (Thailand), had been under foreign colonial domination for generations, whether by the British, the French, the Dutch, the Portuguese, or the Americans. The Japanese conquests of 1940–42 could be seen in some lights as part of the longer-term decolonizing struggle. Hitler, during the same period, unequivocally pursued his invasion of the Baltic States, Russia, Southeast Europe, and the Caucasus as a fiercely ideological war of aggression. He actually refused to market these campaigns as a war of liberation from Stalinist oppression, even though he might have garnered significant local sympathy by doing so. In contrast, the Japanese invaders tended to encourage the natives of the occupied lands to view the Japanese as heralds of forthcoming independence. Within Burma and India, especially, the Japanese had already fostered nationalist movements agitating for independence from the British. In other cases—for example, with the recruitment of Indian prisoners of war into the Indian National Army (INA) after the fall of Singapore—Japanese promises simply preyed on desperation, hunger, and fear. For some—in Burma, for example—the pretense of Japanese solidarity fed the long-standing desire to defeat colonialism. Since before the outbreak of war, Japan had worked to nurture Burman nationalist hopes, leading to the formation of the pro-Axis Burma Independence Army (BIA) under Aung San. Though in reality both the Nazis and the Japanese regarded their respective conquered peoples as subhuman, many defeated Southeast Asians believed the Japanese talk of pan-Asian brotherhood, freedom, and the "Greater East Asia Co-prosperity Sphere," as they branded it. In any case, throughout 1942–43 there was little reason to believe that Japanese control of Southeast Asia would not become permanent.

Conflict and Resistance

In addition to much terrible loss and destruction, the war also served to exacerbate a range of ethnic tensions that had already been present before the war. It was supposedly common knowledge that the Burmans thought of the Indians as covetous and crafty, and that the Indians considered the Burmans unstable and stupid. Both of them, it was said, saw the British as cold and superior.[50] Beyond such trivial stereotyping, the discord between ethnic groups had the potential to become much worse, and there was increasing mistrust and hostility. One very salient point of division in wartime was, predictably, between those who sided with the Japanese and those who fought against them. The Burmese colonial regiment, the Burma Rifles, despite its name, had always consisted almost exclusively of majority-Christian Karens, Kachins, and Chins, serving under British officers. The Karens, who had actually settled in the land called Burma before the Burman people themselves, had acted as guides for the British during the Anglo-Burmese Wars and in the suppression of several rebellions, including the recent one led by Saya San in 1930–32. The ethnic Burmans, on the other hand, had been largely excluded from British military service, being considered neither loyal nor martial enough.[51] As late as 1939, there were still only 432 of them in the army, compared to 1,448 Karens, 886 Chins, and 881 Kachins. The British Army had always hesitated to put weapons into the hands of those who, in their opinion, might misuse them.[52] Those Burmans who did serve in the army were judged to have proven unreliable and even treacherous when subjected to the test of battle.[53] With the onset of the Second World War, the Karens remained loyal to the British, and as a consequence they suffered at the hands of the pro-Japanese BIA, as well as under the merciless Japanese Army itself. Villages were destroyed and massacres were committed disproportionately in Karen areas, with many Christian teachers and lay organizers among the victims, as well as Saw Pe Tha, a prewar cabinet minister, and his family. In the case of Karen Christians, their religion provided an additional reason for their being singled out for attack.[54]

Predictably, the few Burman Christian converts of the central Buddhist heartlands were also earmarked for special persecution. In Shwebo, the Japanese and their collaborators vowed to eradicate Christianity. The most recent Christian convert was a man called Peter Ba Shin, who had been baptized only a few months before the invasion. He was immediately targeted, the theory being that if a prominent recent convert could be forced to publicly recant, then others would follow. But Peter Ba Shin remained utterly impassive to imprisonment and torture, and in the end the fruitless attempt was abandoned.[55] The faithfulness and courage of the clergy, whether Burman, Karen, Chin, or other, proved to be universal. Rev. Henry Ba Tet, a former police officer, had been the parish priest at Prome (Pyay) when the war started. He made sure that his flock got away to safety and then withdrew to a jungle village, where he was hunted down by Burman collaborators but managed to escape. He then bravely decided to move to Rangoon to lend support to the Christians who were stealthily daring to return to the suburbs. Another rising figure in the underground Church was Rev. John Aung Hla, who had been ordained just before the war and had been parish priest of Christ Church, Mandalay. At great personal risk, he began to hold regular Sunday services in private houses, and on his own initiative he expanded this clandestine mission to Maymyo and the surrounding countryside. At one point, he was doing a vast round of visiting twenty-one villages in turn, celebrating Holy Communion in a different place every day for four consecutive months. John Aung Hla even gained entry to the internment camp for Anglo-Burmans at Maymyo. From the Chin community around Prome (Pyay), there were two distinguished young priests: Rev. Ja Bu, who was imprisoned by the Japanese, and Rev. Maung Pay, who made a risky regular round visiting the Christian villages in secret.[56] Another extraordinary underground priest was Rev. Francis Ah Mya, who later came to international attention thanks to Godfrey Winn, a prominent British journalist, author, radio and TV presenter, and war correspondent. Winn wrote in glowing terms about Francis Ah Mya's fearless work as a resistance leader under the noses of the Japanese, describing him as a legend among his people.[57] With good reason, the clergy of Burma were being called patient in tribulation but resolute in faith.[58]

Preparing for Peace: The Church in Exile

The year 1943 brought hopeful signs for the exiled Church, beginning with Bishop West's long-overdue arrival in India after his prolonged forced sojourn in the United States. He had hoped to travel to India via Great Britain, but at the last minute this arrangement was canceled, probably due to a surge in U-boat activity in the Atlantic, and he sailed by another route.[59] Once in India, West started to reorganize the diocese in exile, appointing a new archdeacon, Rev. George Appleton of the SPG, and Mr. H. Smart as diocesan secretary. He established a diocesan office at St. James' Hall, Delhi, and duly informed the RDA of these developments by telegram. Shortly after the arrival of that cable, a cryptic Airgraph (or V-mail) was received from Rev. (later Canon) Hugh McD. Wilson, MC, which hinted at a tour of inspection somewhere inside Burmese territory that he and the bishop had been able to make together.[60] Both men, coincidentally, had been decorated while serving in the Royal Artillery during the First World War, though Wilson had been an officer and Bishop West had been a junior NCO. Wilson had arrived in Burma in 1924 after recovering from being seriously wounded in the war. After six years, he became principal of St. John's College and held a number of senior posts in the diocese before taking part in the evacuation into India in 1942.[61] The two veterans were now stealthily getting nearer to the front. West would later follow hot on the heels of the advancing "Forgotten Army" in the wake of the key battles at Imphal and Kohima.[62]

The mood in exile was therefore increasingly optimistic. There was much talk of greater unity and solidarity in the diocese but also of ecumenism.[63] Indeed, the Church's exile in British India actually provided opportunities to reflect, liaise, and look to the future of the Christian community and Christian missions in what was widely foreseen as an independent postwar Burma. In the first two days of July 1943, the Burma Christian Council (BCC; later Burma Council of Churches and today renamed the Myanmar Christian Council) met for the first time at Forman Christian College, Lahore. Rev. D. O. Smith of the American Baptist Mission was the chairman and Rev. George Appleton, now archdeacon of Rangoon, was the secretary. While the BCC meetings covered a wide range of general discussion topics and getting-to-know-you between the exiled Churches, talk soon focused on how this newfound cooperation might be taken forward to face the many anticipated challenges of postwar Burma.[64] The main concern boiled down to this: the security and freedom of the Christian minority in a country where the government would be largely in the hands of the Buddhist majority.[65] The BCC correctly observed that the Christian community consisted predominantly of Karens and Anglo-Burmese, and the overwhelming majority of the members of a new government would surely be Burman Buddhists.[66] Tensions between Karens and Burmans were already a sad reality, and violent wartime clashes were an unfortunate sign of things to come.

Ethnic diversity and tension had long been a fact of life in Burma, which has never been one people or nation but a cohabitation of peoples, each with their own language, traditions, culture, and history. Religious differences are normal in Burma and perhaps even more widely accepted than in more advanced multicultural societies, though these differences are not always mutually respected in Burma and they can give rise to hostility and violence.[67] The biggest challenge when contemplating an independent postwar Burma was how to assert and preserve the different ethnic identities, with the free exercise of their religions, in the face of a powerful majority movement promoting strong central government, backed by a philosophy of "true" nationhood tied to one militant religion.[68] Groups like the Karens hoped that the British would exercise whatever authority they had left to ensure an autonomous and peaceful future for their most loyal former subjects.[69] And in the midst of all this, the Anglican Church, which represented significant numbers of Karens, had to prepare to operate with something resembling normality. The new archdeacon, George Appleton, appealed for an inclusive approach based on taking responsibility for the whole country and the whole population, identifying with their problems and needs. Burmese Anglican Christians, Appleton argued, were as Burmese as anyone else, and they were just as concerned with Burma's welfare as the most vocal nationalists.[70] Appleton idealized that the Christians of Burma must be fully involved in the national life and must insist on playing a full and equal part in the future of the country: "Our ideal for the future must not be little island compounds of Christian life, but a stream of life flowing into the national life, cleansing, healing, enriching."[71]

The Anglican Church had historically been strongly identified with the minority peoples, and the war had exacerbated the political connotations of these links as well. The Church risked being cast as partisan—pro-Karen, pro-British, anti-Burman, anti-nationalist, anti-Independence. Possible solutions were seen in a return once more to the charism of Rangoon as a missionary diocese with a renewed missionary spirit, breaking out in new forms to meet new needs and conditions: "In the work of reconstructing the country—Appleton wrote—we shall be judged by the insight that we bring to the common problems and the quality of our service more than by our professions and sermons."[72] The time of new needs and conditions and reconstructing the country felt ever closer, as the German and Japanese losses of 1944 made an Axis victory look increasingly unlikely. The campaign for the recapture of Burma brought some of the most memorable British and American military heroes to the fore: the maverick generals "Bill" Slim and "Vinegar Joe" Stilwell (names that could be taken straight from a prewar British boys' adventure story) and the eccentric, brilliant, and controversial genius Orde Wingate (the T. E. Lawrence of the Second World War), as well as uniquely audacious and courageous fighting units such as Wingate's Chindits, Merrill's Marauders, and the legendary Gurkhas of Nepal. An uneasy peace was just around the corner, but at least it would be peace.

The Return to Burma

Burma's Anglicans and their families played a big part in retaking the country. Bishop West's own brother, in fact, was serving right alongside General

Bill Slim, and for some the war signified a return to Burma after a long absence: Christopher Norman Tubbs, son of Bishop Norman Henry Tubbs, had been born in Burma in 1926, when his father was bishop of Rangoon. Christopher had gone to school in England and then been evacuated to Canada to escape the Blitz, but he returned to Britain in 1944 to train as an infantry officer in the Royal Welch Fusiliers. He was sent to India, and from there he made his return to the land of his birth, where the life expectancy of an infantry officer was four days, as the Japanese fought a bitter retreat.[73] Tubbs survived the war to follow his father into the priesthood. His brother Peter also served in the army in Burma and also survived.[74] Other members of the Church paid the ultimate price upon their return: the now-thirty-three-year-old army chaplain Rev. David Alexander Patterson, MA (Cantab), CF, former vice principal of St. John's College, Rangoon, finally succeeded in his ambition of returning to Burma. This had been his goal since making the three-hundred-mile trek to India, where he had immediately volunteered for the army. Sometime between 5 and 6 April 1944, the glider transporting him on active service into the Burmese jungle crashed, and Patterson was killed. His death was felt to be a great loss to the Church and to education in Burma, to whose services he had dedicated his life.[75] Rev. Patterson's final letters "always spoke of his longing for the war to end so that he might return to his missionary work among the people he loved."[76]

After a three-year absence, Bishop West found himself on Burmese soil again, "in a bamboo hut amid green-clad mountains standing at a homemade altar celebrating Holy Communion."[77] As more and more territory was retaken by the Allied forces, the returning exiles came to understand the reality of Burma under the invaders: "The picture of Burma under Japanese rule," *Burma News* reported, "is a somber one . . . devastated cities, no transport for the few goods that remain to be sold at exorbitant prices, disillusionment at the complete failure of Japanese promises of prosperity, and over all the shadow of the Japanese Gestapo."[78] This was the reality of the fictitious independence granted to Burma by the Japanese.[79] Much of the material patrimony of the Anglican Church had been destroyed. Some churches had been burned to the ground, not only by the Japanese but in violent clashes between resistant Karens and pro-Japanese Burman nationalists. As the tide of battle definitively turned, Aung San's Burma Independence Army (BIA) renamed itself the Burma National Army (BNA). At the twelfth hour, the BNA reconsidered its support for the Japanese, and although it was too late for their contribution to have any effect, Aung

THE ANGLICAN CHURCH IN BURMA

San and his nationalists switched sides and joined the Allies. On 20 March 1945, Mandalay was liberated, and at the start of May, Prome (Pyay) was taken by Bill Slim's "Forgotten" Fourteenth Army. With the liberation of Rangoon on 3 May 1945, the war in Burma was virtually over. Rangoon once again justified the name it had been given by King Alompra in 1755, when, to commemorate the conclusion of the war against the Talaings by the capture of the village of Dagon, he changed its name to Rangoon (*Ran* meaning "war" and *goon* meaning "ended").[80] With pockets of Japanese still resisting all over Southeast Asia, the chilling news of the atomic bombs came in August, but in Burma nothing could match the sense of relief and the desire to get back to normal.

Peace

Getting back to normal would certainly be dependent on a great deal of convalescence, recovery, and rebuilding. Former prisoner of the Japanese Rev. Vick Kemp wrote: "Well, it is all over now, and how thankful I am to have escaped, when so many thousands perished. I saw Bishop West in Rangoon and he told me to have three or four months' rest to recover. All prisoners were in a shocking state owing to semi-starvation and beriberi."[81] But there were deep mental wounds to heal as well. When the Anglicans returned to Car Nicobar, where, among others, a medical missionary (recorded simply as Dr. Jones) had been murdered in front of the village, they discovered the depth of their bond with the locals. A returning official, identified only as Mr. Scott, wrote: "As soon as the poor Nicobarese women saw me, they rushed forward crying and saying, 'We are your daughters and the cruel Japs have killed your sons.' We could not start the [Holy Communion] Service for some time because these poor women would not let go of me. After the service the same thing happened again and I completely broke down. I thought my heart would break."[82] The two British officers accompanying Scott stated that they had never in their lives seen such a sad sight and had no idea black people could love a white man so much.[83] At the start of the Japanese occupation, Nicobarese Christians had been accused of spying for the British, and their leaders had been burned to death.[84] At the end of the occupation, the retreating Japanese had randomly murdered hundreds more people on their way out of Car Nicobar.[85] The village of Mus, where Scott had settled before the war and built the mission from scratch, had been wiped from the face of the earth: "There is not a stick to show

"PATIENT IN TRIBULATION BUT RESOLUTE IN FAITH"

where my house, mission buildings and lovely little hospital were."[86] The wreck of his church survived, damaged in the intervening years not only by the Japanese but also by Allied naval bombardment. A small band of Christians had carried on the good work on Car Nicobar Island as best they could, in spite of the Japanese. Mrs. Jones spoke very highly of the Nicobarese and the way they had stood by her in a time of need, risking their own lives after her husband, Dr. Jones, had been put to death.[87]

VJ Day was announced on 15 August, and on 16 October the governor of Burma returned. On 31 December 1945, military government in Burma ended, and peacetime civilian rule was restored, though British battalions would remain in Burma for some time.[88] Smooth as the transition may sound, uncertainty and trepidation characterized the mood of the time. The Anglican Church, especially, was under no illusions about the challenges that the years ahead would bring. Did they feel ready to face Independence, the departure of the British, the struggle to balance ethnic rivalries, the assertion of Buddhist dominance, and more? Surprisingly, the spirit of the Church at the close of 1945 was still resoundingly optimistic: "From December 7th, 1941, till August 15th, 1945, for four long years, the Church of Burma passed through a fiery furnace. But though there has been grievous material loss and many of our most faithful Christian people have perished, the soul of the Church has been untouched: indeed, in many respects, it seems to have been tempered and refined by the fiery trial which it has endured."[89]

Summary

In assessing the role, conduct, and experience of the Church during the Second World War, we see both its strengths and its weaknesses being revealed. We can identify both the sum total of the Church's formative experiences up to that point being put to the test—and also the embryo of the Church it was yet to become, culminating in the one we see in our times. In the late 1930s, the Church in Burma was aware of the war in neighboring China, but along with the rest of Burma's society it was woefully unprepared for the approaching global conflict. Even when the world war was underway, expatriate congregants were more worried about the bombing back home in Britain and the soldiers in North Africa than the threat of Japanese invasion. December 1941 brought a decisive end to the tennis matches and cocktail parties.

The war was ruthless on the people of Burma; civilians were bombed, persecuted, impoverished, executed, and starved. There were reprisals and vendettas, summary executions, forced labor, wanton destruction, and theft of property. Some British Anglican leaders regretted having fled from Burma, but what option did they have? Stories of phenomenal bravery and incredible solidarity among Anglicans are deeply touching, but within the war narratives even more enduring themes emerge. The war highlighted the ethnic divisions in Burma, but it also revealed local Church members' qualities of resourcefulness, leadership, and courage—qualities that would go on to shape the future of the Church and the country. The absence of the British clergy contributed to the emergence of a vision for a future autonomous Church, led by a generation of young clergy schooled in running the Church with desperate limitations and the threat of persecution. They were bitterly aware of the fragility and precarity of the Church's considerable material patrimony, having seen much of it destroyed, and they placed more faith in their (clandestine) networks of personal relationships and small pockets of worshippers. Such was the Church they rebuilt under the noses of the Japanese. It would come as no surprise that this generation of young clergy would become the leaders of the postcolonial Church and go on to face renewed persecution and privations under new regimes.

Nationally and regionally, too, the war acted as a powerful catalyst for future political independence. The Japanese had tried to market their annexations on the promise of liberation from the colonial masters, but any trust they won was violently and totally abused. If postwar Burma, Burmese people, and even Burmese Christians have been accused of isolationism and circumspection toward foreigners, could this not in part be explained by the dual imperial experience, first under British colonialism and then under the supposed liberators from that colonialism, the Japanese? The apparent Burmese reluctance to effectively relate and reach out internationally could be seen as a barrier that institutions, including the Church, may learn to overcome, and the same might be said of persistent interethnic rivalry and discord. All of this forms part of the wartime legacy, which acted both to reinforce these obstacles and to sharpen people's appetite and aptitude to surmount them. The Church we observe today is one very clearly eager for productive international relations while still being self-assured, resolute, and even dogged in preserving its values and identity. It is visibly the heir of the wartime Church.

Chapter 6

"THIS LAST STEP IN THE HISTORIC TASK"

Independence and the Challenges of Postcolonial Burma

In early October 1946, Holy Cross Theological College (HCTC) reopened with just three theological students: two deacons preparing for ordination to the priesthood and a Chinese-Burman who had actually been a student at HCTC before the Japanese invasion and was now attending the nearby university as a day student. The temporary warden of HCTC for the first few months was Rev. Canon William Rolfe Garrad, who also did most of the teaching, assisted by weekly lectures from Miss J. Chapman and Canon Wilson. Canon Garrad had been in Burma since 1910, working with the Winchester Brotherhood in Mandalay except for service in the First World War. Following the evacuation, he had spent the Second World War in India, where he served as an army chaplain once again.[1] Miss Chapman had previously taught at the Kemmendine mission center and was a fellow survivor of the evacuation of 1942. Also living at the college were a dozen or so Christian students from Rangoon University, which had reopened the previous month. These students could not afford the high boarding fees of the university (the cost of living in Rangoon was more than three times the 1941 level), so they were living more frugally at HCTC. The college buildings had survived the Japanese occupation almost undamaged, but every single piece of furniture had been looted or destroyed, and in the desperate postwar economic situation looting was still going on.[2] Holy Cross church, beside the college, had been used as a dining hall by the Japanese. When the British first returned to Rangoon after the war, the Army Chaplains'

Department took over HCTC as a retreat house and training center, and they had got the place up and running again. The man behind this was the archdeacon, the venerable Donald Moxon, MC, a member of the prewar clergy who had won his Military Cross tending to the wounded during the 1942 evacuation and spent the whole war as an army chaplain. Sunday services were once more being held regularly in the church, with a small but lively congregation of mostly prewar faithful.[3]

Holy Trinity Cathedral had also benefited from the British Army's helping hand, after being discovered in an abysmal state after the departure of the Japanese. Captain Peter Tubbs, son of the former bishop of Rangoon, was among the first troops to arrive and investigate the damage. Externally, the cathedral seemed normal, but the inside had been stripped of every fixture or fitting of the remotest value, and the whole space had been crudely partitioned and converted into a distillery, of all things. The foul stench of fermenting yeast was topped off with the aroma of huge dead rats lying around. One of the partitioned areas had been used as a cattle stall and another was used for storing brewing ingredients, and by contrast this area was occupied by huge live rats rather than huge dead ones.[4] The mammoth task of refurbishment was taken on by Major R. D. Hill of the Royal Engineers, who arranged for an altar and sanctuary fittings to be located and installed, as the whole altar area had been gutted. Hill's unit, 517 Independent Artizan [sic] Works (AW) Company, Royal Indian Engineers, completed the restoration in December 1945. In ways such as this, the Church visibly declared its comeback after 1945 and gratefully marked the close of the war years. Bishop West had been eager to get back to work and reconnect with his local native clergy, and he sought to bring as many of them as possible to a reunion meeting in Rangoon. This was not a simple task, however, as large tracts of the Delta area were under the control of dacoits (bandits) who had filled the power vacuum left by the departing Japanese.[5] A generally unsettled and uncertain atmosphere in Rangoon continued, and a series of strikes illustrated widespread discontent.[6]

Peacetime Hopes and Peacetime Fears

Peacetime civilian rule had returned to Burma at the very beginning of 1946, but the air was filled with the sensation that this was merely an interim period, not a return to normality. The war, and the wave of nationalist unrest that had preceded it, had paved the way for Burma's independence, and the countdown had now begun.[7] The Anglican Church had survived the war, but for its constituent peoples, ethnic minorities in a Burman-dominated nation, the jubilation was tempered. They sought reassurance from the British, alongside whom they had fought and sacrificed so much, and the official position appeared to be unequivocal, as King George VI's official message to them seemed to state:

> To the hill peoples of Burma, who have with such steadfast courage maintained for three long years the fight against the enemy, I wish to say a special word. Separate arrangements will be made for your administration so that special care and attention may be given to your welfare and your indigenous institutions may be developed. I hope that the day is not far distant when you, too, will desire of your own free will to take your place in a self-governing Burma, and my Government will do all in its power to forward this last step in the historic task of the unification of Burma.[8]

The Church echoed these sentiments, urging everyone to hope and pray that the Burman majority would cooperate alongside the Karens, Chins, Shans, Indians, Anglo-Burmese, and other minority communities, whether Buddhists, Christians, Hindus, or Muslims, to work out together the future destiny of the country. Church leaders hoped for a pragmatic vision to emerge and unite this comparatively small country locked between giant neighbors, predicting that Burma could become a vital multicultural bridge between India and China and thereby play a crucial role in the postwar world by linking two great and diverse civilizations.[9] The main threat to this vision was clearly the nature, leadership, and mass following of the extreme nationalist parties. In Burma's past life as a colonial backwater, exclusivist nationalism and intense isolationism were understandable, it was argued, but in the global world of the future it would be suicidal.[10] The Karens, as the largest of the minority groups, having the highest number of Christians and a history of support for the British, became the focus of Burman tribal antipathy. The Karens reaffirmed their expectations of full rights in the emerging national order, and as a result their deadly wartime enmity with the Burmans would unfortunately soon be revived. Furthermore, the leadership and personnel of the extreme nationalist parties had not substantially changed since the days of the pro-Axis BIA with its church burnings, destruction of farms, and murders of innocent villagers, all with Japanese endorsement.[11]

THE ANGLICAN CHURCH IN BURMA

The process of achieving national independence was to have the paradoxical effect of severely weakening the minorities' attachment and sense of belonging to the supposed nation while strengthening their feeling of being part of a separate ethnic group. On the one hand, this separate status would mean restrictions and limitations—on freedom of movement, social mobility, and career opportunities—and on the other hand, it would mean strengthened internal identity and solidarity with other ethnic groups, with whom they would be far more likely to share religion, culture, ideals, and aspirations.[12] Ordinary members of all the largely Christian ethnic groups were uneasy about the prospect of coming under majority Burman rule with its militant nationalist take on Buddhist identity. These fears would be realized in many cases of discrimination and a widespread feeling among young people that their freedom, safety, and future opportunities could be seriously jeopardized by their identification as Christians.[13]

Recovery from the war was a painstaking process for the Church. Service books started to be reprinted from photographs of an original copy taken long before, and some clergy were investigating the possibility of producing a joint hymnbook with the Methodist Church of Burma.[14] Such examples of cooperation between denominations hinted at an emerging vision of the future Church. Anglicans had always faced the difficulty of navigating Burma's complex multiethnic and multireligious society, but the war had unexpectedly pushed Church leaders toward greater solidarity and openness. They did not shy away from harsh realities, and, to their credit, they showed intelligence and sensitivity with regard to the coming social and political changes. The biggest coming change, of course, was national independence and all that it entailed. The Church foresaw itself being, for many years to come, a very small minority of the population of Burma existing under difficult circumstances in an environment that would be unfavorable in the short term with the potential to become actively hostile.[15] The Church's response was both realistic and optimistic, maintaining that even with this grim forecast the Church need not give up on its vocation to be an important and decisive influence on the spiritual and social progress of the Burmese people.[16]

A Changing Church

One of the immediately forthcoming effects of the postwar Church scenario, as already mentioned, was greater cooperation among Burma's various Christian denominations, for which the ground had already been prepared

"THIS LAST STEP IN THE HISTORIC TASK"

during the war. Archdeacon Appleton outlined a vision of the Church's future in a booklet published by the SPG, *The War and After*, calling for the postwar Church to be autonomous, pastoral, philanthropic, local, cooperative, and ecumenical. "It is possible," Appleton wrote, "that the Church in Burma will move towards unity in a new way, namely, by denominations thinking and working together."[17] With a view that was sympathetic to this outlook, the American Baptist Mission suggested that their Judson College could become a united Christian college, with the Protestant denominations sharing its staffing, support, and governance. But forward-thinking Anglicans like Appleton would go further, suggesting that if Judson College could also promote the sympathetic study of Buddhism and Burmese culture, it would be doing a great service not only to the Christian Church but to Burma and Buddhism generally.[18] He foresaw a series of two-way benefits in this, allowing missionaries to "gain a deeper insight into Buddhism and learn to see in it a preparation for the fuller revelation of the Christian Gospel" and permitting Buddhists to "learn to see in the Gospel the fulfillment of all that is true and best in their own religion."[19] Bishop West may not have subscribed to such a radically ecumenical outlook, but he did explicitly encourage all Christians to find commonality with adherents of other religions, viewing them as people with similar aspirations and needs fighting against the same difficulties and temptations. Rather than seeing Buddhism as a rival for the religious loyalty of the people of Burma, West believed, religious rivalry itself should be seen as the real enemy, along with religious enmity and the politicization of any religion. West and Appleton felt that the militant Buddhist nationalism of the time was as much a disservice to Buddhism as it was a menace to Christianity: "I would like," wrote Appleton, "to see a spiritual revival of Buddhism so that it became not merely a nationalistic sentiment, as opposed to the religion of the West, but a real dynamic in the daily lives of the people."[20]

Developing needed medical missions in villages and planning for Christian school funding after the imminent loss of government grants were concrete expressions of the new pragmatic outlook, focused on the daily lives of the people.[21] It was not yet clear what the new government's attitude toward Christian education was going to be, though to many it seemed only sensible for them to continue to encourage mission schools in some way.[22] Few would have seriously tried to deny their great worth and considerable historical contribution to the education of the country. Retired bishop of Rangoon Rolleston Sterritt Fyffe wondered just how many of those who formed the new government had themselves been educated in Christian schools: "Our own St. John's College [alone] could probably claim a fair proportion."[23] Education and medical care were only two of many pressing concerns, but it was widely felt that active engagement in social issues was the way forward. Appleton admitted that the Gospel had made little progress in Burma and that the Christian community had to shoulder the corporate responsibility for this. Thinking non-Christians, he said, increasingly judged Christians by their actions, not only as individuals but as a society, and by the contribution they brought to the national life.[24] This shift could perhaps be seen as one of the more positive outcomes of the war, which had necessitated a great deal of initiative and improvisation from Burma's oppressed Christians. The whole Church had been transformed into a practical grassroots network of social, medical, and teaching missionaries, and whatever distinction there may have previously appeared to be between mission and Church had become happily blurred.[25]

Another manifestation of change was the advancement of native clergy to positions of real leadership. The Rangoon Diocesan Association (RDA)'s Annual Report for 1946 called it a revolution in the life of the Church, comparable to the revolution taking place in the political life of the country.[26] This Church revolution was marked by the rise of a generation of Anglicans who had led the Church at enormous personal risk during the war.[27] The local Church had truly proven itself under the wartime occupation, when it stood alone, suffered, and came through the test without failing, in the assessment of those clergy who had been forced to flee.[28] The local clergy had passed some of the toughest tests of all, and it was clear that foreign missionaries could not just walk back in as if they had the right to resume authority and control.[29] Here was the recognition of these facts: 1946 saw the appointment, for the first time, of three local native archdeacons, Rev. John Aung Hla for Mandalay, Rev. John Hla Gyaw (sometimes spelled Kyaw) for Taungoo, and Rev. Luke Po Kun (who was also appointed a canon of the Cathedral) for the Delta. All three had distinguished themselves for their loyalty, courage, and faith during the war: John Aung Hla's record of bravery has been described; Luke Po Kun had remained steadfast despite losing his brother and several other family members to Japanese atrocities.[30] John Hla Gyaw had been arrested by the Japanese along with Francis Ah Mya, imprisoned, tortured, strung up from the prison ceiling by his wrists, and beaten until it was feared he had lost the use of his hands.[31] Supporting the appointments of these men, the RDA did its best to promote the idea that the Church was no longer primarily a Church of European missionaries, who were then small in number anyway, but rather a Church of the nationals of Burma, under their own priests and archdeacons. The obvious next step would be to appoint a Burman, Anglo-Burmese, or, much more likely, a Karen bishop in preparation for becoming a completely self-supporting and autonomous part of the worldwide Church.[32] British bishops would remain until 1966, however, and this vision of handing over total leadership to local clergy was not yet universally supported—and the political situation arguably did not yet provide the best occasion to implement it.[33]

The reality was that despite the support of some visionary SPG missionaries and bishops, native Church leadership had only seen a limited advance in the first four decades of the century. Even the pioneering SPG's practices did not always match its fine words about promoting local leaders. The ordination of local men was indeed encouraged and celebrated, but there was, in general, reluctance on the part of the British to give them any higher responsibility. This general rule—and in the case of the British response, the exception, too—was illustrated in the case of Karen priest and war hero Francis Ah Mya. He had been put forward for the job of assistant bishop of Rangoon by Bishop West as early as 1938, but West was overruled. But things had changed dramatically in the intervening years, and Francis Ah Mya would finally be consecrated as assistant bishop in 1949.[34] The attempt to promote local leadership would remain a defining feature of West's tenure.[35] He was one of a small number of Anglican missionaries who had taken a fairly critical and progressive view of colonialism, espousing some elements of the old "atheism of empire" philosophy. This controversial theory, it will be recalled, cast doubt on the supposed rightness and Godliness of imperialism and tended to evoke support for greater local stewardship of the Church.[36] The wider Church was largely coming around to a similar point of view, while recognizing a continuing need for European input in the training of clergy, teachers, and nurses, but under the direction of diocesan authorities rather than the missionary societies. The mood was improving, and at the first postwar diocesan council, held in Rangoon during October 1946, there was a new spirit of self-confidence and self-reliance among the local clergy.[37] But with the dawn of 1947, the year of Indian Independence, the wider national situation in Burma continued to be one of uncertainty.

The Panglong Conferences

March 1946 had seen the first Panglong Conference take place, with the overall aim of addressing the question of future cohabitation among the constituent peoples of Burma. The first conference was called primarily in order to discuss the future of the minority Shan states after independence, but there were also Kachin, Chin, and Karen representatives in attendance. Burman majority representatives spoke at the conference and a message from the British governor was read out. The Chins and Kachins expressed concerns about the anti-British tone coming from the Burmans, doubting the sincerity of their declared aim of equal rights for all. The Karens demanded a separate state, but a Karen goodwill mission to London in August failed to tease out any British encouragement for these separatist aspirations. In November 1946, the Supreme Council of the United Hills Peoples was formed, and minority leaders continued to lobby London directly. As Archdeacon Appleton observed, this was the most difficult matter before the conference because the Shans, Kachins, and Chins had enjoyed varying degrees of autonomy under the British, enhanced by the social mobility and professional opportunities offered by Christian education. All of the minority peoples, Appleton believed, would generally have preferred to remain in the British sphere of influence in some form or other, but most of them lived their lives inextricably mingled with the Burmans, rather than in ethnic enclaves that might be viewed as easy to partition off.[38]

Aung San and his Burman majority delegation were received in London in January 1947 for talks with Prime Minister Clement Attlee and his government. Rollestone S. Fyffe, former bishop of Rangoon, welcomed this development, seeing the potential of "reasonable and able men" like Aung San and Tin Tut to command the support of the whole people of Burma, without denying the difficulty of their task.[39] Aung San secured the support and confidence of the British government, having already secured the endorsement of Burma's nationalists, who gave him a free hand to negotiate an amicable deal with the country's minorities. Attlee had done well to support Aung San, in Fyffe's assessment, and this augured well for the second Panglong Conference the following month, at which Aung San and the majority Burman representatives would hope to make real progress in discussion with the other ethnic groups.[40]

At the second Panglong Conference, the breakthrough seemed to come in the form of an agreement between the Shan, Kachin, and Chin leaders and Aung San on 12 February 1947. Twenty-three signatories expressed their willingness to cooperate with an interim Burmese government in order to achieve national independence speedily, and they agreed in principle to the formation of a new "Union of Burma." The Panglong Agreement recognized the important role of the Supreme Council of United Hills Peoples, and in

"THIS LAST STEP IN THE HISTORIC TASK"

principle full autonomy in internal administration of the frontier states was accepted. A separate Kachin state was agreed to be desirable, and all citizens of the frontier areas were to enjoy the rights regarded as fundamental in a modern democratic country. Aung San, who had the confidence of the Attlee government since his London meeting, had fulfilled his promises and demonstrated to the British that he was able to successfully mediate with the minority ethnic peoples, though he would never win the trust of some Whitehall detractors, including Winston Churchill.[41]

The agreement was by no means flawless; the Karens and Karenni were excluded, and the Mon and Rakhine were not even considered; the Pa-Oh, Palaung, and Wa peoples were subsumed under the heading of the Shans, despite protests. There were a further fifty assorted ethnic groups represented jointly as the "hill peoples," but even under this broad umbrella term the Delta-based Karens, the Mon, and the Rakhine peoples were excluded. By May 1947, a revolt had already started in Rakhine state, and in July the Karen National Defense Organization (KNDO), a paramilitary force, was formed by the Karen National Union (KNU). As tensions increased, Aung San and several members of his cabinet were assassinated on 19 July. This devastating event sparked decades of theorizing about foreign and domestic conspiracies, from possible Whitehall plots to internal Burman power struggles. The socialist faction leader Nu would become the first prime minister of the independent Burma as a direct consequence of the assassination of Aung San, who is still widely considered a national hero in Burma. Sao Shwe Thaik was elected as the first president for a four-year term (he would later be arrested during the 1962 coup, and he died shortly afterward in custody). The intrinsic shortcomings of the agreement, the assassination of Aung San, and the consequent inadequacies of the Constitution promulgated on 24 September 1947 combined to completely unravel the promise of Panglong, which some feel is still awaiting implementation today. The Church declared its sympathy and solidarity to be very much with the Karen people, who were considered the most prominent and most exemplary Christian community of Burma in terms of numbers, character, and commitment.[42] Archdeacon Appleton observed that the Karens were distinctly uneasy about their future.[43] They seemed to face an unenviable choice between amalgamation and isolation, in the words of Bishop West.[44] Church leaders struggled to be optimistic about the situation, though they did not doubt the vision and courage of the Karens, nor their ability to discern God's purpose in these developments, both for themselves and for the whole of Burma.[45]

THE ANGLICAN CHURCH IN BURMA

Independence

The Union of Burma came into being at exactly 4:20 AM on 4 January 1948. The British governor immediately departed, ceding to the new prime minister, Nu, and the last British regiment, the King's Own Yorkshire Light Infantry, was transferred to Malaya.[46] The very specific timing of independence was not left to chance; it was the most propitious moment, according to the Burmese astrologers who meticulously selected the exact time and date. The moment was greeted with an early morning cacophony of factory sirens, train whistles, gongs, hooters, bells, and amateur pyrotechnics by way of jubilation, but what actually unfurled was a year of intense discord.[47] The new national flag showed one large star symbolizing the Burman people and five small stars representing the "other" peoples, but there was hardly even any clarity as to which peoples were considered part of this symbolism and which were excluded.[48] By February 1949, the Karens were in open insurgency, and the Mon and Kachin were on the point of revolt as well. The Anglican Church took the precaution of closing its mission schools and also HCTC, aware that the strong association between Anglicans and Karens might lead government forces to see Anglican institutions as foci of Karen revolt. Within a few months the prospect of a peaceful unification of Burma's diverse peoples had disintegrated, giving way to the ongoing struggle that would become sadly iconic of Burma. The country's biggest and most enduring challenge is the struggle of communities to assert and preserve their identities, the free exercise of their religions, the free use of their languages, and the promotion of their culture and traditions, versus an uncompromising ideology of centralized governance with a concept of supposed "true" nationality distinct from the "others." Even when the proponents of this centralized ideology have adopted the framework and vocabulary of democracy in order to promote their vision of unity, the struggle has repeatedly descended into violence.[49]

With the partition of India and the creation of Pakistan in 1947, the Anglican CIBC had become the CIPBC, the Church of India, Pakistan, Burma and Ceylon. This period would see the first native bishops consecrated for Burma, a turning point that had been foreseen seventy years previously, when the first bishop of Rangoon, Jonathan Holt Titcomb, wrote that "it is only through the development of a native pastorate [that] we shall ever be able to extend mission work on any sound and proper basis, or to raise up native Christians into habits of self-reliance and strength."[50] Rev. Francis Ah Mya and Rev. John Aung Hla were consecrated as assistant bishops of Rangoon in 1949, and another experienced Karen priest, Rev. Stephen Taw Mwa, was added to the cohort of native archdeacons.[51] Bishop West recalled first meeting Francis Ah Mya in 1921, the year West arrived in Burma and went to work in remote Kappali, where no foreigner had ever previously lived. Francis, as a young Anglican schoolteacher, went along as well. He was already married to Catherine and had been educated in Rangoon and trained for the ministry in Calcutta. West recalled being immediately impressed by Francis's burning passion for his people, his opposition to anything that divided his people, and his idealism and ambition for his people.[52] Both Francis Ah Mya and John Aung Hla commanded far-reaching respect for having served the Church and the people with such distinction during the Japanese occupation.[53]

The decade of the 1950s began with the Church disjointed and largely incommunicado, as insurgent battles swept the country. HCTC and many other institutions were once again closed, and there had been no diocesan council since 1948. A council would finally be held in 1953, once the insurrection subsided and life took on a semblance of normality again. Gradually, schools for catechists recommenced, and in 1954 HCTC reopened; such was the disruption that between 1946 and 1954 only six ordinands were produced.[54] During this period, as international travel started to become easier, the Church did make every effort to send local priests (and some laity) to England for short training courses, theological studies, pastoral experience, and, in the case of Assistant Bishop John Aung Hla, to manage the printing of the revised Prayer Book (and later to attend the Lambeth Conference in 1958). Assistant Bishop Francis Ah Mya was also able to attend some international gatherings and conferences. The number of laity sent to England was still small, but it was the beginning of an attempt to further broaden the knowledge and outlook of native mission workers in theology, Christian education, and social work.

In 1954, Burma said goodbye to Bishop George A. West, MM, whose contribution to the Church in war and peace had been immense, spanning twenty of the most turbulent and transformative years in Burma's history, as bishop, and a total of thirty-four years spent in Burma. In 1955, Rev. Victor G. Shearburn, CR, became the seventh (and last foreign) bishop of Rangoon. Bishop Shearburn was a member of the monastic Community of the Resurrection (CR), known as the Mirfield Fathers because of their home at Mirfield, West Yorkshire, and he took to his new role with impressive energy. In the first years of his tenure, he introduced a Summer Bible School for all ages, at the diocese's expense, to improve laypeople's knowledge of the faith. In 1957, he launched the Archdeaconry of Moulmein (Mawlamyine), with headquarters at Hpa-an, and this would be the foundation of the future Diocese of Hpa-an. Bishop Francis Ah Mya was appointed Archdeacon of Moulmein, and he oversaw both short- and long-term projects of cottage industry—cash-crop planting, animal husbandry, a printing press—and created student residences, a high school, and a Bible school. He oversaw the construction of new churches and the publication of a Hymn Book and a Prayer Book in the Sgaw Karen language, as well as other Christian literature. From 1960, Bishop Shearburn did much to encourage and promote the development of a dynamic local clergy, especially after 1962, when the countdown to the expulsion of foreigners, including Shearburn himself, began.[55]

The Burmese Way to Socialism?

By the start of the 1960s, the initially small Burma Army had ballooned to a hundred thousand men, up from a few thousand in 1948. The architect was General Ne Win, one of the original "Thirty Comrades" who had been trained by the Japanese before the Second World War. Ne Win had controlled the army since Independence and had also devoted himself to eliminating his rivals in the army command. By 1956, independent Burma had seen years of insurrections and discord, giving Ne Win a pretext to float the idea of a military takeover—all in the name of preserving law and order and keeping the fragile union together.[56] He took temporary power in 1958–59 at the invitation of Prime Minister Nu and ceded power back to Nu after the elections of 1960. But tensions began to rise as Nu's rule became increasingly divisive. Nu announced a decree making Buddhism the state religion, a move widely seen as superfluous considering the undeniable influence of Buddhism—already the official religion in all but name—and criticized by some as being provocation.[57] The Anglicans, along with the Baptists and Methodists as part of the Burma Christian Council, made clear their displeasure at this move, while the Roman Catholic Archbishop Victor Bazin, MEP, had previously pledged not to interfere. The Roman Catholics enjoyed a better relationship with the government during this period, and Nu had described it as the "model church" in Burma.[58] The declaration of Buddhism as the state religion triggered a decades-long revolt by the Christian-majority Kachins.

Two years later, in March 1962, Ne Win once again seized power in a coup, and Nu was arrested. Ne Win, who proved to be an incorrigibly superstitious and amoral man, established a dictatorship that would last three decades and worked for a desensitized acceptance of the military's unelected role in governance that endures until today. His single-party rule made use of the term "socialist," but in reality the new regime only paid lip service to authentic socialist ideas. Despite the regime's so-called Burmese Way to Socialism program, the generals established a nationalist authoritarian form of government.[59] It seems likely that the utilization of the word "socialism" was largely calculated to attract sympathy and support in international political circles. The supposedly socialist program was received with a mix of feelings within Burma, and not all of those feelings were negative, by any means, including among many Anglicans. Bishop Francis Ah Mya noted that villagers were optimistic but bewildered by talk of agrarian reform and nationwide socialized services.[60] Ne Win's nationalism hinted at equal treatment in the eyes of the state, but the reverse of this coin was that the leader was violently opposed to federalism and any kind of regional or ethnic autonomy. He set out to enforce a highly centralized vision of the union. The Shan Federal Movement was one example of the more moderate and accommodating ethnic organizations, which had aspired to form a loose federation of states rather than full separatism, but Ne Win's hardliners condemned the Shan Federalists as a breakaway movement. They in turn responded to the general's coup d'état with a further Shan rebellion.

Ne Win's coup also signaled the final demise of the 1947 Constitution, and it extinguished the few remaining hopes of enacting the Panglong Agreement. In addition to the Kachins and Shans, the Chins also launched a rebellion in the 1960s. Ne Win was a notoriously contradictory character, a vitriolic xenophobe who was himself ethnically Chinese; he chased foreign women and loved to travel abroad, though he ostensibly loathed everything non-Burmese. His secret police targeted Indians with particular cruelty, and many were violently expelled from the country in overnight raids. A further insurgency in the Shan substate of Mong Pai was triggered by the regime's absurd "demonetization" decree of 1964, which had its roots in the general's stupefyingly superstitious nature. Ne Win, whose petty obsessions had spread to black magic and the occult, had been convinced by astrologers and numerologists that only numbers divisible by nine would bring him good luck, so he declared the 100-kyat and 50-kyat banknotes worthless overnight, wiping out the meager savings of struggling farmers as well as everyone else in the country.[61] That was only the first of several demonetizations, each one bringing cripplingly dire economic consequences for individuals and the country. A 75-kyat banknote was later introduced just

THE ANGLICAN CHURCH IN BURMA

to mark Ne Win's seventy-fifth birthday. On the further advice of numerologists, 15-, 25-, and 35-kyat banknotes were created, only to be withdrawn overnight in another demonetization, making 75 percent of the nation's currency worthless. Much later, the introduction of the notorious 45-kyat and 90-kyat banknotes (divisible by nine, Ne Win's special number) should have been the luckiest of all, but the resulting economic upset would instead eventually contribute to the coup that (ostensibly) ousted him.

Autonomy or Isolation?

Parallel to such abject lunacy in the early 1960s came sweeping nationalization, and this included education. All Christian and other mission schools were to be nationalized together with all other private schools.[62] Religious teaching was to be strongly discouraged, which was to have a severe effect on the Church's ability to develop its lay staff, teachers, catechists, and future clergy. Alongside these moves came the introduction of complex criteria for claiming Burmese citizenship, leading to the large-scale deportations of non-Burmans—including Indian, Eurasian, and Chinese Christians, among others—whether they were born in Burma or not. Reentry visas for foreign workers, including missionaries, began to be restricted.[63] Speculation grew that it would not be long before the government moved to expel the foreign missionaries and clergy altogether, and work urgently increased in order to prepare the local Church for this new reality. The Church's presence in Kachin state had been undergoing strengthening for several years, and the rudimentary structure was in place for a potential future diocese.[64] Growth was also recorded in Shan areas neighboring Kachin state. The key was to put in place frameworks that could serve as bases for the future dioceses of an autonomous Church. The Moulmein Archdeaconry at Hpa-an was one very good example of this, already being a functioning diocese in all but name, as well as Mandalay. Development was too slow for some Kachin Anglicans, however, and they broke away to launch their own "Christian Freedom Church."[65] All of the Anglican bodies in the Southeast Asian region were increasingly developing in their own ways and asserting different degrees of independence. This placed strains on relationships both internally and internationally, as groups of Anglicans, previously held together by the CIBPC, for example, found that they had less in common with one another than they might have previously thought.[66]

"THIS LAST STEP IN THE HISTORIC TASK"

In 1964, the government ceased to renew missionary visas, and then the year 1966 was given as the final date for them to leave the country. This move, as drastic and unfair as it may seem, must be seen in context; Burma was just one of several decolonizing Asian countries to adopt broadly similar measures around that time, with greater or lesser degrees of urgency and hostility.[67] The expulsion of foreign Christian missionaries, clergy, and bishops was particularly dear to the regime in Burma, led by the nominally Buddhist but in fact fanatically superstitious Ne Win. The hardline Burman Buddhist nationalists of the regime harbored resentments dating back to the Anglo-Burmese Wars and the Saya San Rebellion, and they still longed for revenge against the British and their disruptive, invasive religion.[68] They dismissed Christianity as a Western imperialist philosophy and denounced it as a pseudo-religion consisting of the "three M's"—first the invaders came as *merchants*, then as *missionaries*, and finally as *military* conquerors. This outlook also identified those ethnic minority peoples with an attachment to this Western belief system as highly suspect, considering them instruments of the colonialists.[69]

Rangoon's last British bishop, Victor G. Shearburn, CR, was thus finally forced to depart in 1966, giving way to the first ever native diocesan bishop in Burma, Francis Ah Mya, who up to then had been assistant bishop of Rangoon and archdeacon based at Hpa-an. For the twenty years since the war, there had clearly been a need to prepare local Church leaders to take full responsibility, but it was only with the final departure of the British remnant that the "scaffolding" was finally removed, leaving the local Church standing without external aid.[70] At the last moment, there seemed little time to prepare for the handover, and the transition was somewhat hurried. This meant that the new bishop was overwhelmed with urgent work, and all in the context of suddenly reduced manpower with the expulsion of all the foreigners. The Church still faced several ongoing problems, including a great lack of Christian literature (especially in Burmese) aimed both at clergy and laity for the furtherance of religious knowledge and personal development. There was also a lack of proper teaching aids and materials for Sunday school classes, which further frustrated attempts to offer a consistent Christian education service. Importing any non-Buddhist religious literature into the country became near impossible, and local language translations of the Bible were banned. All publications, in fact, religious or not, had become subject to control and censorship.[71] The Printing and Publication Department of the Church was up and running by the middle of the 1960s, but its remit was severely limited both by law and resources. Its focus was the publication of liturgical books, hymnbooks in several languages, calendars, and a monthly newsletter.[72]

Bishop Francis Ah Mya inherited an ambitious vision for the Church in Burma. He himself was a great advocate of a self-supporting Church, and he continued the micro-industry initiatives in the Hpa-an region that he had launched under Bishop Shearburn. At the same time, he was conscious that the new political order left Burma's Anglicans isolated and disconnected from the wider world Church, so increasing self-sufficiency in every sense was no longer a choice but a necessity. The bishop's three-point plan to deal with this new reality was as follows: (1) self-propagation of the Church, through the development of lay ministry, the development of a mission-oriented clergy, and the promotion of ecumenical fellowship among Christian denominations; (2) self-support in finances, through self-supporting micro-industry projects and a new investment policy; (3) self-administration, through the reorganization of the parish structure, the promotion of higher education in church leadership, and ultimately making preparations for the formation of a separate Church of the Province of Burma.[73] The implementation of this vision created both the need and the opportunity for dynamic lay leaders to distinguish themselves. The most prominent of these lay leaders is the genial figure of Wilfred Aung Hla Tun—U Tun—an unassuming polymath whose many and varied contributions have earned him the esteem of several generations in the Church. U Tun has been a teacher, organizer, historian, and general problem-solver, counting among his credits the foundation of a clinic, a pharmacy, a printing press, and the creation of many lay training programs and teaching materials. The capacity to effectively carry through projects such as these increased people's confidence in the Church's autonomous future.

Autonomy Despite Isolation?

Bishop Francis Ah Mya would become the first archbishop of the new autonomous province of Burma when the overdue reorganization of the old CIPBC was finally to be concluded in 1970. For neighboring India, the end of the CIPBC was a particularly fraught and controversial process, seeing the creation of two "united" Indian churches. Both of these new churches drew together multiple preexisting churches, each with differing traditions, worship styles, ecclesiologies, and polities. The prospect of autonomy also

"THIS LAST STEP IN THE HISTORIC TASK"

presented problems for Burma: the Church had participated in the CIPBC, along with the other constituent parts that were now gaining autonomy, but the new political situation in Burma was clearly not going to make any further international cooperation easy. An organization named the South East Asia Church Council had been at work throughout the 1960s, with Burma's active participation, in order to negotiate the transition after the breakup of regional Churches. The council's other specific aim was to lay the foundations of a new Church of the Province of Southeast Asia as an independent part of the Anglican Communion, but in itself the council was not an executive or administrative body. The Church of the Province of Southeast Asia did eventually become a reality, but Burma's participation in the preparatory council's work revealed no particular grounds for supporting its absorption into this new province. In Burma, what would emerge would be the Church of the Province of Burma (CPB), founded partly because not doing so would have left Burma as the sole remaining component of the old broken-up CIPBC.[74]

The canons of the Anglican Church stipulated that there must be at least three dioceses in a territory in order to form a province, with each one having a certain amount of endowment. Therefore, Bishop Francis Ah Mya made concrete preparations for autonomy: (1) he demarcated the boundaries of *four* dioceses, created out of the original Diocese of Rangoon; (2) each new diocese finalized its preparations to meet canonical requirements such as key staffing, financial arrangements, and so forth; and (3) draft canons of the new province were prepared in Burmese, based on the CCR (the canons) of the CIPBC. In 1969, the new dioceses were launched—namely, a much-reduced Diocese of Rangoon with new boundaries, the Diocese of Mandalay, and the Diocese of Hpa-an, with the Diocese of Sittwe as a missionary diocese. Other missionary dioceses would soon be created in Taungoo (dependent on Hpa-an) and Myitkyina (dependent on Mandalay) before becoming full-fledged dioceses by the 1990s. The province effectively came into being with the appointment of a bishop for each of the four original dioceses in 1969, to be formally ratified and inaugurated the following year.

The granting of autonomy was probably right and possibly inevitable, but it was not immediately clear whether autonomy would positively empower the Church or isolate it further, in tandem with the political isolationism of the state.[75] Overseas cooperation had obviously played a large part in the development of the Church over the years, but its international relations would struggle to survive the political changes of the 1960s. Becoming an autonomous province on its own certainly allowed the new

CPB to organize itself more freely, but it did not instantly change the fact that, in 1970, it was still effectively one big diocese in a country still trying to recover from the Second World War. No one could deny that the CPB came through the test of war and reached maturity as a result, but the challenges of peacetime required solutions that proved even more elusive.[76] Real development and growth in the Church, rather than mere survival, would be considered almost stagnant for around sixty years after Burmese independence, and countless issues went unaddressed for decades.[77] The CPB was also still paying the price for the mistakes of previous generations of Church leaders: "One of our weaknesses in Burma—and this applies to all denominations, though the Baptists were ahead of the rest of us—was that we had not trained nationals in administrative posts, so that when the foreign workers left, the corporate and administrative work could not be carried on as usual."[78] Archdeacon Appleton had pleaded this case back in 1946, but it was equally and starkly true twenty-five or even thirty-five years later: "Whatever else we do, the training of leaders must be our main aim. . . . The time is past when missionaries had to do everything."[79]

With the creation of the CPB, the bishop of Rangoon also became the archbishop of the province, and the Rangoon diocesan headquarters effectively became the new provincial headquarters overnight, placing an enormous additional burden on staff and resources. Archbishop Francis Ah Mya reportedly overheard a remark that "Bishopscourt office has become a Secretariat," which he chose to interpret as a favorable comment on their efficiency, rather than meaning that they were unnecessarily multiplying in terms of staff and bureaucracy.[80] But it was clearly an inadequate arrangement, as the Church's workload and membership were increasing. Growth necessitated the creation of a new Lay Department to coordinate the work of the main lay organizations already existing and organize a comprehensive Lay Leadership Training program.[81] This unwieldy concentration of offices on the diocesan premises would endure for many years before the inauguration of a dedicated provincial headquarters. Among other emerging challenges, the type of support offered by the foreign missionary societies such as SPG (now USPG) began to evolve at the world level. The transformation of the world after the colonial era had prompted huge discussion about the future role of missionary groups, resulting in them moving away from traditional models of support and toward increased mutuality and partnership-based forms of aid. This meant that the Church could no longer take for granted that cash grants would continue to arrive, to be regarded as a source of regular income to use as they determined.

"THIS LAST STEP IN THE HISTORIC TASK"

The radical series of name changes in Burma in 1989, most famously of the country's name itself but also of the major cities, towns, streets, and rivers, had its obvious effect on the Church, which was renamed the Church of the Province of Myanmar (CPM). In central Burma, meanwhile—in Mandalay and Bagan, for example, the heartland of the dominant Burman (Bamar) ethnic group—the use of "Burma" is still very widespread, and the use of "Myanmar" is seen as anomalous rather than controversial. The Church's name change has caused some consternation among militants of minority groups who resent this demonstration of central government power. In a few places, the signs outside of churches do not read "Church of the Province of Myanmar" but simply "Anglican Church" in order to circumvent the political issues but perhaps also as a subtle act of defiance. The national name change is widely regarded as a matter for the Burmans, as it ultimately concerns the name of a state to which many among the ethnic minorities do not aspire to belong. The whole state of affairs is in stark contrast to the shattered postwar vision of a peaceful, multiethnic Union of Burma.

Summary

Peacetime had begun with feelings of confidence and optimism alternating with uncertainty and apprehension, in what seemed like a brief interlude of relative calm before the storm of national independence. Hope came from a concerted effort to carve through the uncertainty with interethnic cooperation and compromise, but wartime enmities, ancient rivalries, and the assassination of the most able postwar statesman would conspire to jeopardize this. The two postwar conferences held at Panglong sought to establish a fair and effective working basis for the many ethnic communities of Burma to cooperate after independence. Though flawed, the Panglong agreements appeared to provide the best hope for peace, but these hopes suffered early derailment with the elimination or sidelining of the most likely and most balanced future leaders. The proposed models of union and unity for an independent Burma began to sound more and more like the suppression or elimination of ethnic, cultural, and religious differences. The fear of this outcome would encourage a strengthening of those ethnic identities and a surge in militancy.

For Christians of various denominations, however, this was also a period of greater cooperation, building on links forged during the war.

THE ANGLICAN CHURCH IN BURMA

They shared resources and opened the door to ecumenical work, and this allowed more benevolent attitudes toward Buddhism to develop. In contrast to earlier entrenched positions in the Church, Anglican leaders had begun to posit that a deeper understanding of Buddhism could surely be of benefit to a Christian Church rooted in the soil of a Buddhist culture. It was a viewpoint that sought to see the practical, secular ends of all religions as harmonious, and in terms of practical aims there was much work to be done in the medical, social, and educational spheres. For the Anglican Church internally, this era of openness and cooperation also meant the promotion of local native clergy to senior positions in the Church. The Church did well to try to evolve in its thinking, because this would be an age of changing relationships among institutions, religions, and international organizations. The Churches in the region, previously relating to one another on the basis of common participation in the colonial family or the CIPBC, began to discover that they had little else in common after all, and this prompted an exploration of their own particular identities. But do processes like this lead to autonomy or isolation?

Independence had come hand in hand with ethnic division and armed conflict, which led the way to a succession of authoritarian rulers. The Church was almost forced to go underground once more, but this time its leaders were better prepared. By the 1960s, a wide range of social initiatives and pastoral works were established when a new dictatorship clamped down and banned religious instruction, nationalized religious schools and hospitals, declared Buddhism the state religion, and vowed to expel all foreigners, including missionaries. With all British clergy expelled by 1966, the Church was left completely in local hands. Hurried preparations were made for the final breakup of the old Church of India, Pakistan, Burma and Ceylon (CIPBC) and the inauguration of the Church of the Province of Burma (CPB). It is perhaps ironic that the Anglican Church, which had been brought to Burma by the British, was suddenly left alone among the ashes of the hopes of independence. Britain had pledged that the minority peoples of Burma would never be forced to accept a constitution or a settlement that did not suit them, and all sides had agreed that the goal was to find a form of union that would be freely agreed to and mutually supported.[82] At the time of writing, that free consensus has yet to be reached, and the British guarantee has not aged well either. But of all the colonial-era institutions and organizations that had so much at stake at Panglong, the Anglican Church—transformed but intact—has been one of the few to survive.

Chapter 7

"A LAND AND PEOPLE OF PROMISE"

Intercultural Theology in a Southeast Asian Context

The two main Protestant colonizing nations in Southeast Asia, the Dutch and the British, went into the region as a commercial capitalist venture. As such, the management of the colonies was at first entrusted to private companies, who raised their own private armies and also relied on the armed forces of their respective monarchs for protection. Both Dutch and British colonists took Protestant religious representatives with them, but the authorities generally discouraged missionary activity because of its potential for interfering with trade relations—for example, with the devout Muslims of modern-day Malaysia. In the case of both the Dutch and the British, it was only after these private companies were replaced by a proper colonial government apparatus that Protestant missionaries began to make progress in the colonies of Southeast Asia.[1] Once the Churches had achieved a degree of freedom to operate, though still within certain limitations, they did not abuse that freedom, generally speaking. The spread of Christianity in Southeast Asia never depended on an organized campaign of coercion, and although there were instances of coercion, these were usually the initiative of particularly zealous individual colonial officials rather than a matter of Church or government policy.[2]

As peaceful and nonideological as its introduction may have been intended, Christianity in these parts of Southeast Asia would remain culturally wedded to the capitalist Protestant worldview by virtue of its origins. Across the region, Christianity would often be seen as imbued with a "thick

Western accent" or dismissed as a pseudo-religious philosophy imported from the West.[3] Church life in Burma, for example, would be unequivocally Western oriented for much of its history, including in its theological expressions, its forms of worship, its church polity and organization, and its approach to doing missionary work. Even after many decades, when, for various reasons, foreign missionaries began to depart from Burma, the native Christians would be seen as products of a missionary compound mentality that looked to the West alone for its model of life.[4] Despite this picture of the Church as an incongruous and insensitive intrusion on local culture, it must be acknowledged that the history of the development of Christianity in Southeast Asia suggests that it was widely welcomed. Christianity showed consistent growth during the later colonial era but also after the end of colonialism; conversions tended to occur in uneven clusters among different peoples in different areas rather than in sweeping uniform patterns or waves of conversions, and active involvement in Church life and the development of native community leadership tended to occur organically and spontaneously (albeit gradually) from an early stage. All of these facts point toward the conclusion that Christianity was adopted enthusiastically—though certainly slowly and in piecemeal fashion; there was rarely a "boom" of conversions—rather than through some form of obligation.[5]

Two hundred years ago, enthusiasm for doing tough missionary work, spreading the Gospel around the globe, and trying to emulate the Roman Catholic missionaries tended to come from the more orthodox or High Church Anglican tradition. Many Anglicans felt that the historical moment was ripe to reclaim certain aspects of their Catholic heritage, such as the concept of the Universal Church, the monastic and missionary lifestyles, and an orthodox appreciation of church order and ecclesiology. An ordered society, both within the Church and in the world at large, was the ideal of High Church Anglicans. They revered the bishop and the monarch and wished to see Western Christian civilization extended throughout the world. This was at the heart of their understanding of colonial expansion, and it was a perception that sat in harmony with the political understanding of colonialism as well.[6] "Accompanying [their] high ecclesiology," as Daniel O'Connor wrote in his history of the SPG, "was a political theology which saw Church and state intimately associated, theologically and practically, two aspects of a single national community."[7] This close association of Church and state was a reflection of the well-established societal form then prevalent in continental Europe. In the Catholic sphere of influence, it was referred to as Christendom, in which society was seen as being governed by two universal and parallel powers: the secular and the spiritual, or "the Pope and the Prince."[8] The espousal of this political theology clearly presented problems and contradictions for Anglican missionaries in the colonies, including the fact that they obviously did not have universal powers even by proxy—they could only work within the confines of the state's colonial and imperial domains and not beyond them.[9] While and wherever the missionaries did work, however, they were usually welcomed and enabled by individual colonial administrators, who were happy to see spiritual and temporal powers coalescing in the best traditions of Christendom.

Education as a Missionary Tool

As well as receiving faculties and facilities to operate, therefore, it is clear that Christian missions in Southeast Asia were enabled and encouraged by a sociopolitical order in which missionaries could move with confidence and security. They were able to implement a range of socially useful medical, welfare, and especially educational projects.[10] Their works may be counted among the most positive by-products of colonialism, and the benefits they brought were enduring and far-reaching.[11] In Burma, the initially very small Anglican presence achieved a certain amount of stability, which, with the expansion of the colonial administration, encouraged and facilitated the arrival of other Protestants, such as the Presbyterians in 1852, mainly to cater to the significant contingents of Scots and Irish working in the colonial bureaucracy. The presence of the well-established American Baptists was eventually followed by the arrival of the American Methodists in 1879, and in 1887, after the colonial annexation of the whole of Burma, British Methodists also arrived to tend to significant expatriate flocks. Protestant missionaries of all types viewed education as a way of expanding Christian influence, though it was not overtly part of a strategy to push for conversions. This would not only have been unrealistic and controversial but could also have provoked a hostile response. The aim instead was to create the conditions for possible conversions in the medium or long term by making the presence of Christianity acceptable, agreeable, and ultimately attractive. Anglican educators acknowledged what was framed as the government's supreme duty of absolute impartiality, not showing favor to any one religious body, but they were also confident that their educational provision was objectively the best. They accurately foresaw both a strong public following for their schools and a degree of preferential treatment from the administration.[12]

THE ANGLICAN CHURCH IN BURMA

The poor state of education in most of Southeast Asia meant that the Church was indeed very welcome to get involved, as colonial governments in general were not prepared to invest money and resources in the basic education of native children for its own sake. The Anglicans, Methodists, and Presbyterians, in addition to the already prolific Roman Catholics, were particularly zealous in establishing comprehensive networks of educational institutions, often spanning the whole spectrum from preschool to university or seminary, from the most basic one-room village schools to well-equipped high schools and vocational colleges in major cities. In the countries of Southeast Asia under British control, such as Burma, mission schools gained fame for providing a modern English-language education that prepared the student for a potential career in government service, the professions, or commerce, instilling in them an unmistakably Western and European philosophical outlook. Alumni of Anglican institutions who went on to achieve prominent positions in society would often further enhance the fortunes and reputations of such schools through direct and indirect means.[13] Schools also provided the most obvious and visible meeting point for the different ethnic groups; the first bishop of Rangoon listed Burmans, Karens, Shans, Siamese (Thais), Talaings, and Eurasians among the strictly local scholars at St. John's College, as well as Muslims, Tamils, and Bengalis originating from India.[14] Many of these young men would later go out to every part of the country as clerks and officers of almost every government department.[15] There can be little doubt that in promoting multiethnic integration and facilitating access to employment and positions of leadership, the Anglican Church's education work helped to pave the way for a fairer society and ultimately the end of colonialism.

Emerging Christian Identities in Southeast Asia

When Westerners contemplate Christianity in Asia, they might expect to find the most striking differences in the external features. They may assume that elements such as worship style, music, dress, gestures, greetings, and so forth will display distinctive local characteristics. At the same time, they might think that the basic ideas and philosophical concepts underpinning the Christian religion are bound to be fundamentally the same everywhere; otherwise, it would be difficult to call it the same religion. In reality, the reverse of all this is more likely to be true, because having a universally similar external appearance, especially with the help of Western liturgical books to follow, is much easier than assimilating content that may be socially, culturally, and philosophically alien. Colonial-era Christianity, a distinctly Western religion with its own social and cultural concepts and language, did not arrive in Southeast Asia to find a blank slate; it encountered a range of ancient, preexisting, and deep-rooted social and cultural concepts and language relating to spirituality and supernatural belief. Proponents of Christianity gradually accepted that it was hopeless to try to uproot local philosophies and religions, because even with the roots gone, the very soil of Southeast Asia was steeped in these local ways and worldviews.[16]

It is regarded as neither inappropriate nor unusual in Southeast Asia to believe and practice elements of more than one religion in conjunction with one another, especially when there is no explicit contradiction; the Christian scriptures, strictly speaking, do not address reincarnation, for example, and many Confucian and Buddhist principles sit well enough alongside Christian ones or even mirror them.[17] There may also have been elements of the European missionaries' approach to teaching religion that directly reflected colonialist attitudes and values rather than Christian ones, and that local converts explicitly wanted to discard. Converts could take ownership of the religion in their own way, because just as the Christian scriptures do not rule out reincarnation or honoring the ancestors, they also do not contain an explicit justification for colonialism or a condemnation of national liberation movements. The churches with a strong Eurocentric model, such as the Anglicans and Roman Catholics, were sometimes seen as too colonial and domineering in their outlook and intolerant of local expressions of faith. In some cases, they were perceived as seeking to quash local characteristics and push for uniformity, which actually meant *con*formity with the European ways, even in matters unrelated to faith itself.

The Christian churches in Southeast Asia all had to address similar conflicts, though for Protestant denominations that customarily used, on principle, the vernacular languages of wherever they were present, incorporating local characteristics was inevitable. The Roman Catholics, with their universal use of Latin in worship, were unique in having a policy expressly opposed to diversity and not open to more than the most minimal adaptation. However, at least some members within each of the colonial churches agitated for a native clergy, in anticipation of the European missionaries' departure.[18] Younger European clergy themselves would eventually begin to question the logic of importing external forms of their religion that were unthinking copies of Western things while expecting local Christian converts to jettison their traditions.[19] Archdeacon George Appleton longed

THE ANGLICAN CHURCH IN BURMA

to see Anglican churches modeled on Buddhist pagodas, and he argued for sweeping away what he described as the Anglican Church's "monstrous collection of pulpits, pews, faldstools, alms bags, and discarded bells from worn-out steamers!"[20]

Local Beliefs: Competition, Conflict, Cohabitation?

Christian organizations in Southeast Asia, such as the Anglican Church in Burma, faced certain challenges inherent to being largely made up of recent converts. Among these challenges was the need to deal with the hangovers of previously held beliefs and superstitions, which could be extremely deeply rooted, resilient, and influential. Most of the people in Burma followed a rural way of life that depended on nature and the elements; life revolved around fishing, planting, harvesting, hunting, and raising livestock, and having recourse to supernatural powers to sustain and protect these endeavors was ingrained. *Nat* (spirit) worship or animism pervaded the daily life of much of the population, along with ancestor worship, venerating deceased forefathers and actually involving them in family affairs and decision-making. It was (and still is) common to consult astrologers: when a child is born, a horoscope chart of the child's birth is made and becomes an important personal document, by which the individual's future is planned and predicted. Many Burmese people treasure their personal horoscope document, and they take it with them when they go back to the astrologer for consultation, as and when required.[21] By the time the main Christian churches were properly established in Burma, the country's cultural landscape was made up of a full range of indigenous, pre-Buddhist, Buddhist, and even some post-Buddhist elements.

Nat worship, for example, predated Buddhism in Burma, and it seized the imagination of many early Christian missionaries.[22] By the time the Anglicans arrived, Buddhism was unquestionably the prevailing religion of the country, but *nat* worship did not appear to be any less popular as a result of the spread of Buddhism, and the two belief systems peacefully coexisted. Anglican missionaries, by contrast, approached spirit worship with near-zero tolerance, at least until the early twentieth century. Rev. Alexander Salmon, one of the most successful missionaries in the last two decades of the nineteenth century, tried to explain some of the complex issues involved in converting a local person: "The people are not, as yet, very far removed from heathenism, and many superstitions still abound. The

"A LAND AND PEOPLE OF PROMISE"

world, the flesh, and the devil still have a very powerful hold over even the best of them," Salmon wrote. "[Will] they give up all their ancient superstitious ceremonies, incantations, charms, etc. etc. and destroy all the visible emblems thereof? Some wish to delay and do these things at a more convenient season—others can hardly bear the idea of giving up their cherished modes of propitiating evil spirits."[23] But for the conversion to be accepted, the destruction of charms and emblems had to be systematic; "the [local] Christians with us go round to each house and bring out for destruction all the emblems of their old superstitions; chicken bones, jawbones of pigs, withered branches of trees, leaves, etc."[24] There were also those who, while showing a genuine interest in Christianity, actually made a living out of crafting and peddling charms and paraphernalia for animist rituals, making it difficult for the missionaries to know what to do and what to advise. A keen convert was highly prized, but this victory could be soured by making it conditional on losing a livelihood.[25]

The old beliefs remained very influential. Christian converts would sometimes completely lapse, even after, in the more dramatic cases, the old superstitions had been publicly denounced.[26] Aside from such extremes, and even after decades of missionary work, it seemed clear that some Burmese converts were only capable of a casual attachment to Christianity, but as the twentieth century dawned this was no longer considered the worst possible scenario.[27] The fact that some local converts continued to cling to old beliefs was no longer seen as a particular impediment to advancing the Church's overall mission, and these fears gave way to a greater acceptance of a more pluralistic reality.[28] Archdeacon George Appleton was part of a new generation of missionaries, born around the turn of the century, who had grown up with the sobering and disillusioning experience of the First World War, and several missionaries of that generation had actually served in that war. For one thing, these newcomers were more likely to see themselves in the context of their role in *Burma* rather than as part of the *empire*, and this led to a more generous reassessment and reevaluation of "this land and people of promise" called Burma.[29] In contrast to earlier, negative assessments of Burma, the new generation saw it as a land of beauty, of plenty, of ample hospitality, and of graciousness. They were also less scandalized than their predecessors to see Christianity cohabiting side by side with local religions and traditions. "In the past we have set Christians and Buddhists as rivals," Appleton wrote, "[but] Buddhism is a noble way of life, with a founder whom all men may rightly revere, and a standard of ethics which approaches closely to the Christian."[30]

THE ANGLICAN CHURCH IN BURMA

From the middle of the twentieth century onward, missionaries began to realize that the fundamental challenge facing them had changed; mission was no longer a question of winning converts for this religion or that religion but of promoting the idea of the religious life itself to an increasingly doubtful modern world. If greater "cross-fertilization" between belief systems was what was needed in order for religion itself to survive, then this would have to be accepted. This realization, coming first from the practical mission field and feeding back to the world of theory, soon took shape as a tendency within intercultural theology to recognize and accept "symbioses" of religions. A symbiosis of religions could be seen as the lesser of other evils such as syncretism (a cocktail of religions in which each one loses its specific flavor) or a synthesis of religions (a totally new creation emerging from a mix in which the component religions lose their specificity).[31] And even these could be seen as preferable to total secularization and what some saw as the impending collapse of religion. By 1945, the first generations of the twentieth century seemed to have comprehensively lost not only their innocence but also their faith in many of the institutions and ideas that had previously seemed to underpin civilized existence. In the modern world, nothing could be taken for granted, as, increasingly, George Appleton observed, the struggle was not between individual religions but between the spiritual outlook on life and the secularist one.[32]

Accepting the cohabitation of different and well-established local beliefs alongside Christianity would unwittingly create a theological space in which to formulate a challenge to the legitimacy of this "Western" faith's presence in Southeast Asia. After all, could colonial Christianity itself not be seen as a strategic fusion of Church and state ideals, or a political theology used for advancing Western interests? In recent decades, the fact that Christianity in the region did eventually demonstrate a capacity for bonding with other belief systems has made it easier to accommodate newer expressions of Christian worship imported from other parts of the world, such as Pentecostalism. Some particularly strong historical attachments to animism (e.g., among the Chin people of Burma) may account for their tendency to prefer Pentecostal styles of worship. Even some more mainstream churches, in certain parts of Burma, have put considerable emphasis on praying for miracles, performing healing rituals, banishing evil spirits, chanting, trances, speaking in tongues, and other supernatural manifestations.[33] However, it should not be assumed that these locally adapted hybrid forms of Christian worship make the religion more acceptable to Christianity's detractors; in fact, these more eccentric and theatrical Christian rituals are more likely to attract attention, antagonize non-Christian neighbors, and thus further exacerbate discord, as well as appearing to justify all the suspicion and distrust of Christians.[34] As a generalization, progressive and liberationist-leaning theologians in Asia have approved of the fusion of Christian and local beliefs, as even some early European missionaries did, refusing to see the religions of the region as competitors but see them instead as cohabiters.[35] But for the detractors of Christian and Western thought in Southeast Asia, this shift would also effectively signal Christianity giving up its claim to supremacy among religions.

Third World Theology and Liberation Theology

By the 1970s, the postcolonial experience had begun to produce a theology that could rightly be called a third world theology, often seen as sitting alongside liberation theology, both chronologically and in spirit. "Third world" in this case does not indicate negative connotations such as being third rate or in third place after the capitalist "free world" and the old Soviet bloc. Especially in Francophone regions, "third world" recalls the original French meaning of "tiers monde," indicating an alternative world to be aspired to, or a third way of doing things. This also invokes the language of the Greek Fathers of the Church when they applied the word *triton* (*genos*) to Christianity; this was in order to emphasize that their religion was neither a Judaic nor a Hellenistic religion but a tertium quid, a "third something."[36] Christians in Southeast Asia were able to embrace this thinking, having experienced one way (namely, colonial domination and military occupation) and then facing the prospect of a second way (namely, becoming a satellite state of one or another of the superpowers, or an outpost of economic imperialism). Southeast Asia had experienced the one and rejected the other, so a third way, politically and ideologically, meant exploring a potential form in which to be truly self-determining. This defiance also explains Asian liberation theology's reluctance to embrace Marxism too completely; the emerging Asian nations did not want to repel the Western colonizers only to fall under the spell of Moscow instead.

The decolonized nations of the 1950s and 1960s, whether in Africa, Asia, or the Mediterranean, similarly aimed to resist the threat of becoming mere satellites of one world bloc or the other, which would risk being just another form of colonialism. The Asian third world had shown its potential and might since the Second World War. Indonesia had won its

THE ANGLICAN CHURCH IN BURMA

independence from the Dutch, and Malaysia had concluded a protracted and painful separation from Britain. Vietnam in this period defeated *two* world powers, first France and then America. China's steady rise to the level of economic, political, and military giant also gave a boost to Asian consciousness. As emboldened Asians gained confidence, they rejected the idea of "being developed" from without, and they were able to see the big world powers critically, often as sources of domination rather than sources of development.[37] Burma made a comparatively peaceful break from the British Empire, asserting its own commitment to a third way by other means, such as declining to join the British Commonwealth, refusing to keep the British monarch as a figurehead, gradually rejecting all things British, and eventually expelling supposedly undesirable categories of persons seen as being linked to the colonial past, including the Christian missionaries. Furthermore, although Burma reached the end of the colonial period in a state of peace, there were so many unresolved internal problems that decades rather than years of conflict would ensue. Burma's defiant assertions of autonomy frequently went to the point of isolationism, still without addressing the very real and urgent calls for autonomy from its own constituent peoples. Diversity and independence are crucial matters for all of Burma, but they are unresolved ones, and their quest for an elusive third way remains frustrated.[38]

The idea of navigating a corresponding alternative theological route between competing global influences was not new for postcolonial Asian Christians. They had already managed to reconcile the Christian and Southeast Asian worldviews and were therefore able to look beyond any apparent contradictions to find a harmonious third way. Though the term "third world" need not be seen in a negative light, it is evident that for multiple historical reasons the third world has indeed been left in third place in many senses; it has been distinguished both by its mass poverty and for its being exploited by the other two worlds. The so-called third world is also, however, numerically superior, including, crucially, in numbers of Christians, which has prompted some to refer to it as "the two-thirds world."[39] In the wider Christian world, a series of experiences turned the Churches' attention, and their theologies, toward the poor and oppressed. The worker-priest movement in Europe after the Second World War, the modernization of the Roman Catholic Church at the Second Vatican Council, significant advances in ecumenical theory and dialogue, and the empowerment of local Church leadership in Latin America, Africa, and Asia all combined to revitalize debate on the worldwide Church's social mission.[40]

"A LAND AND PEOPLE OF PROMISE"

Specific local experiences, such as a succession of brutal dictatorships across Latin America and the apartheid system in South Africa, transformed the worldview and also the theology of a generation of clergy. Among the most famous of these would be a number of bishops: the Roman Catholics Hélder Câmara and Oscar Romero in Latin America, and the Anglicans Trevor Huddleston, CR, and Desmond Tutu in South Africa. As well as liberation theology and third world theology, and for starkly similar reasons, this historical period saw the emergence of black theology. For Christians in Asia, it was a subtly different theology of liberation that took shape, less pointedly inspired by (or opposed to) specific political philosophies but marked by its opposition to the retreating colonial powers and Western interference, and by its wariness of new, emerging forms of imperialism. But throughout all of this, there has been a broader ongoing struggle for a Southeast Asian Christian theology to gain acceptance. Asian liberation theology continued to be less concerned with Marxism than its counterpart in Latin American countries, which had experienced their own anti-colonial struggles many decades earlier. Even so, the opposition to unbridled capitalism (or Mammon-worship) professed by socialist governments often led to Asians having greater sympathy for the communist worldview than for the capitalist one.[41]

Perceptions of the Church in Burma

The Burmese people have a very long history of plurality of religions, whether it suits them all or not.[42] In terms of the variety of religions being practiced, Burma is just about as diverse today as it was one hundred or two hundred years ago, though this does not imply that the freedom to practice a religion is in any way guaranteed. Buddhism, the longtime dominant religion, is believed to be practiced by 89 or 90 percent, Christianity by about 6 or 7 percent (some estimates suggest a higher figure), Islam by 3.5 to 4 percent, and Hinduism by 1 percent of the population. Some fairly long-established communities, such as the Jews, are now reduced to a tiny handful. The spread of Christianity is not geographically even, and it remains an alien religion in large tracts of the central plains. Historically, the appeal of Buddhism has been connected to social mobility, status, and opportunity, because the "authentic" Burman (Bamar) people and their kings were Buddhists, and for much of history non-Buddhists, though often tolerated to varying degrees, have been considered second-class citizens or worse.[43]

Christianity in Burma has suffered from being portrayed as the religion of the invaders, a political cult used for justifying the Western socioeconomic worldview and subjugating the "ignorant heathens."[44] Some Burmese people deeply resented what they saw as the attempted imposition of Christianity as part of the "three M's"—merchants, missionaries, military—of colonialism.[45] But as colonialism has now almost completely faded from public consciousness, recent years have seen attempts to expose Christianity for just being intrinsically bad; it can be portrayed and perceived as an exclusivist, selfish, insidious, and intolerant sect, responsible for encouraging the use of "inappropriate Western clothing" by Burmese teenagers.[46] Wariness of Christianity runs deep in the Burma military establishment, for example, where conspiracy theories portray ethnic minority Christians as sleeper agents for the West. The British, it is said, knowing that they would eventually have to abandon Burma, converted the minorities to Christianity in order to maintain Western influence. The growth of Christianity in Burma, therefore, means the growth of Western influence.[47] This may strike us as a somewhat naive and sensationalist (not to mention historically problematic) analysis, but it is not the only evidence of Christians still being viewed as puppets of the West.[48] In recent years, even though the Christian churches are now fully under local leadership, suspicions are exacerbated when Christians develop good links with worldwide religious organizations, stoking fears of an international Western Christian conspiracy.[49] Within the Christian community of Burma itself, however, more constructive and critical debates are taking place. The leading institution of theological education, the Myanmar Institute of Theology (MIT), has a track record of strong ethnic minority representation, including Chins— notably the president, Rev. Dr. Samuel Ngun Ling, and Rev. Dr. Cung Lian Hup. These theologians represent modern pluralist and multiculturalist approaches, recognizing the importance of mission as the bedrock of Christianity in Burma but pointing out that without ongoing dialogue, mission has "often taken the form of militancy and cultural imperialism."[50] Ngun Ling promotes the important contemporary discourse of still working to decolonize Christianity in modern Myanmar.[51]

Anglicanism in Burma has suffered more than other denominations from associations with all forms of colonialism, since even its everyday local name identifies it as "the English Church." When Anglicanism arrived in Burma, there was little expectation that one day the theology, worship, and organization of the Church would be completely driven by locals, and in any case the main missionary organizations tended to bring a clear

"A LAND AND PEOPLE OF PROMISE"

ecclesial identity with them. In the heyday of the Church, the Society for the Propagation of the Gospel in Foreign Parts (SPG) brought a distinct Anglo-Catholic character and tradition with them, which endures today in the many churches they founded in Burma. Their Anglo-Catholicism manifested itself as a strong focus on liturgy and sacraments, especially Holy Communion, which for some missionaries seemed to be the beginning and the end of what the Church could offer.[52] Other needs, such as the formation of catechists, the development of local leadership, and general Christian education for adults, sometimes fell by the wayside, because of the sacramental emphasis inspired by the Catholic theological outlook. This was especially so in rural areas, where clergy assiduously conducted Holy Communion services every Sunday and then departed, traveling in rotation to the clusters of Christians under their care, with as many as twenty villages in one parish. They would effectively touch base to deliver the all-important sacraments and then swiftly move on. Many of the difficulties of the modern Church are seen as having roots in the failure to lay comprehensive foundations and nurture a culture of more holistic participation, especially in those "sacraments only" rural chapels of many decades ago.[53]

The Church's growing tendency toward self-sufficiency became an obligation rather than a choice when the government banned foreign religious missions from operating in the country in the mid-1960s, a ban that also prohibited individual foreign religious representatives from settling in the country. At the same time that the foreign missionaries were expelled, private schools and hospitals, which were mostly affiliated with Christian organizations, were nationalized, meaning that foreign Christians involved in those occupations had to leave as well. Even today, the government continues to prohibit *any* Christian clergy from proselytizing in certain designated areas, with no explanations offered. Of course, practically all Christian groups in Burma have at some point invited foreign clergy, consultants, health and social workers, conference speakers, and guest lecturers to visit, though they enter the country legitimately as tourists. They have been cautious to ensure that the government does not perceive their activities as proselytizing, and visitors' activities tend to be limited to having contact with those who are already official members of churches, not potential converts.[54] A number of charity organizations working in Burma (e.g., in education and sanitation) have religious affiliations or inspiration, and their activities are similarly restricted. These restrictions are compounded by a generally unreliable and underdeveloped culture of communications and associated technology, meaning that the self-sufficiency of the Anglican

Church continues to be dictated by circumstances as well as being something that is desired.

Global South, Global Anglican Future

Asian theology and Asian ecclesial visions are nowadays eager for independence from the old imported models. Within the Anglican Communion, the transition to a postcolonial world was apparently fairly smooth, but it was widely assumed that the same old binding ties between home and abroad would simply become longer, and that the former colonial churches would remain on the same old leash that led to Canterbury. The strength of these churches' aspirations for self-determination was unforeseen. Their commitment to doing theological discernment for themselves while nourishing an authentic Anglican identity has found expression in recent years with GAFCON. The quinquennial Global Anglican Future Conference, which started in 2008, is widely seen as an alternative international conference and gathering of conservative Anglican bishops opposed to the direction taken by the official Anglican Communion on several issues. GAFCON's supporters, however, may dispute the word "alternative," pointing out that it is not *they* who have deviated from the biblical foundations of the Church.[55] Far from being a fringe group, GAFCON bishops represent tens of millions of Anglicans, with a heavy focus on the global south. It would seem that many of the real long-term questions arising from the postcolonial transition were not quietly addressed after all, but quietly postponed.

Archbishop Stephen Than Myint Oo, Burma's current archbishop, attended GAFCON 3 in 2018 and had previously participated in the enthronement of Archbishop Foley Beach for the Anglican Church in North America (ACNA), the alternative non-Anglican-Communion body that adheres to GAFCON and enjoys good relations with Burma. Burma's Anglican leaders have also participated in other international conservative gatherings, such as "Global South" (which unites no fewer than twenty-five of the forty provinces of the Anglican Communion in conservative-oriented discussion) and the Fellowship of Confessing Anglicans (FCA). Archbishop Than Myint Oo and the other bishops' stances appear to faithfully represent the feelings of other Anglicans in Burma, whose outlook accords with the orthodox Anglican vision. This orthodox vision corresponds, culturally, to several aspects of wider Southeast Asian society—opposition to women's ordination, for example, is a common, if not universal or mandatory, stance

"A LAND AND PEOPLE OF PROMISE"

among GAFCON and Global South adherents—and this also conforms to the traditional Anglican understanding that was first planted in Burma. GAFCON adherents do not actively encourage the use of not-always-helpful terms like "conservative" or "traditionalist," preferring the definition "orthodox," while appreciating the need to explain "orthodox Anglicanism" to the untrained ear.[56] It is actually a term with a long history in Asian Anglicanism. Three hundred years ago, "orthodox" was used within Anglicanism to indicate the High Church tradition—church order, apostolic succession, liturgy, and sacraments—of which missionary organizations such as the SPG and SPCK were flagships.[57] Given the huge influence of these organizations in Southeast Asia, it is little wonder that modern Anglican orthodoxy finds an attentive audience there, where the practice of Christianity has not been subject to the gradual reforming effect of the rolling social and cultural revolutions of Western societies.

GAFCON describes itself as springing from the search for an agreeable solution to the human sexuality controversy in the Anglican Communion, though it is usually stressed that the issues are wider than just homosexual clergy and same-sex unions.[58] The fundamental problem is seen as being the challenge to the authority of the Bible in all matters of faith and practice, both within the Church community and in personal morality.[59] These concerns reached international attention in 2003 when Gene Robinson, a practicing homosexual, was consecrated as an Anglican bishop in the United States. The case is seen as a watershed moment, or as symbolic of the beginning of a headlong decline, according to different points of view. Deep rifts were opened up among the Anglican Churches regarding, among other things, the Church's sources of authority, the interpretation of scripture, theological pluralism, and postcolonial power relationships, as Anglicans turned this way and that looking for consistent answers. The Anglican Communion, GAFCON contends, has yet to fully appreciate the reality of postcolonial Anglicanism, not just in terms of the continued existence of national Churches in the non-Western world but in terms of flourishing Churches on several continents with increasing memberships and the power that attends such growth.[60]

GAFCON struck at the heart of the postcolonial Church dilemma that may be summed up as "who should be listening to whom, and who should be taking direction from whom?" All of the long-established global Christian churches, in fact, are seeing their memberships capsize in favor of the global south, where the churches are bursting at the seams instead of standing empty. But the sources of administrative authority, the nerve centers, and the power bases are still obstinately entrenched in the north of the world, in the ancestral homes of colonial Christendom, even though the historical churches are almost minority religions bereft of members, in their original homelands at least. Anglicanism, it is argued, harbors elements that are vigorously resisting the need to adjust and relate to the new realities, while other elements embrace change.[61] It may be seen as ironic that the socially and politically progressive forces within Anglicanism could be seen as resistant to change in this case, while the conservatives are all focused on shifting power bases and radical institutional reform. GAFCON has predictably harvested accusations of being openly schismatic, deliberately divisive, and seeking to create a parallel church, but the truth is that the questions it raises are not purely Anglican problems.[62] With the issues at stake reaching well beyond the frontiers of the Anglican Communion, and with real ramifications for the worldwide Christian community, the Anglican Church in Burma is positioned on several of the active fault lines of global Christianity's future.

These fault lines are not always obvious or clear. As mentioned earlier, GAFCON bishops do not all hold the same view on the issue of women's ordination, and the body will not condemn it. This means that there is also a considerable body of traditionalist, conservative, or orthodox Anglican groups, strongly opposed to women's ordination, who in conscience feel that they must sit outside of both the official Anglican Communion and GAFCON as well. They are usually called Continuing Anglicans. The clergy in Burma are largely sympathetic to the Continuing Anglicans' objections to women's ordination and their consequent rejection of GAFCON's ACNA, which does tolerate women's ordination. But the clergy in Burma are proud to be associated with GAFCON and are prepared to accept that the archbishop of Canterbury's role as head of the Anglican Communion is open to question. With a few exceptions, strictly Continuing Anglican groups have no institutional contact with the Anglican Churches of the global south, though some may sometimes attempt to launch their own missionary ventures there. There are no such initiatives in Burma. In Burma, Church members are often curious about other Anglican Churches in the region, keen to know about their worship and churchmanship. Orthodox Anglicans are well represented in Burma, Malaysia, and to some extent Thailand, but it would be a mistake to imagine that orthodox sympathies have gripped Asia's Anglicans entirely. There appears to be some skepticism among Burma's Anglicans about the heavy Pentecostal influence they have heard about in the Church in Singapore. The Anglican Deanery of Nepal is

"A LAND AND PEOPLE OF PROMISE"

also considered to be distinctly Pentecostal, while the neighboring Church of North India (CNI), anecdotally, seems to have an unfortunate reputation for being both unorthodox and allegedly corrupt.

The Anglican Church in Burma, for its part, has been able to avoid the innovation of women's ordination, at least in practice. In earlier times, as we have seen, the Church in Burma was pioneering in its range of roles and opportunities for women. The Woman's Mission Association was active as early as 1868, and the Church strongly encouraged the YWCA to come and work in Burma. Women were always among the most distinguished and influential educators in Burma, including Mary Chapman, the first principal of the school for the deaf and dumb, which opened in 1919. Women began to play a part in training future clergy, and in later years female teachers and social workers were sent to England for further study and to gain pastoral experience. The refusal to accept ordained roles for women in the Church would not therefore seem, historically, to be a matter of denying women pastoral responsibility or even leadership roles. The avoidance of the ordination issue is more likely to stem from a combination of several factors, including the powerful influence of Burman culture and specifically Burman Buddhist religious customs, which prohibit women from setting foot on sacred sites or from entering monkhood. It is argued that both religion and culture have marginalized Burmese women, limiting their standing and dignity both in society and in religious spheres. In recent decades, some Christians in Burma may also have been influenced by conservative views on women and society promoted by well-resourced international Protestant organizations.[63] As in all parts of the worldwide Church, Anglicans have generally turned to the Christian scriptures for guidance on the topic of women's ordination.

Within the Anglican Church, a traditional interpretation of scripture survives that has not necessarily evolved or dialogued with modern progressive scholarship. Other elements of the colonial inheritance have inevitably survived into the modern Church, not least the widespread use of the often gender-specific English language, and this may be responsible for some vestigial skepticism about the recognition of women in the highest levels of leadership and ordination. Broader cultural influence, but also regional cultural sensitivity, may also contribute to an explanation of the status of women, as the Churches in Pakistan and Bangladesh also refrain from ordaining women out of respect for the Muslim majority, it is understood.[64] A more simple explanation put forward is that the independent Church in Burma is still relatively young and quite slow to change; it may also be pointed out that the issue is not a done deal, and, in fact, the possibility of ordaining women was approved in theory as far back as 1973.[65] It is worth noting that in Karen society, from which so many Anglicans in Burma hail, men and women traditionally have equal landowning rights, equal property and inheritance rights, and they maintain strong ties to the maternal family.[66]

Christianity and Buddhism in Burma

As appropriate and important as it is to discuss Christian relations with the largest religious community in Burma, it is necessary to reaffirm that the version of Buddhism that has most impacted the Christian population is actually a political instrumentalization of Buddhism. Instead of the hoped-for democratic union of the peoples of Burma, the dawn of independence in 1948 gave way to a centralized authoritarian nation driven by militant Burman Buddhist nationalism, to which non-Burman ethnic groups could feel little attachment.[67] Members of the largely Christian ethnic groups were uneasy from the start, fearing a stark choice between amalgamation and isolation.[68] The installation of the majority Burman nationalist dictatorship was sealed by the proclamation of Buddhism as the official state religion, a move widely regarded as both unnecessary and a political blunder, even by regime insiders.[69] Buddhists' domination in politics, in the professions, in the military, in popular culture, and in sheer population numbers was a plain fact, and it did not really need to be asserted by law. The Burma Christian Council (BCC), composed of Anglicans, Baptists, and Methodists, took a firm stance against this adoption of Buddhism as the state religion, while the Roman Catholic Church had pledged not to interfere.

Considering the state's vindictive restrictions and active discrimination toward other faiths, its threats and inducements to convert to Buddhism, and its campaigns of state terrorism against non-Buddhist minorities, it is clear that the supposed exaltation of Buddhism has nothing to do with the religion itself. The ideology behind decades of horrific torture, punitive rape, material destruction, burning people to death, and mass murder cannot by any definition be considered Buddhism but rather a politically expedient perversion of Buddhism.[70] Recent research demonstrates that the successive military regimes since 1962 have used Buddhism as a political weapon, with the junta's generals making a public show of attending Buddhist festivals, visiting monasteries, giving alms, and building pagodas in order to craft an image of being faithful Buddhists. They have also gone so far as to plant military intelligence operatives inside the Buddhist religious leadership in order to watch for signs of dissidence and to ensure that the religious authorities continue to accept the regime's superficial piety as a credible legitimization of their rule.[71]

This opportunistic use of Buddhism is mirrored in the superficial, politicized understanding of Christianity touted in some Burmese circles, which holds that being a Christian and being a Westerner, or a Western-oriented stooge and traitor, are the same thing. Christianity is presented as being inseparable from both old and new forms of imperialism and as a foreign religion that threatens the stable, peaceful, and Buddhist Burmese way of life.[72] This propaganda creates distrust between Christians and Buddhists and breeds skepticism among Christians when Buddhists do convert to Christianity, thereby jeopardizing their commitment to the Church.[73] The pressures, misinformation, and misunderstanding facing potential Christian converts are therefore formidable, but some of the blame can also be leveled at the churches, who have arguably not yet found a way to communicate the Gospel in a way that Buddhists readily understand.[74] The first generation of Anglican missionaries held mixed opinions of Buddhism and had difficulty moving away from the labels of heathenism and atheism. Some were impressed by what they saw as the gentleness and openness of the Buddhists, however: Dr. Marks considered Buddhism to be "thoroughly tolerant" and said that neither the laity nor the monks objected to missionaries teaching the precepts of Christianity to old or young.[75] Nevertheless, it remained perennially difficult to envisage, much less achieve, significant numbers of conversions from Buddhism, though the fire of optimism never completely died out. Rev. "Tim" Houghton of the BCMS would not accept that "the God of the impossible should call us to this work without the intention of achieving results," though he admitted that "the day of rejoicing might be delayed."[76] The twentieth century brought a generation of missionaries who were more able to dialogue successfully with Buddhists, often resulting in lifelong positive impressions of Buddhism. Such was the case with George Appleton, who went on to have a prolific career as an SPG missionary bishop, and who would forever fondly recall "the gentle, tolerant Buddhists of Burma"[77]—epithets that would unfortunately be disputed by many today.

Christians in Burma are sometimes said to have remained, perhaps as a defensive measure, locked inside the old missionary compound mentality. Their Christianity is sometimes accused of not having fully shaken off the

Western ideals and accessories it is thought to have retained from colonial days. The teaching of the Gospel, it is argued, must now be reformulated so that it comes through to local people with a local accent.[78] The gulf in understanding is illustrated by a possibly apocryphal story about the missionary Ann Judson, wife of the great Adoniram Judson: as she explained the Gospel to a group of Burmese women one day, some of them responded by saying that they would rather spend eternity in hell with their families and ancestors than spend it in heaven by themselves, as they presumed they would have to do if they alone converted to Christianity. The question of life after death is not a crucial one for devout Buddhists, whose priority in life is to live in peaceful communion with supreme beings, with their relatives, with their friends, and with the forces of nature, in the harmony of the moment. This obstacle to understanding exemplifies the type of barrier faced in seeking to spread Christianity among Buddhists, and it is a perspective that earlier generations of missionaries may have failed to approach sympathetically. It is widely felt that Christians have never since found a way to communicate the Gospel in a way that Buddhists understand, and cooperation with Buddhists has sometimes been considered de facto off-limits. The following is a summary of observations and suggestions put forward by two scholars of Tahan Theological College in Burma, Theodore Lim and Dengthuama, who aim to challenge a number of preconceptions about Christian–Buddhist dialogue and interaction:

1. Christians fail to communicate the Gospel to Buddhists when they fail to distinguish between Christian traditions that are actual Gospel teaching and traditions that are Western cultural add-ons and fail to exorcise the latter.
2. Poverty, illness, family separation, and social exclusion are rampant in Burma, and the Gospel must be made to speak to immediate needs: where will the next meal come from? How can people avoid sickness? How can they get a job? How can they escape oppression?
3. There are few efficacious routes to serious employment in Burma, and many people leave the country to work in unskilled jobs in other parts of Asia. Founding training centers or micro-industries can provide employment opportunities and could be a first point of contact with the Gospel for young people in Burma.
4. Medical work, sanitation work, and education ministry in rural areas could still be an effective means of doing Christian witness in majority Buddhist environments.

"A LAND AND PEOPLE OF PROMISE"

5. There are many social development programs established by Buddhist intellectuals, and for Christians to get involved in these programs is seen as acceptable among Buddhists.
6. Ordinary Burmese Buddhists tend to be hospitable and generous; charity is regarded as a key virtue, and nondenominational works of charity can provide common ground for positive Christian–Buddhist interaction.
7. People can best be understood by spending time with them; until Church members understand the Buddhist mindset, they will not be able to play a significant part in the culture of Burma.
8. Churches in Burma, geographically remote at the global level and politically disenfranchised, have long felt the pain of isolation. Christians must explore possible cooperation with Christians abroad in witnessing the Gospel to the Buddhists.[79]

These observations touch on a range of very pertinent topics, old and new. They reflect many of the concerns that oriented liberation theology and third world theology away from the historic centers of power, established in the West and the global north, and toward the poor and marginalized. These points suggest that putting the Gospel into action is both the best way to communicate it and the best way to learn about the Buddhists, because doing social works of mercy allows for the discovery of much-needed common ground while actually fulfilling Gospel commands in the process. Archdeacon Appleton arrived at similar conclusions in the 1940s, writing that "preaching is no longer the dominating evangelistic activity" and calling for Christians to step up their practical contribution to society.[80] Buddhists in today's Burma actually engage in all the types of social work that the old Anglican missionaries initiated and that many local Christians have also continued. The first of Buddhism's Four Noble Truths is *Dukkha*, the noble truth of suffering. It states that life is all suffering and pain. The word *Dukkha* relates to the *Pyithu*, or the one who suffers the most—a life of poverty, illness, family separation, social exclusion, and so forth—in what could be called a "theology of suffering" for Burma (*Pyithu-Dukkha*). It would be difficult to present a Gospel that promises a better afterlife in response to suffering when this concept does not feature on the Buddhists' horizon. However, a Gospel that has something concrete to say about their social and economic reality and works to address these problems may be more accessible and inspire more understanding.

There may be, some would argue, more similarities between following the Christ and following the Buddha than people realize: both Christ and Buddha are models of faith for their followers (Christ by his death and resurrection and Buddha by his enlightenment); both Christ and Buddha faced and defied temptation, both renouncing worldly power and wealth; and as the Christian inherits the sinful condition, so the Buddhist inherits the suffering condition, according to Karma.[81] What is more, promoting and sustaining the orthodox practice of Buddhism in Burma meets with some of the same difficulties and frustrations as Christianity, since Buddhists as well as Christians continue to seek other kinds of supernatural assistance in their daily lives. Superstitions and *nat* worship famously predate Buddhism and have run parallel to the development of all other religions in Burma, both before and since the arrival of the Anglican Church. This seems to demonstrate that the actual spiritual needs of the people involve sensing the presence of a saving power, receiving a helping hand to endure this world of suffering, and having a source of hope, health, opportunity, and prosperity. Across the generations, these fundamental needs clearly continue to transcend exclusive attachment to this or that religion.[82]

Summary

Protestant Christianity in Southeast Asia tended to retain significant aspects of its European character, which eventually gave rise to a conflict in which local converts could be seen as siding with the West, the colonizers, the invaders. But that inherited character also tended to be conservative and orthodox, a nature that could be seen as compatible with Asian culture and that makes Christianity less of a violent departure from local values— these are all obvious starting points for further discussion rather than neatly packaged conclusions. For at least its first century of presence in Burma, the Anglican Church was representative of official government thinking on most, if not all, issues, and this conformity won it the concessions and freedoms to do as it wanted. This included a wide range of beneficial works, not least the provision of education, which in turn directly benefited the government, too. Thus, we could say that from its earliest days this story became a story of trade-offs, and the main theological discussion to emerge would concern fusion; to what extent did effective evangelization and missionary success hinge on the Church accepting fusion with other beliefs, allowing the accommodation of non-Christian customs, and tolerating dual or triple affiliation in its members? What demands would or could the Church make on its converts in these regards?

The early approach had been to seek to eradicate and destroy all traces and paraphernalia of other belief systems, demanding from the individual convert a total adherence verging on complete submission. Anything less was described as a mere "loose attachment" to Christianity. Over time, however, elements of fusion would be seen as inevitable, then increasingly as acceptable, and ultimately even as desirable. Realists among the Anglican leadership began to see the modern world as a "last chance saloon" for religious belief itself, the final standoff being not between the different religions but between the religious mindset and the secularist one, forging a kind of solidarity between all religious exponents. This line of thinking would be expressed later in Pope John Paul II's assertion that the great enemy of faith in our times is not so much atheism as indifference.

The desirability or undesirability of fusion with other religions is open to debate, but is it not, on the other hand, simply what happens always and everywhere when a new religion is introduced? The *linguistic* translation of religious texts and ideas is a universal practice, and it inherently involves the *cultural* translation of the religion too. Two points must be borne in mind about translation: it is nearly always a two-way process in which the produced translation sheds new and different light on the meaning of the original text, rightly or wrongly; also, language in all its forms is inseparable from culture in all *its* forms. This not only helps us to understand the indelible imprint of "Italianness" or "Irishness" on Roman Catholicism and vice versa, for example, but also goes a long way to explain tendencies, in some religions, to insist upon linguistic purity as a guarantor of theological purity. This is observable in the retention of Arabic, Latin, or Greek as official, liturgical, canonical, and theological languages of some religious bodies.

The willingness of some progressive Anglicans to interact with other religions may have looked like an admission of guilt to Christianity's detractors—it was a foreign import and even its proponents apparently knew that it did not truly belong, they may have concluded. The development of global capitalism had run parallel to the colonization of Southeast Asia, and the region became a trove of all kinds of resources and commodities for the Western powers to pick at. For many reasons, this came to an end, and Asia's role in the capitalist world system came to be reassessed, clearly not as a mere adjunct to the system but as a major player. This liberation called for a liberated postcolonial theological expression. Christianity found

THE ANGLICAN CHURCH IN BURMA

a degree of acceptance among the well-established religious diversity of Burma, and the relative size of the Christian quota of Burma's society has changed very little. But whereas Christians arguably represented a privileged caste in colonial times, they later became targets of discrimination and persecution.

Anglicans suffered from connotations of colonialism and elitism that were in some ways reinforced by ecclesiological and theological principles regarding sacraments and rites. Christianity could be framed as the religion of the invaders and Christians portrayed as unpatriotic, subversive infiltrators. The theological pushback has grown stronger in recent decades without denying the Western heritage, and some Burmese Christian theologians currently seek to decolonize the religion and rehabilitate it. When forced to become self-sufficient and autonomous, in times of both peace and war, the Anglicans in Burma rose to the challenge, further supporting the case that the Church was not just an appendage of the British Empire. The identity and orientation that they affirmed has paid some homage to the origins, however, and the current Church's alignment with global conservative and orthodox streams within Anglicanism clearly has firm roots in history. The challenge of identities in the Anglican Communion is far from just a historical curiosity, though. The nature of the divisions within Anglicanism suggests that it never properly adapted to the postcolonial world and that this transition remains unfinished business.

Another outstanding matter is the Church's relations with Buddhism, which have a checkered history. It is a difficult discussion that begins with a difficult question: which Buddhism? "State" Buddhism in Burma has denied, ignored, enabled, and justified state terrorism and genocidal atrocities, and its devotees have perpetrated every war crime and human rights abuse imaginable. "True" Buddhism, on the other hand, has always posed a theological challenge for any Church to dialogue effectively with. Currently, theologians in Burma emphasize areas of communality, or at least lack of conflict, and the old idea that the social or secular ends of all religions converge is still around. The perennial social, economic, and political problems of Burma have not only endured but worsened, and members of all faiths are increasingly drawn to humanitarian projects, often in education and health. There could be no better time for Christians to put aside theological differences for the sake of a practical ecumenism grounded in meaningful social endeavors, with a common and urgent goal of survival.

Chapter 8

"CARRYING THE CROSS"

Perspectives on the Church in Burma Today

There are an estimated sixty thousand to seventy thousand Anglicans in today's Burma, now called Myanmar.[1] Christians are still a fraction of the national population, but in an increasingly well-connected Southeast Asia they are aware of being in a not-so-distant second place (approximately 22 percent of the population) at the regional level.[2] The region, furthermore, has its share of Christian-majority countries, states, and territories, meaning that Christians can feel quite well represented overall. In addition, there is increasing interaction with big neighbor China, where Christianity is experiencing growth despite myriad problems. One part of this evolving regional picture is the Church of the Province of Burma (CPB) and its unexpectedly significant voice in an evolving worldwide Anglicanism, even indirectly representing tens of millions of Christians. These facts combine to make the study of Christianity in the Southeast Asian region, and of the Anglican Church in Burma, essential for understanding global religious developments in general and for understanding the future of Christianity in particular.[3]

The advent of autonomy for the Church in Burma coincided with the start of a period of uncertainty and identity crisis in the Anglican Communion. Just when much of the historic instability in the small Church began to subside, the wider foundations of Anglicanism began to tremble, and the tiny CPB would come to play its own role in facing this broader crisis. The whole world seemed to be in a state of flux by 1970, the year of the final breakup of the old CIPBC and the subsequent creation of the CPB.

THE ANGLICAN CHURCH IN BURMA

The Church of India, Pakistan, Burma and Ceylon had been in existence for just forty years, the blink of an eye in retrospect, but what a forty years it had been. The world had been transformed at every level and in every sense, and its very boundaries seemed to have been pushed back. In those forty years, empires had fallen and risen, despots had come and gone, and the limits of human cruelty and cupidity had been redrawn over and over. The planet's energy had been harnessed to facilitate mass destruction, while astronauts had symbolically exported our supposed civilization to other parts of the solar system. The task of communicating the Christian message in this brave new world had been complicated anew countless times, with problems of all magnitudes and dimensions.

The disintegration of the territorially vast CIPBC posed a wide variety of immediate organizational problems for its constituent members. The specific challenges of the Church in India led to a solution that highlighted the progressive thinking of the Anglican world. The southern dioceses of India had already formed a "united church," and the northern dioceses would now do the same. These united churches would remain within the Anglican Communion, though without using the word "Anglican" in their names. They would be both united and uniting Churches in the sense of drawing together several small Protestant denominations into one new Church. They faced prickly theological problems of contrasting church polity, as among the various uniting denominations there were long-held and fundamentally varying approaches to the ideas of episcopacy, ordination, apostolic succession, and the sacraments. This was an age in which the phrase "historic compromise" came to be used in a variety of contexts around the globe, and it was no less applicable to the case of the new united churches of North and South India. And with every historic compromise comes historic controversy. The now-separate Churches in Pakistan and Ceylon (called Sri Lanka after 1972) faced considerable challenges and difficulties arising from their specific sociopolitical situations, not least the militancy of other, dominant non-Christian religions. In this sense, the experiences of Pakistan and Ceylon were similar to Burma's, but for all of them the actual process of transition to ecclesiastical independence was in itself fairly smooth.

The Church and the World

Bold pragmatism and flexible negotiation within the Anglican Communion were to be thanked for securing successful transitions to small national

Churches after the final dissolution of the CIPBC. It is perhaps ironic that the ongoing crisis in today's Anglican Communion can clearly be seen to stem from the fact that modern Anglicanism, objectively, has successfully adapted to and kept up with the modern world. Whether this is to be applauded, accepted, derided, or deplored is the point at which division of opinion largely occurs. The 1970s began with a progressive and ecumenical approach to the question of the old CIPBC, but the decade also saw the first real waves of women's ordination in the Anglican Communion, though there had been isolated precedents. Women's ordination then gained momentum in the 1980s, leading to its widespread adoption and ratification by the 1990s. The early 2000s saw the initial signs of acceptance of same-sex relationships, including for clergy. All of these developments have been met with large-scale organized opposition as well as the formation and growth of rival Anglican bodies calling for a halt to the revolution.

For those who oppose these developments and try to call the Anglican Communion to orthodoxy, the problem is not just a question of a misplaced social conscience or an ill-considered strategy for keeping up with the times; it is a question of moving away from core, biblical principles and values, of choosing the profane over the sacred and deliberately shifting the magnetic pole of Church authority away from the Bible and away from Christianity's two-thousand-year tradition. There is a veritable panoply of opposition organizations and contesting groups, including those with both feet still firmly in the official Anglican Communion, such as the Global South network and the FCA. The panoply also includes bodies with one foot placed firmly *outside* of the official structures, such as GAFCON. There are also a large number of now-independent worshipping bodies who view themselves as part of the legitimate spiritual and sacramental continuation of Anglicanism, but with both feet placed well outside of the official Anglican Communion organogram, and these are the Continuing Anglicans. This spectrum of Anglican resistance represents, combined, tens of millions of Anglicans around the globe, easily constituting the majority of the world's Anglicans. This indicates not only the extent of the contestation to official Anglican policy but more importantly the varying modi operandi of the different organized protests. The Anglican Church in Burma, for its part, relates strongly to the first camp, the Global South conservatives, and also to the second camp, the GAFCON bishops and their adherent Churches, including the influential and growing ACNA (Anglican Church in North America), which is not (or not yet) part of the Anglican Communion. But the sympathies of the Church in

Burma seem to be with all contesting Anglicans, who in turn frequently look to the support of the CPM and cite Burma as a clear example of Anglican orthodoxy and solidarity.

In England, where this author was born, the Anglican Church projects an air of being a timeless and unchanging feature of the community. Despite obviously diminished social standing, the Church's historic buildings, civic ceremonies, seasonal events, charitable works, services, and hymns are still part of the fabric of life in England. But this very English view of Reformed or English Catholicism is not only subjective; it is also skewed, for there is little that is stable and unchanging in today's worldwide Anglican Communion. The Anglican Church stands on very loose tectonic plates, and a modern glossary of Anglican terms—realignment, Global South, ACNA, AEO, FCA, GAFCON—has little that is timeless and unchanging about it. All of this underlines the fact that the Anglican Communion has actually come a long way in the relatively short period of time since the end of the age of empire. For many people, the great turning point was the ordination of women. The Anglican Church in some parts of Asia, such as India, does ordain women, while in others, such as Burma, it does not, though even in India the work of ordained women may be limited to ministry to other women and children.[4] But since the women's ordination debate, the Church has also seen the advent of same-sex unions, challenges to traditional family values, debate about sexual orientation and gender identity, extensive changes to language and liturgy, and postcolonial identity struggles in much of the world's traditional Anglican heartland, and this list is hardly exhaustive. One clear feature of the colonial period was the need to patiently understand and sensitively accommodate local culture, from which the Church cannot live in isolation. Similarly, the Church today cannot exist in a state of brooding hostility toward decadent mainstream society, which, as in missionary territory of former times, the Church must either effectively engage with or shrink from the public stage. But a question immediately arises as to the extent to which this engagement means the Church adopting or conforming to society's values, if at all.

The Church and the "Nation"

In Burma's society, Anglicanism is a minority denomination of a minority faith that is most popular among the country's minority ethnic groups. To be a minority group in Burma—whether religious or ethnic, or in the case of most Christians in Burma, both—means to be discriminated against, persecuted, or, again, both. The Independence of Burma from Britain had high hopes of a democratic union of autonomous minority regions, each with its own language, traditions, and history.[5] But this potential was derailed in the hands of those who sought a strong, centralized nation, a false construct that in any case was perhaps not very sincerely intended. The effect of that push toward centralized governance and control was that the minorities experienced little sense of attachment or belonging to this supposed nation and, conversely, a strengthened feeling of being part of their ethnic group, with their shared language, religion, and culture.[6] It was a situation that many had feared, a false two-way choice between amalgamation and isolation for the ethnic groups.[7] Choosing amalgamation might at least have kept the peace, one may think, but there was no socialist vision of equality on offer, despite the government's terminology. Being subsumed into the Burmese idea of nationhood meant accepting a permanently low rung on society's ladder, with no contingent freedoms of worship or expression. Members of the largely Christian ethnic groups were rightly uneasy about coming under majority Burman rule with its militant Buddhist identity, which is actually a corruption of Buddhism for political ends.[8] These fears would be borne out in countless cases of discrimination and persecution, leading to a widespread feeling among young people that their opportunities and future in the country may be severely limited by their identification as Christians.[9] From the false choice of amalgamation or isolation, both actually came to pass: effective amalgamation by coercion and force and political and social isolation by stealth.

Today, at the political level, ethnic minority groups still pine for the "spirit of Panglong" and for the promise of that postwar agreement to prevail: a federal democracy in which the peoples have equal rights and a significant degree of autonomy within a Union of Burma.[10] But that hope seems ever more remote in recent years, despite the supposed turn to democracy, and as ever, religion is at the center of the concerns. Every single year for the past two decades, the United States Commission on International Religious Freedom (USCIRF) has identified Burma as a "country of particular concern" for its "systematic, egregious, and ongoing violations of religious freedom as defined in the International Religious Freedom Act of 1998."[11] The USCIRF cites the long history of religious freedom violations across several faiths (including cases to the detriment of Buddhists within some ethnic minorities), and it encourages reform and respect for religious freedom and related human rights.[12] The combined impact of two very different events in close succession—the pro-democracy Saffron Revolution in 2007 and the devastating Cyclone Nargis in 2008—placed huge internal and external pressures on the military regime. These pressures prompted the regime to enact reforms and shed their uniforms but retain power, establishing a nominally civilian government. But, to quote a Kachin proverb, a tiger cannot change its stripes, and the former generals continued to perpetuate grievous abuses despite some encouraging signs of progress such as the release of political prisoners, the relaxation of social and media restrictions, and the pursuit of meaningful ceasefires with armed rebel groups.[13] The year 2015 saw the democratic election of a new civilian government, with the leader of the country's democracy movement, Aung San Suu Kyi, as de facto leader. But hopes of a new era of democracy, in which human rights and peace accords would be respected, faded after just three years in office. Repression and human rights abuses continue, and lasting peace now seems further away than ever. Instead of the trumpeted democratization, Burma has witnessed new and renewed genocide, crimes against humanity, and de facto military rule.[14]

Christians and Human Rights

The horror of the Rohingya humanitarian and human rights crisis, for many people around the world, exposed Burma's long pattern of religious persecution for the first time.[15] Any notion that Burma's inoffensive and peaceful Christians have never faced or could never face such a sudden and violent crackdown is dangerously mistaken, and the Anglicans there are under no illusions. Even in the days before the divisive national independence of 1948, the Church speculated that before long the open practice of Christianity, and conversion to it, would be violently discouraged or forbidden outright.[16] The current archbishop of the CPM, Stephen Than Myint Oo, is a Karen who has known persecution personally: he was imprisoned for two years on a typically vague charge of harming the state, though in reality he was being held hostage for his brother, a resistance fighter.[17] Today, discrimination is an ongoing reality, and young ethnic minority Christians are aware that their religion will bar them from getting top jobs, promotions, or just decent employment in a branch of public service, including education.[18] But the result, fortunately, is not hatred for Buddhists or Buddhism, and young Christians are quite aware that the regime uses and abuses religion as a political tool.

Burman Buddhist nationalism continues to be behind much of today's religious intolerance in Burma, being one of four principal drivers, according to Christian Solidarity Worldwide.[19] First, this brand of nationalism promotes the idea that to be Burmese is to be Buddhist, and it encourages a visceral hatred of Muslims in particular and Christians to a lesser extent. This is fueled by the preaching of some influential Buddhist monks. Second, the military has long utilized both ethnicity and religion to stoke conflict and increase their power, in a classic divide and rule. Third, marketplace competition has led to resentment toward Muslim businesses, and there have been calls to boycott them. And fourth, this is all enabled by politicians of various parties who either share the Buddhist nationalist agenda or who lack the political skill, will, or courage to confront it. The most overt and violent forms of persecution against Christians occur among the nonurban "hill people" ethnic groups, especially the Chins, Kachins, and Karens, in states where Christians make up a significant proportion or a majority—as much as 90 percent—of the population. These Christians can routinely face physical attacks and the destruction of churches and crosses. This persecution is arguably not always a question of Christians being singled out because of their faith alone, but they are often targeted for both their faith and their ethnicity, which for Chins, Kachins, and Karens go completely hand in hand. The faith dimension is a strong and clear factor in the discrimination.[20]

The Church and the Rohingya

The Church's accumulated experience of human rights abuses has not necessarily left it well equipped to engage with further major human rights crises. This is revealed in the light of the humanitarian catastrophe taking place in Burma's Rakhine state, affecting the Rohingya ethnic group.[21] The Rohingya crisis has rightly attracted worldwide attention, and this has prompted a search for a coherent response from the other faith communities inside Burma. It is fair to ask whether the apparent lack of a strong response from Anglican circles is attributable to an actual decision to remain silent, or a sign that the Church is or aspires to be apolitical. The answer lies in better understanding the institution's limitations and in precisely which areas the Church has historically not yet achieved maturity. Part of the Church's general lack of development is the absence of mechanisms, forums, and resources for conducting an effective critique of major internal and external issues. Such vehicles or forums might one day include theoretical journals, dedicated committees, academic conferences, research centers, or communications agencies. It is within such a critical framework that lines of argument and analysis would usually be expected to develop. Without this reflective tool kit that we have come to expect in modern and complex organizations, it can be difficult to identify the Church's stance on extremely complex issues that are also cloaked in misinformation, and it is perhaps unrealistic to expect that this stance would be uniform. Without the necessary institutional and cultural apparatus, the Church has never developed a culture of systematic criticism or contestation of the government's various repressive campaigns.

It may be true that underdeveloped institutional structures do not promote a coherent critique of events, and there could be a temptation to conclude that the Church has chosen to play it safe, so to speak, by not developing these critical functions. But in reality, there is little that is socially, politically, or humanly safe about being a Christian in Burma.[22] The Anglican experience in Burma must be understood in relation to a number of observable contextual factors:

1. If Church members have erred on the side of caution, it is because they have direct, multigenerational experience of actual persecution, torture, and the physical liquidation of family and neighbors. This collective experience, much of it still within living memory, has been at the hands, crucially, of a variety of opposing forces rather than one single identifiable adversary, such as the army.[23] Christians in Burma may be well aware of the complexity and ultimate ineffectiveness of seeking to apportion blame, and it can also be true that Christians' speaking out is limited by genuine and reasonable fear.[24]

2. The Church is aware of its own frailty and lack of influence, but it has nevertheless consistently shown solidarity for persecuted groups, chiefly when these consist, partly or largely, of Christians. This bias may be due to the fact that the Church inherited fluency and dominion of an established values framework—the Christian religion—through which to express this solidarity, and it is more likely to have the knowledge, vocabulary, and information (which cannot be taken for granted) in order to construct an appropriate response when commenting on the Christian experience.

3. The country's situation of notoriously poor access to education is disproportionately worse for minority groups, and it cannot be assumed that Christians, including clergy and senior lay staff, are

necessarily well informed or well equipped to pursue an effective, sensitive, and safe discourse around complex sociopolitical issues. It must not be taken for granted that know-how with regard to technology, communications, language, law, research, and analysis is available in the local talent pool.

4. The existence and persistence of this Church, with its significant foreign contacts and Anglophone patrimony, can be perceived as an act of defiance in itself, standing in quiet opposition to the regime. To what exact extent this watchful presence has had a tempering or restraining effect on the regime is impossible to assess, but there are reasons to believe that some repressive government campaigns could have been worse without the presence of foreign-linked Churches keeping watch, with an admittedly tiny cohort of foreign visitors and volunteers observing. It is also true that foreign Anglicans are present in the many and varied humanitarian organizations working and watching in Burma.

5. It can be difficult for observers from some Western and other Asian societies to appreciate the extent to which communities can live in isolation and without integration in a medium-sized country like modern Myanmar. Internal diversity is a feature of the Church, but this does not mean that it has developed sound strategies for promoting diversity or even a strong aversion to being isolated. The same could be said of modern Myanmar society itself, which is both diverse and isolationist, but this does not mitigate the lack of a convincing response on the Rohingya. The Church cannot be blamed for not being a champion of integration, and the same could be said of the Rohingya themselves, whose justifiable isolation and strong identity have generally prevented them from engaging effectively with other groups.[25]

Within the Christian and Anglican community, sadly, there are also some perceptions, fueled and nurtured by convincing and intimidating voices in wider society, that the Rohingya do not even *want* to integrate and have never wanted to integrate. These perceptions, when considered alongside genuine cases of armed militancy practiced by the Rohingya, lead to an impasse that naturally prompts some diffidence.[26] But analyzing the Church's response to the crisis reveals inadequacies in institutional infrastructure, systems, and communications rather than individual moral failings. At the same time, it must also be asked whether the international

THE ANGLICAN CHURCH IN BURMA

Anglican community has actually discharged its duty to support the Church in Burma in effectively engaging with the Rohingya crisis, or whether this has been presumed not to be a matter for Christians, except for them to remain silent. A balanced view may be achieved by considering the Church's response to a different type of crisis, Cyclone Nargis in 2008, without question the worst and deadliest natural disaster ever to strike the country. The Anglican Church in Burma responded pragmatically, effectively, and with indiscriminate solidarity and compassion, operating across all ethnic and religious communities, but this fact is barely recorded anywhere. We may search in vain for evidence in print or other media of the CPM's disaster efforts, though anecdotally, talking to the survivors on the ground, the history is unequivocal. Because of the organizational and communications deficiencies outlined previously, the Church has been similarly "silent" in terms of communicating its considerable efforts and achievements to the world.

The Church and Its Own Ethnic Minorities

The northernmost diocese of the modern CPM's six dioceses (and two missionary dioceses) covers Kachin state (also known as Kachinland), including areas of active armed conflict, as the Kachins have long and vigorously asserted their independence.[27] The Kachin capital and diocesan seat is Myitkyina, a low-profile city of around three hundred thousand people. Due to its relative proximity to China and India, and the strategic value of this location, history has made Myitkyina ethnically and religiously diverse—descendants of all parts of the old Indian empire reside here, including ethnic Gurkhas (Gorkhas, or Gorkhali), and there is a fairly large ethnic Indian township to the east of the city. In Myitkyina city, the Anglican congregations include a mix of ethnic groups, including Shans, Anglo-Indians, Anglo-Burman, and Nepali, as well as the local Kachins. The diocese covers a vast territory, divided into only nineteen parishes, four of which are located in and around Myitkyina city. Thanks to the historic input of two very different missionary organizations, the diocese has parishes of both Anglo-Catholic and low-church evangelical styles, the latter of which the local Anglicans describe as being similar to the Baptists. The majority-Christian state is thought to be 45 percent Baptist, 40 percent Roman Catholic, and 15 percent other, but despite this small share, the Anglicans of Kachin state are visible and active. Their membership is dwarfed by the

"CARRYING THE CROSS"

numerical and cultural dominance of the Baptists, and the link between being ethnically Kachin and being a Kachin Baptist is considered to be strong. There is a general tendency to venerate heroic Baptist figures, such as Ola Hanson, as the bringer of Christianity to northern Burma, but the Anglicans also take care to give credit to early Karen catechists who accompanied the missionaries and brought the Gospel to the region.

Among the minority ethnic groups such as the Kachins, the Anglican Church is recognized as an inclusive Church, and Kachin Anglicans, as well as Chin and Karen Anglicans, are happy that they have good numbers of Tamils and Nepalis in their congregations. Marriage outside of one's own ethnic group is perceived as being more common among Anglicans than among Baptists or Roman Catholics. Whether there are clashes or quarrels between any of the Kachin Christian denominations is disputed. A young Baptist Church worker I spoke to seemed genuinely shocked by this suggestion, while his Anglican counterpart was less surprised; she explained that when mixed Anglican/Baptist couples intend to wed, the Baptist pastors invariably insist that the non-Baptist partner be rebaptized (the Baptists generally considering only an immersion baptism to be valid). The Myanmar Council of Churches (MCC) had actually reached an accord on the mutual recognition of baptisms, but this has not stopped some pastors demanding fresh baptisms in mixed families, it is said. My Baptist interviewee admitted that this may be the case with conservative pastors, suggesting that newer pastors (and future pastors) may be developing a more ecumenically friendly outlook in line with the MCC accord. What about relations with the Roman Catholics? They do not demand that non–Roman Catholic spouses be rebaptized, but their priests will not set foot in Anglican churches for weddings, even though Roman Catholic Canon Law makes provision for precisely such cases of mixed marriages in non–Roman Catholic temples. Between Roman Catholic foibles and the Baptists' intractability, the Anglicans try to avoid conflict and good-humoredly consider themselves the easygoing denomination.

Low-church Anglicans can feel slightly out of place at Myitkyina's Cathedral of Christ the King, which has distinct Anglo-Catholic touches mixed with local flavor. The chief celebrant wears full counter-reformation-style vestments, including the lesser-spotted amice and maniple, as well as the alb, cincture, and stole (but he is barefoot, as are all the clergy concelebrants), and the consecration of the gifts is done facing the main altar, not the congregation (ad orientem rather than versus populum, in Catholic liturgical terminology). The cathedral seats five hundred, but at services

THE ANGLICAN CHURCH IN BURMA

like Christmas there can be a thousand communicants. Alternate Sundays offer services in the Burmese and Kachin (Jingpho) languages. The *English Hymnal* in use at the cathedral is a reprint of the 1906 University of London edition, and at least one hymn in each service is sung in English. The use of English among Christians, obviously a visible part of the missionary inheritance, acquires additional significance in places like Kachin state, where the local Kachin language is *lingua non grata* to the central Burma government and its regional outposts. Take the example of Christian faith schools, which are now allowed to exist as independent initiatives as long as their curricula conform to the prescribed government one. This applies to the parts of Kachin state controlled by the central Burma government, like Myitkyina, while other areas of the state are controlled by the Kachin Independence Organization (KIO), where none of the schools are recognized by the Burma government. Government approval for Christian schools is necessary both for their very survival and also so that school-leavers may access employment and further or higher education, but the government demands that instruction be in Burmese, not Kachin (Jingpho) or any other ethnic minority language. For peoples with their own distinct culture, history, and language, like the Kachins, the suppression of local languages is one more powerful threat to their identity. This is, after all, a government that has in recent years gone to extraordinary, bizarre, and barbaric lengths to erase minority identities, seeking to subjugate and homogenize the population.

The Church and Language

The Church in Myanmar preserves the use of the English language at many levels, not out of slavish imitation of its parent Church, nor just to pay homage to the founding missionaries, but because the English language and the English hymns and prayers are as much part of their identity and patrimony as they are part of anyone else's. Identity is, of course, no trivial issue in Burma, nor is it a question of mere pride. The use and tradition— in the original Latin sense of passing on—of the English language persisted in defiance of the dictatorship's very real efforts, over many years, to wipe the language out. With church resources including the use of some quite ancient books and a distinct preference for older language and hymns, there may be some residual attachment to colonial missionary days, but the preservation of English can also serve to make a statement of identity.

For some Christian communities, using English provides a neutral ground between the politically charged use of ethnic minority languages, which is forcefully discouraged, and the use of Burmese, which is imposed in many quarters. There is nothing surprising or illegitimate about Burmese having become the lingua franca and the de facto official language, given its currency and diffusion even in colonial times, but the ideological imposition of Burmese in tandem with the ideological eradication of English have defied all educational benefits and common sense. The discrimination against *all* minority languages has been such that it is easy to interpret their use as an act of defiance, in the sense that to assert minority culture itself is to oppose the regime.

The Kachin people, whose identity is closely bound up with the Christian faith, are a case in point. The Kachins enjoyed an affinity and camaraderie with the rank-and-file British, and the same could be said for Christians in other ethnic groups. The history and use of the Kachins' Jingpho (or Jinghpaw) language are so entwined with Christianity, especially in worship, prayer, and education, that government censuring of the language may also be perceived as religious discrimination in effect. Some Christian educators may have found a solution, and experiments in increasing the use of English as a medium of instruction may provide a route to circumvent the imposition of Burmese, and while English is not their language as such, it is certainly not the language of the Burma military either. English is a language of which they can claim ownership, especially in consideration of its religious and cultural history, within which, as a people, the ethnic minority Christians have certainly played a part. It is certainly ironic that the language of the former colonizers now becomes a language of liberation and an important weapon in safeguarding ethnic identity. The case has much to say about the subtle power of language as a political resource. Christ the King Cathedral, incidentally, is currently looking to introduce another service in addition to the Jingpho and Burmese services—an English-language one.

Within the parish territory of Myitkyina's cathedral, a former township chapel has become a full-fledged separate parish, St. Matthias. Situated in the Shatapru quarter, the parish buildings consist of a smallish traditional red-brick church (around 1,700 square feet or 160 square meters), a similar-sized hangar-style covered area for meetings and celebrations, and a modest two-story vicarage. A full-time catechist lives at St. Matthias, but she is also tasked with teaching and training future catechists in all the parishes of the huge diocese, having had the benefit of four years' training at Holy Cross Theological College (HCTC) in Rangoon. The vicar of St. Matthias lives nearby in the township, while the on-site priest's house is home to around twenty families of internally displaced persons. It is fairly common for parishes to host families of internally displaced persons, who are sadly a very common feature of Burma. Large areas of Kachin state are controlled by the Kachin Independence Organization (KIO) and home to armed groups opposed to the central government, but any part of the state can be subjected to an attack by the Burma Army. In KIO areas, and in Kachin state in general, the full name of the Church of the Province of Myanmar, or the shorter Church of Myanmar, are not popular, and parishes tend to use the term "Anglican Church."

Kachins seem to care little about the change of name from Burma to Myanmar—it is generally regarded as a Burmans' affair—but the KIO may object to the new name in as much as the change is a reminder of the Burma government's power. While the Anglican Church is absolutely seen as welcome to be in Kachin state, the government's imposed name is not. Younger Christians from the ethnic groups—Kachins, Chins, Shans—see the national name change as potentially confusing but not important to them. They regard both "Burma" and "Myanmar" as names for a country they do not fully belong to. In the Jingpho language, the word "Myen" means Myanmar, just as it meant Burma previously, so there has been no change for them, except when it comes to using English. This does make one wonder to what extent the "Burma to Myanmar" name change was calculated to make a statement to the outside world rather than to the people of Burma. In most of the languages of Burma, like in Jingpho, the name has not changed at all. As for criticism of the old "colonial" name, Burma, there is not much support among the historically British-friendly Kachins for the idea that Burma was a name imposed by the colonialists, and they regard it as an appropriate transliteration.

For many minority Christian people with their own (suppressed) languages, the "Burma to Myanmar" changes are immaterial, even though it may appear to be a major hot-button issue to outsiders. There is also some support for the change, though: one student I talked to pointed out that the name Burma originates from, and privileges, one ethnic group— the Burmans or Bamar—while the name Myanmar at least does not. The use of the name Burma is currently thought to be more widespread in central Burma—in Mandalay and Bagan, for example—where the overwhelmingly dominant ethnicity and culture is original Burman (Bamar). "Myanmar" purports to be an inclusive name embracing all the peoples of Burma, though this explanation is widely rejected as a fudge, including by some democracy leaders. Young people are unsure of the etymological arguments behind the change, and in any case, they are often doubly unconvinced, as young ethnic minority Christians are reluctant to be embraced in such a union under the same old dominant group. Similarly, young people support the principle of replacing the old British street names with local names, but by the same logic they feel that Kachin, Chin, Shan, and Karen streets should have names in those local languages and relevant to local culture and history rather than having names in Burmese relevant to Burman culture and history. Paradoxically perhaps, it is in Burma's urban areas, where Burmans and Buddhism are these days more likely to be dominant, that the persecution of Christians is less common. Physical destruction of churches does not occur, and parishes function with less interference than in the ethnic minority states. However, they do face restrictions in building, extending, or renovating churches, or in starting any kind of house church, and there are frequent legal disputes over land, nearly always to the detriment of the Church.[28]

There are considerable restrictions in producing Christian literature.[29] When the translation of the Prayer Book into Burmese was last updated in 1992, the Anglican Church encountered problems with the censors. The phrase for "Almighty God" is translated as "Myatsaw Phayar" in Burmese, but this is the same phrase used by Buddhists for the Buddha. The censors ordered the Church to change it to "Ah Pha Phayar," meaning "Our Father God." The dispute was evidently not just linguistic but political. According to some observers, they did not want the Christian God to be on the same level as their Buddha.[30] Biblical translation has quite a long and impressive history in Burma, starting with Judson's Burmese translation, which was later thoroughly updated in the 1920s by Rev. William Sherratt and Rev. Charles E. Garrad. Sherratt was a Wesleyan minister working with the Burma Bible Society, and Garrad was a missionary of the SPG; their translation was published in 1926.[31] Rev. Dr. Josiah Nelson Cushing, a Baptist, produced a Shan translation and others completed versions in Sgaw Karen and then Pwo Karen. As mentioned previously, Dr. Ola Hanson translated the Bible into Kachin (Jingpho), and Rev. Ernest Francis, an Anglican, translated the New Testament into Khumi Chin in the 1950s.[32] There is also a translation into Lisu for the Lisu Christians residing mostly in Kachin state and also over the border in China. The meticulous 1926 translation, occasionally referred to as the "Geratt" version (a possibly accidental conflation of the names Garrad and Sherratt), has proven the most influential.[33] Garrad would continue making handwritten corrections and improvements to this work for the rest of his life, long after he had retired to England due to ill-health.[34] The bishops of those years, Fyffe and then Tubbs, were enthusiastic about translation, and Tubbs requested a Burmese version of the main services from the new 1928 Prayer Book when it appeared.[35] By 1970, Rev. Canon A. T. Houghton estimated that 90 percent of the people of Burma, if literate, could read the Word of God in their own language.[36]

The Church in the Burman Heartlands

The Anglican Cathedral in Mandalay can prove difficult to find for first-time visitors, as it is tucked away in a residential neighborhood, and city visitors are more likely to catch sight of St. Mary's Church, on the south side of the palace square. The comparatively modest cathedral congregation of around seventy is ethnically mixed, including many Kachins and Karens, but services are in Burmese. English translations of both the liturgy and the hymn book are available. St. Mary's has a similar attendance of about seventy. The town of Pyin Oo Lwin, also known as Maymyo, as in colonial times—literally May's town, named after a Colonel May—used to have four Anglican churches. Maymyo was very much a military town, but it was a hill station, somewhere to go and rest in the pleasant climate, much like the role of Simla in the life of British India. There is only one Anglican church in Maymyo now, with a congregation of around one hundred. The congregation participates in Bible study groups outside of services, while the services themselves are solely Holy Communion, in either English or Burmese. Maymyo's congregation is also ethnically mixed, having Kachins, Karens, Burmans, Tamils, and Anglo-Indians among them. The style of churchmanship throughout Burma, especially outside of the main cities, tends to be old High Church or Anglo-Catholic, with a few exceptions, observers agree. Exceptions include those parts of Kachin, Chin, and Shan states that were pioneered by the evangelical BCMS, making Kachin, for example, a distinctly "mixed" state in terms of churchmanship. Charismatic-style worship is said to have made some inroads among Anglicans in Burma, but it seems to be an elusive phenomenon if it exists.

Karens continue to predominate among Burma's Christians in general and the Anglican Church in particular. Understandably, Karens have long been well represented at the Church's senior levels. The Anglican Church's episcopal model of governance has often recognized Karen clergy as the most able candidates to become assistant bishops and then move on to take the reins of the various dioceses in both Karen and non-Karen areas. This appears to have caused a little discomfort in the past among some non-Karen Anglicans, especially those from ethnic minority groups that are not particularly well represented in senior positions. As a result, there has been a drive in recent years to elect, as far as possible, bishops from the respective ethnic community they will then lead. This idea may not have been proclaimed as official policy, and the election of bishops is ethnically nondiscriminatory, but Anglicans at the grassroots level have sensed positive moves in the direction described. It is not that simple, of course, as it is clear from the aforementioned observations that practically all congregations are ethnically mixed, even in ethnic heartlands. Clergy from all backgrounds and across the whole country tend to be theologically conservative, mirrored by the attachment to the old High Church worship style. They also tend to be quite studious and attentive to wider developments in the Anglican Communion, of GAFCON, ACNA, and the Continuing Anglican bodies.

The Missionary Societies Today

The Bible Churchmen's Missionary Society (BCMS) first reached the far north of Burma, at Mohnyin in Kachin state, in 1924. BCMS continues to be involved in Burma under its new name (since 1992), Crosslinks. The society supports two local theology students—"study partners"—and now runs annual workshops as Crosslinks School of Biblical Preaching in Rangoon and occasionally in several other locations. The old name "BCMS" lives on in a less auspicious fashion up in Mohnyin, where the name was appropriated by a breakaway group of the congregation in the 1990s. This group had been in conflict with the diocese, whose heritage is strongly SPG and Anglo-Catholic. The evangelical "BCMS" parish broke away, it is understood locally, and anecdotally they claimed to be "no longer Anglican, we are BCMS." A number of meetings took place in both Mohnyin and Myitkyina, seeking reconciliation between the Church, in the form of the Diocese of Myitkyina, and the so-called BCMS breakaway group in Mohnyin. The group was explicitly instructed by the Crosslinks mediator and the Crosslinks mission director at the time, Rev. (now Bishop) Andy Lines, that they were not to style themselves "BCMS" since they are not part of that organization's work and have no endorsement from them. Mohnyin was also home to what became the Emmanuel Bible (or Divinity) School, founded in December 1931 as a simple Bible school, the fruit of years of missionary effort.

Rev. A. T. Houghton, his wife, Coralie, and his sister were the first BCMS missionaries in Burma in 1924, and they began the work in Mohnyin that year, first founding Emmanuel Church. Within ten years, there were no fewer than thirty-seven BCMS missionaries at work in the country.[37] The early years (recounted in Houghton's *Dense Jungle Green: The First Twelve Years of the B.C.M.S. Burma Mission*, 1937) emphasized healthcare work rather than the stock-in-trade education mission. Houghton coldly but accurately appraised that the history of educational missions in Burma was not encouraging from the point of view of converts.[38] The BCMS mission came into contact with a variety of ethnicities, as well as the indigenous Kachins, and encountered all the challenges that come with multiple languages and traditions living side by side. Burman Buddhist converts would remain exceedingly rare, though Shans and Kachins who had been brought up mainly with spirit beliefs rather than Buddhism could be more receptive. Some of them had already had a little cultural exposure to Christianity, which helped. Those from a spirit (or *nat*) worship background were less likely to be viscerally hostile to Christianity at least, and they would not necessarily see the two belief systems as incompatible: "until our message was really known," Houghton recalled, "we were frequently invited to *pois* (*nat* festivals) for marriages, funerals, and other events."[39] Houghton's grandson, Tim, whose father was the first "mission baby" born at Mohnyin, is involved with Crosslinks and acted as the mediator in the Mohnyin BCMS dispute. Tim's uncle and aunt, Peter and Rachel Thompson, were also BCMS missionaries in various parts of Burma, including Mohnyin, from the mid-1950s until their expulsion in 1966. Emmanuel Bible School, now in the hands of the breakaway group, will hopefully be soon replaced by a new Anglican Bible college for the north of Burma.

The modern heir to the SPG, now called United Society Partners in the Gospel (USPG), still works in partnership with the Church in Burma. As was foreseen from the middle of the twentieth century onward, the SPG's role shifted away from direct "parachuting-in" interventions and moved toward working in targeted partnerships to empower local organizations. These models contributed to the fact that Church-led primary health care in Burma, for example, had actually expanded by the 1990s.[40] From 1997, the society reaffirmed its support for the Karen people, including the vast numbers then fleeing across the border to Thailand to escape a new wave of ethnic cleansing.[41] The USPG currently focuses on training volunteer health workers to send into remote rural areas, with particular emphasis on isolated and marginalized communities. USPG works in all the dioceses in Burma, helping to support 270 health workers who are often a community's only access to health care. Health challenges in Burma are legion, and the country ranks 145 out of 187 countries in the UN's Human Development Index. It is one of the world's most underresourced health-care systems, especially in rural areas. Malaria, though partly preventable with nets, is still a main cause of sickness and death. Tuberculosis (TB) is also a big problem, especially drug-resistant TB and TB linked with the spread of human immunodeficiency virus (HIV). Health workers travel huge distances, and journeys can be long and difficult. In the Dioceses of Hpa-an, Yangon (Rangoon), and Mandalay, the USPG's WASH (Water, Sanitation, and Hygiene) program gives rural communities access to safe water (for people, agriculture, and livestock) and improved sanitation and health; it also promotes community resilience to disasters. WASH increases access to clean water by improving infrastructure such as water pipes, water tanks, and latrines. Training is also given in water management, hygiene, climate change effects, and climate-related emergencies and disasters.[42]

Christians and Social Problems

At local levels, Anglicans participate with other Christians in a range of social works, including the campaign against drug use, which is a significant problem among disenchanted young people with limited prospects. Families often send their children to work abroad in low-skill jobs in Thailand, China, and even South Korea or Japan in order to escape the lure of drugs and a dead-end future—clearly not an ideal solution, to put it mildly. Pat Jasan is a grassroots Christian antidrug movement with local cells in churches of all denominations, founded in Kachin state in 2014.[43] By local estimates, Kachin state alone is home to ten thousand hectares of opium production.[44] The government of Burma and the Burma Army are seen to be actively *opposed* to the antidrug fight, and they encourage a perception of Pat Jasan as a group of "sickle-wielding vigilantes" or quasi-paramilitaries, because some Pat Jasan activists wear combat fatigues on duty.[45] No one denies that Pat Jasan's methods have been controversial: destroying poppy crops, restraining and forcibly detoxing drug users, and apprehending and beating known dealers.[46] The name Pat Jasan translates as "banning and cleaning."

To the argument that it sounds drastic, activists respond by pointing to the drastic nature of the crisis. Coercion into drug use is famously rampant in one of northern Burma's most dangerous and lucrative industries, gemstone mining. Young workers can be lured into using drugs to make the appalling working conditions temporarily tolerable, in order to earn comparatively good wages but at enormous risk. Powerful financial interests are anxious to keep jade mining cheap and secretive, with desperately poor miners being an additional captive target market for the drugs business. Activists from Pat Jasan argue that the whole drugs crisis is an extreme situation requiring extreme measures, and that the crisis also serves to expose the institutional corruption and violence of the military. It is widely believed that the Burma Army's opposition is due to its complicity in the drugs trade, which seems to flourish despite supposed government crackdowns.[47]

The Church and Its Liturgy

In the Church of the Province of Myanmar (CPM), two liturgical books, one old and one new, are currently used, often in combination. One is the Prayer Book (Book of Common Prayer) of the old Church of India, Pakistan, Burma and Ceylon (CIPBC), which has its origins in the colonial Church. The other is the locally produced Order for Holy Communion, written by the province's own liturgical commission and approved in 2001. The CIPBC book provides the framework, lectionary, psalter, and Sunday lessons, as well as liturgies for baptism, ordination, matrimony, and so on.[48] It must be borne in mind that practically every scrap of liturgical or biblical text in print was destroyed during the Second World War, along with the printing presses themselves. The Church had always sustained a strong tradition of translation of texts and dissemination of worship material, and a few earlier text samples survived by chance, as a result of former missionaries taking copies home with them upon leaving Burma. What the Church possesses today results from what could be pieced together from scratch under hostile postwar conditions, at times comparable to the Japanese occupation itself. Depending on the whim and inspiration of government officials, controls and restrictions on Roman Catholic and Anglican churches have often been extended to liturgy, in which traditional Burmese music, arts, symbols, and so on were suddenly not allowed to be used, because these were considered proper only to Buddhist culture and not appropriate for use in the supposedly alien cult of Christianity.[49]

The Church and Its Leader

Stephen Than Myint Oo, current bishop of Yangon (Rangoon) and archbishop of the Church of the Province of Myanmar (since 2008), is the man who today faces the challenge of leading the Church, as Burma's fragile relationship with democracy progresses by two steps forward, two steps back.[50] He was born in a small village on the Delta riverbank in February 1958, into the Pwo Karen people, also called the plains or lowland Karen. They are said to trace their origins to groups who moved down from Mongolia in antiquity and then began to form a majority of the population in the southern part of the Delta area, a huge expanse of perfectly flat land to the south and west of Rangoon. At high tide, water envelops the Delta, while at low tide multiple rivers, inundating the land from the north, turn it into hundreds of islands with no bridges. Over 130,000 people died here in 2008 when Cyclone Nargis struck. The Karens who live here today are true survivors.

The archbishop has few memories of this place because by the age of four he had moved to Rangoon to begin school. But whenever he went back to his village, he saw many dead bodies in the river. Asking his parents about them, he learned that some of them had died attempting the perilous journey by boat to Rangoon, while others were killed by the Burma military, and still others by the Karen militia. When he was seven or eight years old, the Burma Army entered the village demanding rice and chickens, and the villagers were forced to comply. Sometimes there was fighting near the village, but he never saw it. On some occasions, the military pressured the villagers to turn over Kawthoolei (Karen Independence) leaders, using boats to search in and around the large lake behind the village. The archbishop still remembers many stories told around the villages, of so many Karens who were caught and killed.[51] Than's father and grandfather were teachers. His maternal grandfather was trained by a British missionary and became a teacher and missionary among the Karen people, and his father was a school principal.

When he was around four years old, Than's aunt had a vision of the village being invaded and of people being rounded up to serve as porters for the army—sadly, not an unusual occurrence. The omen was taken seriously, and little Stephen and other children were sent to the safety of Rangoon to attend St. John's Diocesan Boys' School.[52] These were the closing years of the tenure of Bishop Victor G. Shearburn, CR, well remembered by the current archbishop, but his hero was Delta Archdeacon Luke Po Kun, who assisted in sending many young Karen children to the school. Several of Than's aunts were teachers there and lived in the bishop's home compound. On his father's side, Than's family were all Christians, and on his mother's side most of the family were Buddhist. He was surrounded by Buddhists both in his extended family and in the areas where he lived. The Buddhists helped the Christians celebrate at Christmas, and, likewise, when the Buddhists celebrated a festival, the Christians helped them. Later, Than was somewhat surprised to learn that this situation was not replicated everywhere in Burma—for example, in the Karen areas near the Thai border. It is significant that the man who would go on to lead the Church was grounded in the principles of a multifaith community, a multifaith family, and the values of education but also exposed to the harshest realities of Burma and its conflicts. After studying at HCTC in Rangoon, he would gain an international perspective at Trinity Theological College in Singapore. Than's background and experiences connect today's Church with the struggles of its past and the challenges of its future, having experienced the peaceful cohabitation of different religious and ethnic groups as well as the violent oppression of the regime. He himself spent two years in prison as a hostage for his brother, a resistance fighter. It is hard to imagine a more apt person to lead Burma's Anglicans.

The Church and Higher Education

Holy Cross Theological College (HCTC), now in its eighty-sixth year, continues to be a vital hub in the life of the Church. At present, it is the only theological college for the whole of the CPM. HCTC offers a bachelor of theology (BTh) degree for students coming from all the dioceses of the province. Its capacity has historically been limited, and it has only been able to take twelve to fifteen new students each year, with two to five places being reserved for the Diocese of Yangon (Rangoon). This number is insufficient for training ordinands and future leaders, even for the relatively modest needs of a sixty- to seventy-thousand-member Church. Although there are currently Bible schools in some dioceses, they are only meant for catechists and full-time mission workers to serve in rural areas, not for the training of ordained clergy. The Bible schools tend to have limited places as well.[53] The BTh program at HCTC was started for the first time only in 1989, and it is destined to be phased out and replaced by the higher master of ministry (MMin) degree, similar to that offered by Myanmar Institute of Theology (MIT).

An ambitious building project is currently underway at HCTC to complement the handsome original red-brick college and provide vital room for expansion. Much depends on the dynamism and vision of the current principal of HCTC, Rev. Canon Dr. Paul Myint Htet, an Old Testament scholar who previously lectured at MIT. Under his direction, HCTC takes its unique role in the life of the Church seriously, and it is truly representative of the whole province. About 40 percent of the students are Karens, as are most of the teaching staff, which is partly aided by the college's geographical location and its accessibility for Karens. Twenty to thirty percent of the students are Kachins, who are also represented on the teaching staff. There are Chins and also some Tamils, often still coming from the Indian-Tamil parish of St. Gabriel's.[54] One of the long-standing limitations of the Church has been the absence of Christian education programs for adult members or adolescent members after confirmation. The only source of advancing in knowledge of the faith for future adult life has generally been attendance at Sunday services, hearing Bible readings and sermons given by the priests, which is obviously dependent on being able to attend regular church services. It remains difficult to guarantee, to every Anglican in Burma, regular access to proper church services with a prepared sermon being preached. While priests affirm that they do realize the importance of delivering a prepared sermon, for a variety of reasons they can feel incapable of doing so.[55] CPM members can be refreshingly open, positive, and sincere about the many difficult tasks facing the Church.

Summary

This chapter has aimed to highlight the sheer range of difficulties facing all Christians in modern Burma—now Myanmar—with a special focus on the Anglicans' situation, especially as expressed by Anglicans themselves. It should be obvious that these difficulties are great not only in variety but also in complexity, including some of the toughest problems facing any modern social group, such as youth and drugs, young people's prospects and aspirations, threatened ethnic identity, social and economic marginalization, human rights abuses, political oppression, and the struggle for religious freedom. There are also what might be called the old problems for the Church relating to education provision, training, and supporting church workers, being a small Church in a multifaith society, being a small Church spread across a vast territory, and not least, of course, the challenge of doing evangelization.

THE ANGLICAN CHURCH IN BURMA

Much of the worldwide Christian churches' relations with the secular world over the past fifty years or so may arguably be read as a story of historic compromise. For Anglican Churches in Asia, the ultimate postcolonial solution meant compromising on church order and polity, but new bones of contention soon started to appear, the first global one being the question of women's ordination. This would lead to a rejection of the compromise path and the growth of a substantial rival Anglican community organizing outside of the official structures of the Anglican Communion. In Burma, the newly autonomous Church had to face the immediate existing challenge of being a minority Church of a minority religion, finding its main appeal among minority ethnic communities. All three of these factors have served as pretexts for discrimination and prejudice, in addition to the persecution suffered by all Christian ethnic minorities. Being a religious minority entails more than simply being underrepresented in Burma, where the dominant Buddhist elite have often put their faith at the service of authoritarian regimes.

For the Church, the constant struggle to show solidarity and support for Christians in ethnic minorities, without simply drawing even more hostility and restrictions upon them, is a balancing act that has contributed to hindering the Church's general development. The Church does lack resources for raising its profile, but would it be desirable to raise its profile anyway? Similarly, effective channels and platforms for delivering a critical commentary on current affairs (such as the Rohingya case) may be missing, but we may wonder to what extent such criticism would have to be carefully rationed and perhaps even self-censored. The possible result of this is that the Church's voice appears weak and immature in an age when we have come to expect strident and sophisticated messaging from faith organizations. There is no highly trained international communications team to marshal the Church's messages on major issues and stage-manage an official response. Outside observers may be forced to pick through individual comments to identify a semblance of a collective opinion, but it would be a mistake to conclude that Church members shy away from the terrifying injustices, social problems, and crises they face.

Language and its political and practical implications pervade every aspect of Anglican life, further complicating matters, but despite this fact today's Church is eager for international cooperation. The work of the historic missionary societies continues in new and reimagined forms, and it is by nurturing its connections with the worldwide Church that the Church of the Province of Myanmar (CPM) hopes to find solutions to many of its most persistent problems. Common ground with the other Anglican Churches, based on faith, heritage, and language, has never been lacking, but the new reality facing Anglicans everywhere in this century—the global south focus and the much-debated global Anglican future—is leading to a radical recalibration in international relations among all Anglicans. Clearly, some of the old frameworks for international Anglican networking, relationships of dependence dating back to the colonial era, can no longer be seen as appropriate, desirable, or compatible with a completely decolonized future. And so, the common ground shifts to discerning the fundamental values that underpin the Anglican Communion, within which, in previous times, no one doubted the member Churches' agreement on those fundamentals. The main source of those fundamental values was, of course, the Bible, in a traditional Anglican—Reformed and Catholic—interpretation, but this can no longer be easily agreed upon. The Anglican Churches now find themselves in an age where nothing can be taken for granted, and the CPM has accepted its role in helping to establish worldwide Anglican communion—*small c*—all over again, as one of Christianity's biggest global organizations completely reconfigures itself.

Afterword

"To anyone interested in religions, Burma is the most fascinating country in the world. Here, side by side, can be seen numerous adherents to all the great religions of the world."[1] This statement, made more than ninety years ago, is a little less true today, for political and historical reasons, but it is still, in essence, correct. Today, the once prominent Jewish and Armenian communities of Burma are reduced to a tiny handful each, and there are far fewer Sikhs and Hindus than in the British Empire days, but all of the world's faiths are indeed still represented. Just as there are many religions in today's Myanmar, there are many more ethnic groups and subgroups, more than 130 by the most widely accepted calculations (see appendix 3), and a similar number of indigenous languages. This complexity is also reflected in the multiplicity of political groups, regional independence groups, and ethnic-national organizations.[2] In the midst of this complex picture, we find the Anglican Church, the old "church of empire," and to the casual observer it could look like nothing more than a colonial relic today.[3] But the story of the Church in Burma did not end along with the empire; it succeeded in the daunting task of surviving Independence from Britain and going on to flourish with an identity of its own. Anglicanism never vied for first place in Burma, even among the other Christian denominations. Of these, the American Baptists were the most successful, having a looser hierarchy, a more practical, reformed approach to church order and ministry, more flexibility, and therefore more adaptability. For the Baptists, crucially, entrusting locals with greater responsibility had no subversive anti-colonial connotations or worrying political implications, as was the case for the Anglicans, so the Baptists' work developed faster. The Baptist Church had no stake at all, directly or indirectly, in the running of the empire, as the Anglican Church did. All of these factors served as advantages for the Baptists and, when reversed, hindrances for the Anglicans.

Looking to the Past

The Anglicans, unlike the other denominations, may be thought to have had a captive audience in the troops, traders, and bureaucrats of the empire,

AFTERWORD

but was this a blessing or a curse? British expatriates were indeed the mainstay of the Church, especially in the urban centers of Rangoon, Mandalay, and Moulmein. These included public servants, teachers, clerks, merchants, and soldiers, and while many of them settled in Burma with their families, sometimes for several generations, the typical colonial functionary was a young, carefree, single British male. Their attachment to decent society and Christian values quickly deteriorated in the mysterious East, where "the ardor of religious life cools," as Bishop Strachan put it, perhaps mildly, and "the lessons of early life are forgotten . . . people lapse into indifference—nay, even into immorality."[4] The Church had little chance of bringing these young, male, and wayward expatriates back from the brink. For many of this cohort, the empire unreservedly meant adventure: the stuff of Kipling, the British Club, gin, sport, and local women and girls as their playthings, but the Church would be left to care for the resulting orphans and abandoned families. This particular type of adventure sport helped to deprive the Church of the priceless time and resources needed to undertake real evangelization, missionary work, and social projects. Even without such worries, the Church had no free rein from the authorities, and the early decades in Burma saw the Church "hindered at every turn by the incredible scruples of the East India Company"[5] and later by the British government's own policy of religious neutrality.

Roman Catholic missionary societies enjoyed similar freedoms as the American Baptists, while also benefiting from much longer corporate experience in Southeast Asia. But the Roman Catholic Church still carried the stigma of having previously won conversions by force and coercion in the region as part of the wider political objective of expanding Christendom. The various components of the Protestant wave of missionaries to Southeast Asia were well aware of these unfortunate precedents, which they sometimes mitigated as having been an excess of zeal, but the Protestants would not completely escape criticism either. In the case of both the Baptists and the Anglicans, genuine missionary zeal and passion were considerable, but the majority of the population in Burma remained impassive: "To gain a convert from Buddhism is like pulling the tooth of a tiger," Adoniram Judson is reputed to have said.[6] None of the other Christian denominations, it must be reiterated, operated under the same gamut of restrictions, limitations, and pressures that the "the poor, unoffending old Church of England"[7] had to endure, but none of them had significant success converting Buddhists either.

AFTERWORD

The evolution of the Anglican Church's role in Burma was not linear but confused, and there were competing understandings of what that role should be. It was not the first Church to arrive in Burma, and when it did arrive it did not do so in orchestrated fashion; there were the army chaplains, the government chaplains, the missionary societies, and the "additional clergy," and at length a diocesan structure was established. But from the start, the Church counted on a radical and "emphatically missionary" element whose gaze went beyond official policy to the higher cause of preaching the Kingdom of God. They were passionate missionaries but also realists who soon saw that not much could be achieved among the "unresponsive Burmans" without more personnel and resources.[8] In their well-meaning naivete, or ignorance, they lost little love for this "atheistic Buddhism," which seemed impervious to the Christian message, and which was generally blamed (along with the other institutional and political causes) for the lack of progress. Despite all this, a great century-long love affair had begun: "British people loved Burma," Bishop West wrote. "After India's arid plains, Burma was rich and green. After Calcutta's gloom, Rangoon was gay. The Shwe Dagon Pagoda was one of the delights of the whole earth."[9]

To the Church's credit, there were skilled men and women in its ranks who understood where progress could be made, such as among the lower-status expatriate communities of Tamils, Telugus, and Chinese, who proved more receptive to the Christian message. There were also the large, marginalized ethnic groups such as the Karens, the Kachins, and the Chins, who felt no compulsion to emulate the higher-class Burman Buddhist elite in their intransigence. Christianity could even provide a liberating contrast to society's pecking order and allow downtrodden minorities to assert their separate identity more freely. Cynicism and frustration gave way to idealism and hope for many second- and third-generation missionaries who could feel that their work was truly transformative and that they were helping to establish "new harmony between man and man and race and race."[10] Anglican schools had always succeeded in bringing together a bewildering number of ethnicities, including Armenians, British, Burmans, Chinese, Eurasians, Hindus, Jews, Karens, Madrassis, Shans, and Talaings, just to mention a selection.[11] Many of the ethnic groups the Church engaged with had no written language before the missionaries' arrival, and it fell to a few of these dedicated pioneers to transcribe the local languages for the first time. They would use either Roman script (as with the Kachins) or the Burmese alphabet, if any of the mission team had mastery of it (as was the case with

AFTERWORD

the Karens). As hard as the missionaries worked, the Anglican Church still did not put enough effort into training native catechists, evangelists, and teachers, as the Baptists had done, adding further to the disparity between the denominations.[12] The one salient Anglican runaway success story was and remains the Church's mutual embrace with the Karen people, beginning a long history of encouraging self-support and self-propagation among the Karens, enabling the Church to grow in their midst, and to persist under impressive homegrown leaders during the Second World War.[13]

There was less conflict between the competing Christian denominations than might be expected because they were mostly careful not to step on one another's toes. The Anglicans had a substantial and theoretically already churchgoing European community as well as several substantial immigrant and ethnic groups to minister to, so they refrained from anything that might look like poaching from the Baptists. Beyond these key groups there was no need, and no use, in pursuing an aggressive evangelization of the Buddhist Burmans, though some of these did convert. The Church's effort was not perfect, and its leaders admitted this; progress was always painfully slow and success was never overwhelming. There were great cultural, physical, and spiritual obstacles to contend with, and there was sometimes great indecision, such as whether or not to accept the conversion of Mrs. Mason's former Baptist Karens. Church leaders often fell prey to discouragement and demoralization. Other clergy and missionaries, and certainly not just Anglicans, may have succumbed to more soul-destroying temptations, as George Orwell suggested in his early writing about Burma. The Anglican Church clearly did make a substantial positive contribution to Burma in many and varied ways, providing education, health care, and social infrastructure, but also pathways to solidarity and enfranchisement for oppressed groups, things that are remembered to this day as being vital for defining national ethnic identities. Young Christian teachers asked me rhetorically, "What kind of schools were here before the British came?" The answer is "There *were* no schools." The overwhelming impression from the writings and recollections of Anglican clergy and missionaries, for their part, is one of profound affection and love for the country and its people.

Looking to the Present

There is no way of avoiding the fact that the modern history of Burma is a staggering tragedy. The forces of government hold an indisputable record of brutality, corruption, and inhumanity, and the challenges directly facing Anglicans have been legion. In the middle two decades of the past century alone, these challenges included exclusion, discrimination, suppression, persecution, the destruction of both material and human resources in wartime, and dashed hopes of true independence in peacetime.[14] And the challenges did not end there; to date, there has not been a time in which Anglicans in Myanmar have not experienced some combination of discrimination, violence, and frustrated hopes for improvement. This all sits side by side with the usual problems related to extreme poverty—poor access to education, poor access to sanitation and clean water, lack of opportunity, lack of facilities, and so forth—that affect an enormous section of the population.

Among some of the ethnic groups, Christianity is the majority religion. About 80 percent of the Karenni people, about 90 percent of the Kachin people, and a similar proportion of the Chin people are Christians. The Chins are one of the most diverse ethnic groups, consisting of many different subgroups, and Christianity is one common thread that provides a measure of cultural consistency and ethnic unity; it is thus at the core of Chin identity.[15] The majority of the Naga people (considered to be a subgroup of the Chins) residing in Sagaing Division are also Christians.[16] Around 40 percent of the Karen people are Christians. Punitive military campaigns against minority Christian groups are far from over, and Burma continues to wage an actual religiously inspired war on several fronts against its own people. Buddhism, in a distorted and perverted form, is still used to justify military aggression.[17] Before the 2020 global pandemic began, a peace process had started between the central Burma government and the Northern Alliance, composed of Kachin, Shan, and Wa (a subgroup of the Shans) Christians. But even as the negotiators sat in session, in September 2019, five Kachin Christian civilians, including three children, were killed when fighting suddenly broke out between the Burma Army and the Northern Alliance. The fighting started at about 6:00 in the morning in the jungle just north of Kutkai town. Alarmed villagers fled to the house of the village chief, and at 12:30 a mortar shell hit the house, killing five people from two families. Two other civilians were wounded on the same day when the Burma Army fired mortars at their house. As the fighting was taking place, Northern Alliance representatives were meeting the government's National Reconciliation and Peace Center representatives to discuss a bilateral ceasefire aimed at ending the recent round of clashes.[18] Such incidents were never atypical, but the subsequent pandemic drew a

AFTERWORD

curtain around already isolated Myanmar, behind which, it is feared by human rights watchers, the regime now operates with the assumption of total impunity.

Christian Solidarity Worldwide points to some symbolic improvements in the status and security of Christians in recent years, such as the surprise appointment of an ethnic Chin Christian as vice president in 2016, who served until his removal by the military in 2021.[19] Non-Burmans, and especially non-Buddhists, have customarily been barred from military or government positions beyond the equivalent rank of major. There have also been some relaxations in the restrictions on church building and the construction of crosses. (A tradition in Chin state is to erect large crosses in prominent public places. This has regularly sparked government reprisals, the crosses being destroyed or replaced with Buddhist symbols). But violence against Christians and the targeting of churches as part of the ongoing war continue despite a few positive omens.[20] Some young minority Christians, conscious of history, regret that stronger links with Britain were not maintained after 1948, and they are keen to preserve the links that do remain, not least of which, of course, is a common religious heritage. Young Kachins told me that they value their shared history with Britain, and one suspects that the old colonial rulers are regarded with more warmth than the current ones. Peace remains elusive for Burma's Christians.

Looking to the Future

As this book reaches its end, it is clear that the story itself is far from over. If you have the privilege of seeing the Anglican Church of Myanmar in action for yourself, you will be touched by the warmth, conviction, aspiration, dynamism, and enthusiasm of old and young members, but especially the young. There is nothing frivolous or throwaway about what they do; their Church is no mere diversion from the cares of the world, nor do they attend out of obligation or habit. There is an earnestness and dedication to their activity: building community, showing mutual care, giving a welcome to strangers, and above all praising God. The modern Church honors the early missionary work that was aimed at breaking down all barriers of race, religion, and social position, and it remains a very diverse entity.[21] There is still much to learn from and about this curious Church.

The Anglican Communion today is marked by heated debate over its composition, its orientation, its structure, its foundations, its future, and its very survival as a worldwide church. The small Church of the Province of Myanmar plays a full part in that debate, punching well above its weight in the world arena. This Church is no relic of the empire, as may be thought; it preserves many customs and traditions of the old English Church, it is true, but it does so almost in a defiant way, long after the bulk of the English Church itself has abandoned many of those same customs and traditions. The CPM also preserves the use of the English language, which can be seen as both a cause and symptom of a still-enduring historical relationship with the former colonial powers. The use of English has almost certainly provided ammunition for accusations of being an unpatriotic, Western-looking Church, and in turn it too can be construed as an implicit (or even incidental) act of defiance, in the face of a regime that sought to denigrate and eliminate all minority languages. For some Christians, maintaining the use of English provides a neutral ground between the politically charged use of ethnic minority languages, which can be a punishable offence, and the use of Burmese, which is forcefully promoted. Opting for the neutral language of English is a strategy that may facilitate and enable Christian education as well.

One important potential outcome of this book is for Anglican readers and students of religion in the global north to appreciate certain aspects of the worldwide recalibration taking place within Anglicanism—with its emphasis on the global south—that may have escaped their attention. This story concerns the rebuilding and reimagining of networks and lines of communication in a world that is postcolonial, post–Cold War, and in some ways postcapitalist, at least in the sense of the unfettered and ubiquitous Western-dominated capitalism that went unquestioned and unchallenged for so long. The world today feels a much greater sense of connectivity and sensitivity to other cultures but also a greater urgency to find common ground on a wide range of crucial issues, such as family, poverty, human dignity, freedom of worship, economic and social justice, health, and the environment. The Churches of the global south, almost without exception, once formed part of something bigger—an empire ruled from the global north—and with the end of empire there came the risk of isolation, becoming an outpost on the fringe *of* the fringe of the worldwide Church. But since God surely does not relegate any local Church or people on the basis of their place in the economic pecking order, that perception could not go uncontested. Anglicans began to query the unspoken power-flow running from north to south and to wonder whether it would prove still fit for purpose.

AFTERWORD

As time progressed, the age-old power frameworks superimposed onto worldwide Anglicanism were indeed shown to be universally defective, with global north and global south being completely out of balance and out of harmony. In a quest to preserve Anglican values, to uphold the traditional sources of authority and moral decision-making, and to reserve the right to discern those values and morals for themselves, new alignments have emerged that transcend the old ones. The worldwide Anglican Church may have to acknowledge with sorrow that the old power structures are fully obsolete. Against the odds, a small minority Church in a half-forgotten corner of the world has come to play a leading role in the regeneration of a worldwide communion, and the voice of the Church in old Burma is heard by and resonates with around ninety million people worldwide. The Church of the Province of Myanmar is both committed to and emblematic of the shift toward a reinvigorated Anglican Christianity with a focus on the global south. This shift takes the form of a historic orthodox and conservative movement, which heralds either the breakup and separation or the renewal and revitalization of global Anglicanism.[22]

Appendix 1
Chronology of the Anglican Church in Burma

This chronology draws on a wide range of sources, all of which are listed in the main bibliography. These sources include the Rangoon Diocesan Association (RDA)'s journals published between 1897 and 1970; numerous contemporary histories, memoirs, and biographies; and Bishop Mark Saw Maung Doe's 2008 doctoral research. Biographical details have also been checked against the records of the Diocese of Yangon (https://yangon.anglicanmyanmar.org) and the library and archives of Holy Cross Theological College (HCTC), Yangon.

1824 Anglican clergy arrive in Burma as chaplains accompanying the British Army during the First Anglo-Burmese War (1824–26).

1825 First Church of England parish established in Burma, at Sittwe.

1826 Following the First Anglo-Burmese War, Anglican clergy are appointed throughout British territory as government chaplains.

1852–54: Second Anglo-Burmese War Extends British Burma

1854 First SPG (Society for the Propagation of the Gospel) missions in Burma with the arrival of T. A. Cockey.

1859 A. Shears (SPG) and his wife arrive from England to direct the missionary school in Moulmein (Mawlamyine).
Arrival of John Ebenezer Marks (later Rev. Dr.), who enlarges and develops the educational mission in Moulmein.

1863 J. E. Marks opens a school in Rangoon (this later becomes St. John's College).
Mang Shwe Zan is baptized by A. Shears as the first Burmese native Christian, in England.
Ms. Cooke (sometimes spelled Cook) establishes a school for women, named St. Mary's Girls' School, in Rangoon.

1868 At the invitation of King Mindon, J. E. Marks goes to Mandalay to begin a school and mission there.

1870 J. E. Marks opens schools in Zalon (or Zalun), Henzada, and Thayet-myo, beginning the Delta missions.

1872 The mission among the Tamils begins in Moulmein.

1873 The mission among the Burmans begins in Taungoo.

1874 James Alfred Colbeck starts the mission among the Burmans and other ethnic groups based in Kemmendine.

APPENDIX 1

1875 Karen Anglican population increases dramatically in Taungoo because of internal division among the Baptists. The Taungoo mission becomes the main Karen mission.

1877 Rangoon Diocese launched on 24 February as part of the Province of Calcutta. Jonathan Holt Titcomb becomes the first bishop of Rangoon (1877–82).
John San (or Tsan) Baw is ordained as the first native Burmese deacon, in England.

1878 Four Karens ordained as deacons; they are the first native Karen clergy.
Samuel Abishe Ganathan ordained as the first Tamil deacon, working as missionary among the Tamils in Moulmein.
Mission among the Chinese already underway in Rangoon.

1882 John Miller Strachan MD becomes the second bishop of Rangoon (1882–1903).

1883 John Fairclough opens the catechetical training school in Kemmendine.
T. Rickard (sometimes spelled Richard) starts the mission in Pazundaung township, east Rangoon, including a girls' school and a dispensary.

1884 John San (or Tsan) Baw ordained priest at Holy Trinity Church (the then-pro-cathedral), at that time on Strand Road (near the intersection with Merchant Road).

1885–87: Upper Burma Is Annexed to British Burma

1888 H. M. Stockings (sometimes spelled Stocking) begins the mission in Shwebo, in middle Burma.

1892 A. H. Ellis begins the Winchester Mission in Rangoon.

1893 John Hackney opens St. Peter's Bible School in Taungoo.

1894 Using Thayetmyo as his base, C. R. Torkington, a layman, begins the mission among Asho Chins.

1899 Based in Prome, George Whitehead begins the mission among Chins.

1900 W. C. B. Purser begins the mission in Kyaiklatt (or Kyaiklat) in the Delta area.

1901 David Po Sa and Po Thet (Burmans) ordained deacon, joining the Kyaiklatt mission and extending their mission to other areas in the Delta.

1901: The Death of Queen Victoria

1903 Arthur Mesac Knight becomes the third bishop of Rangoon (1903–09).

1904 Pwo Karens in the Delta area begin Anglican conversion.

1907 Mission to Seamen begins in Rangoon.

1909 R. S. Fyffe, missionary in Mandalay of the Winchester Brotherhood, becomes the fourth bishop of Rangoon (1909–28).

APPENDIX 1

Pwo Karen in Mhawbe near Rangoon begin Anglican conversion.

1910 Anglican mission spreads to other Pwo Karen areas in the Delta; Nyaungdon, Pantanaw, Wakema, and Shwedaung.

1914–18: The First World War

1914 First Rangoon diocesan council held.
W. C. B. Purser opens Kemmendine Blind School.
Mrs. Mary C. Purser begins mission among mothers in Kemmendine.

1917 W. H. Jackson, a blind priest known as "apegyi" ("great father" to the blind), arrives in Kemmendine to lead the Blind School.

1918 Saya Tawmhwa from St. Paul's Church in Taungoo is sent as a missionary to Kappali in Hpa-an, southeast Burma.

1921 Samuel Tun (an Asho Chin) and Nashone Mahn Own Bwint (a Karen) ordained as deacons—the first clergy for their respective communities.
Peter Khin Maung becomes the first native bachelor of divinity degree holder (Bishop's College, Calcutta) and is later ordained priest.

1924 A. T. "Tim" Houghton from Bible Churchmen's Missionary Society (BCMS) begins the mission among the Kachins in Mohnyin.

1925 New version of the Burmese Bible, translated into Burmese by the Bible Society led by C. E. Garrad, is published.

1926 BCMS begins its mission in Hukong areas in Kamine (or Kamaing), northern Burma.
Rangoon Diocesan Trust Association formed.

1928 Norman Henry Tubbs becomes the fifth bishop of Rangoon (1928-35).

1929 H. Hacking of the BCMS begins the mission among the Khumi Chins in Palawa.

1930 Church of India, Burma and Ceylon (CIBC) is formed.

1931 Emmanuel Bible School (sometimes Divinity School) opens in Mohnyin.

1932 Conference of the clergy held in Rangoon.
BCMS begins its mission in Wontho (or Wuntho) in Shan state.

1934 Construction of a building for the Bible School is begun on Inya Road, consecrated in 1935 and initially named Holy Cross College.
Kukekine Bible School transferred to the new Inya Road site.

1935 George A. West becomes the sixth bishop of Rangoon (1935-54).

1936 Karen national Saya Saw Satphaw ordained deacon at BCMS mission in Mohnyin.

1937: Burma Is Separated from India as a State

1937 First Kachin, Khamawgum, ordained deacon.
Emmanuel Church in Mohnyin is consecrated.

APPENDIX 1

1938   W. B. Johnston opens a missionary hospital in Pinlon, southern Shan
       state.

1939–45: The Second World War

1939   A. T. Houghton is elected as assistant bishop of Rangoon (not carried
       forward due to enemy action in the Second World War).
1941   Japanese forces invade Burma; all missionaries and foreign civilians
       (and their families) begin evacuation northward.
1942   George Appleton is appointed archdeacon to oversee the Burma
       missions remotely from India.
       Native clergy, ministers, and teachers continue serving dispersed
       Anglicans at huge risk to their lives and livelihoods.
1945   Bishop West returns to Rangoon at the end of the war.
1946   West reorganizes the Church, creating three archdeaconries—Delta,
       Mandalay, and Taungoo—led by native clergy: Luke Po Kun, John
       Aung Hla, and John Hla Gyaw, respectively.
       Holy Cross Theological College (HCTC) reopens, run by R. W. Garrad.
1947   First postwar Rangoon diocesan council held.
       Church of India, Pakistan, Burma and Ceylon (CIPBC) formed as a new
       province in the Anglican Communion.

1948: Burmese Independence

1948   G. Tidey takes over at HCTC.
       St. Peter's Bible School transfers from Taungoo to Kappali in Hpa-an,
       under the direction of Francis Ah Mya.
1949   First native bishops, Francis Ah Mya and John Aung Hla, consecrated
       as assistant bishops.
1950   HCTC closes temporarily due to insurgencies.
1951   The Emmanuel Bible School closes for ten years, eventually reopened
       by D. H. Dansey.
1952   Rangoon diocesan council held after a five-year hiatus due to unrest.
1955   Victor G. Shearburn CR becomes the seventh bishop of Rangoon
       (1955–66).
       Ta Hwai is ordained deacon, the first Khumi Chin clergy.
       HCTC reopens with thirteen students and J. Maung Pe becomes the
       first Burmese principal.
1956   Bishop Shearburn launches the Summer School.
1957   Moulmein archdeaconry opens and Bishop Francis Ah Mya is
       appointed archdeacon, launching the self-supporting program in
       Hpa-an.
1958   Assistant Bishop John Aung Hla attends the Lambeth Conference, the
       first native bishop to do so.
1959   Students from HCTC are sent abroad for further study.

APPENDIX 1

Esther Hla Kyaw, teacher at St. Augustine's in Moulmein, is appointed national youth leader, the first native Karen woman in the post.

1960 Youth conference in Rangoon—the Anglican Young People's Association (AYPA)—is launched.
The Religious Education Department is founded—Dorothy Lewis becomes the department head.
Church newsletter launched.
HCTC graduates begin further studies at universities.

1961 Emmanuel Bible School in Mohnyin reopens after ten years. Kushin Hla becomes the first local (Kachin) principal.
Tote Yow (Khumi Chin) and Yone Htow are ordained deacon.

1963 St. Peter's Bible School, which was closed for nearly ten years, is transferred to Hpa-an and reopened.

1965 The Special Evangelism Project begins in Palawa.

1966 Expulsion of all foreign missionaries, clergy, and Bishop Shearburn.
Francis Ah Mya becomes the first native bishop of Rangoon (1966–73).
Rangoon Diocesan Men's Association (MA) is formed, with Ba Than as head.
Daw Nelly, a native woman, is appointed as chief of the Mothers' Union (MU).

1967 The "Three in One" Project begins at Indaw in Upper Burma, with three aims: evangelism, self-supporting income-generating activities, and establishing male and female religious communities.
Reorganization of the Church: the diocesan council agrees to work for the creation of a new Anglican province in Burma.

1968 The provincial council of the CIPBC initially approves the proposal for a Province of Burma.

1970 The provincial council of the CIPBC ratifies the proposal for the Province of Burma in January.
In February, the Church of the Province of Burma (CPB) is created.
Rangoon Diocese becomes the lead diocese of the new province and Bishop Francis Ah Mya becomes the first archbishop of the CPB (1970–73).

1971 The AYPA presents the first of the annual theatrical performances at the Baptist compound memorial hall.
Evening Bible class for laypeople begins at the Anglican Religious Training Centre in Rangoon.

1972 The Central Rangoon Religious Education Committee is formed.

1973 The first summer training course of the Central Rangoon Religious Education Committee begins.
The AYPA and MU support the launch of the Samuel Project for clergy education.
Bishop John Aung Hla becomes the second archbishop of the CPB (1973–79).

APPENDIX 1

A Worker Priests project begins.

1975 Rangoon Diocesan Aid Board formed.

1976 The mission among the Lay Myo Chins begins, led by Tote Yow.

1978 Diocese of Hpa-an is created.

1979 Gregory Hla Gyaw, former bishop of Hpa-an Diocese, becomes the third archbishop of the CPB (1979–87).

1981 The Mindon mission is relaunched, by retired Archbishop Francis Ah Mya.

1982 Catechist training begins at the Anglican Religious Training Centre in Rangoon.

1984 The Partnership in Mission Program is launched.

1986 The mission in Hakhine Hill is launched.

The provincial council approves the creation of Myitkyina Missionary Diocese from the existing Myitkyina archdeaconry.

1988 Andrew Mya Han becomes the fourth archbishop of the CPB (1988–2001).

Andrew Hla Aung becomes bishop of Myitkyina.

Samuel San Si Htay, former principal of HCTC, becomes assistant bishop of Rangoon.

1991 The Decade of Evangelism is launched.

1992 Conferences on evangelism held in every diocese, and mission works launched in new areas.

Taungoo, which was a part of Hpa-an Diocese, becomes Taungoo Missionary Diocese with George Kyaw Mya as bishop.

1993 Bishop San Si Htay becomes general secretary of the Myanmar Council of Churches (MCC).

J. Than Pe, former archdeacon of Yangon, becomes assistant bishop of Yangon Diocese.

Tin Maung becomes archdeacon of Yangon Diocese.

1994 Taungoo Missionary Diocese becomes Diocese of Taungoo—John Saw Wilme, former principal of HCTC, becomes first bishop of Taungoo (until 2019).

1995 Social development projects are started in every diocese.

1999 A new Bible school is opened at St. Michael's Church in Kemmendine.

2001 Samuel San Si Htay becomes the fifth archbishop of the Church of the Province of Myanmar (CPM) (2001–08).

2005 Stephen Than Myint Oo of HCTC becomes the fifth diocesan bishop of Hpa-an.

2008 Stephen Than Myint Oo, bishop of Hpa-an, becomes the sixth archbishop of the CPM (2008–present).

Saw Stylo becomes bishop of Hpa-an.

Full college of bishops of Myanmar attends the Lambeth Conference.

Cyclone Nargis hits—the Church is actively involved with relief efforts.

2009 James Min Dein, former distributor of the Myanmar Bible Society and secretary of AYPA, becomes bishop of Sittwe.

APPENDIX 1

2010 Archbishop Stephen Than Myint Oo attends the fourth Global South encounter in Singapore.
2014 Archbishop Stephen Than Myint Oo joins six other archbishops for the enthronement of Foley Beach as primate of the Anglican Church in North America (ACNA).
2017 Dr. Mark Saw Maung Doe, former principal of HCTC, becomes bishop of Hpa-an.
Dr. Paul Myint Htet becomes principal of HCTC.
2018 Archbishop Stephen Than Myint Oo attends GAFCON III in Jerusalem.
2019 Dr. Saw Shee Shoe becomes bishop of Taungoo.
2020 Coronavirus pandemic hits—Church volunteer teams are actively involved in relief, led by Archbishop Stephen Than Myint Oo.
The Church quietly marks its fiftieth anniversary as an autonomous province.

Appendix 2
List of Bishops Having Leadership of the Church in Burma

Consisting of:
(a) Bishops of Calcutta, 1813–98
(b) Bishops of Rangoon, 1877–1970
(c) Archbishops of the Church of the Province of Burma (CPB), 1970–89
(d) Archbishops of the Church of the Province of Myanmar (CPM), 1989–present (note that archbishops of the Province also hold the position of bishop of Rangoon [Yangon])
(e) Sources and further reading

(a) Bishops of Calcutta

THOMAS FANSHAWE MIDDLETON (28 January 1769–8 July 1822), first bishop of Calcutta from 1813 until his death. The diocese included the entire territory of the British East India Company, eventually including Burma. Upon arrival Middleton learned that he was not allowed to ordain natives. In response, he founded Bishop's College in Calcutta, which admitted Britons, Indians, and Anglo-Indians, some of whom would go on to ordination. Bishop Middleton died in Calcutta on 8 July 1822 and is buried under the altar of St. John's Church, then the Cathedral of Calcutta.

REGINALD HEBER (21 April 1783–3 April 1826) was the second bishop of Calcutta, from 1823 until his death. He had a long-standing interest in the work of overseas missions; he supported not only the SPG but also its more recently formed evangelical sister-body, the Church Missionary Society (CMS), and while still at Oxford he had helped to found the British and Foreign Bible Society (BFBS). Arduous duties, a hostile climate, and poor health led to his collapse and death after less than three years in India.

JOHN THOMAS JAMES (23 January 1786–22 August 1828), known as Thomas James, was bishop of Calcutta briefly from 1827 until his death in 1828. On 20 June 1828 he began a visitation of his diocese, but he was taken ill and was advised to take a sea voyage. He sailed for China on 9 August but died during the voyage and was buried at sea.

JOHN MATTHIAS TURNER (1786–1831) was appointed as the fourth bishop of Calcutta in 1829. He died in post in the summer of 1831.

DANIEL WILSON (2 July 1778–2 January 1858) was consecrated as bishop of Calcutta and first Metropolitan of India and Ceylon in 1832. He founded churches in Rangoon and Ceylon as well as St. Paul's Cathedral, Calcutta (consecrated 1847). He also founded Dhaka College on 18 July 1841 (completed in 1846). He was associated with the Clapham Sect of evangelical Anglicans, the best known of whom is William Wilberforce. In 1835, Wilson was notable for calling India's caste system "a cancer." He died in Calcutta in 1858 and is buried within St. Paul's Cathedral, Calcutta.

GEORGE EDWARD LYNCH COTTON (29 October 1813–6 October 1866) became the sixth bishop of Calcutta and the second metropolitan of India in 1858. He had been a schoolmaster at both Rugby School and Marlborough College, becoming headmaster of the latter. He founded many schools in India; his insistence on his pupils wearing socks, and his habit of blessing the socks prior to being issued to the pupils, is thought to have given rise to the popular phrase "bless your Cotton socks." On 6 October 1866, he had consecrated a cemetery at Kushtia on the Ganges and was crossing a plank leading from the bank to the steamer when he slipped and fell into the river. He was carried away by the current and never seen again.

ROBERT MILMAN (25 January 1816–15 February 1876) was consecrated as bishop of Calcutta and metropolitan of India in 1867 and moved there with his sister in March of that year. The diocese at that time included the Central Provinces, the Punjab in the west, and Burma in the east, totaling nearly a million square miles (2.59 million square kilometers). A talented linguist, Milman learned to speak Bengali, Hindustani, and several related dialects. He caught a chill when traveling from Calcutta to Peshawar and died at Rawalpindi in February 1876. He had never married.

EDWARD RALPH JOHNSON (1828–11 September 1912), known as Ralph Johnson, became bishop of Calcutta and metropolitan of India in 1876. During Bishop Ralph Johnson's tenure, the Diocese of Rangoon was created. He retired in 1898, being the first Bishop of Calcutta not to die in office.

(b) Bishops of Rangoon

JONATHAN HOLT TITCOMB (29 July 1819–2 April 1887) became the first bishop of the new Diocese of Rangoon in 1877. On 17 February 1881, he fell over a cliff in the Karen hills and was so severely injured that he was forced to return to England. He resigned on 3 March 1882.

JOHN MILLER STRACHAN (1832–1906) was the second bishop of Rangoon. He trained as a medical missionary doctor and worked with the SPG in India before episcopal consecration on 1 May 1882. He served until 1902, when he resigned for health reasons.

ARTHUR MESAC KNIGHT (9 July 1864–4 October 1939) was the third bishop of Rangoon between 1903 and 1909. He was a fellow and dean of Gonville and Caius College, Cambridge, and a lecturer in divinity. After his resignation from Rangoon, he became warden of St. Augustine's Missionary College, Canterbury.

ROLLESTONE (sometimes spelled Rolleston) STERRITT FYFFE (1868–3 April 1964) was the fourth bishop of Rangoon. From 1904 to 1910, he was a missionary in

Mandalay, from where he was elevated to the episcopate, serving for eighteen years before resigning.

NORMAN HENRY TUBBS (5 July 1879–2 September 1965) became the fifth bishop of Rangoon in 1928 after five years as a bishop in India. He had arrived in India as a CMS missionary, eventually becoming principal of Bishop's College, Calcutta. He resigned in 1934 to become archdeacon of Chester and later dean of Chester, England.

GEORGE ALGERNON WEST (17 December 1893–25 May 1980) served in the Red Cross in Serbia and then in the British Army in France during the First World War. He spent many years in Burma, first as a missionary for the SPG and then as the sixth bishop of Rangoon from 1935 to 1954. After retiring from Burma in 1954, he became assistant bishop of Durham, England.

VICTOR GEORGE SHEARBURN (28 October 1900–3 December 1975) was ordained in 1924 and held several curacies before becoming a member of the Community of the Resurrection. He served with distinction as an army chaplain during the Second World War, including at Dunkirk. In 1955, he became the seventh (and last British) bishop of Rangoon, and also the last person to hold the post without also becoming archbishop of the province. He was in post for eleven years.

FRANCIS AH MYA (6 July 1904–8 June 1998) became the eighth (and first native) bishop of Rangoon, and the last person to hold the post on its own before also becoming archbishop of the province. He devoted his life to the Church and served with great distinction in the Second World War. He was made assistant bishop in 1949. His tenure as bishop began in 1966 and included the period of transition to an autonomous Anglican province in 1970.

(c) Archbishops of the Church of the Province of Burma (CPB)

FRANCIS AH MYA (6 July 1904–8 June 1998) became the first archbishop of the Church of the new Province of Burma in 1970, keeping the post of bishop of Rangoon alongside the new role. His tenure had begun in 1966, included the transition to an autonomous Anglican Province in 1970, and ended in 1973, when he returned to missionary work.

JOHN AUNG HLA (8 June 1915–19 December 1987), assistant bishop of Rangoon, became the second archbishop of the Church and ninth bishop of Rangoon in 1973, serving until 1979. He was ordained priest in 1939 and continued to serve with exceptional courage during the Japanese occupation of Burma. Along with Archbishop Francis, he represented the original old guard of pioneering native clergy who survived all of the upheavals of the twentieth century.

GREGORY HLA GYAW (17 June 1933–6 December 1987), formerly bishop of Hpa-an Diocese, became the third archbishop of the Church and tenth diocesan bishop of Rangoon in 1979, serving until his death in 1987. Archbishop Gregory was another member of the original group of highly distinguished native clergy who oversaw all of the difficult transitions from the colonial Church through to the Independence period and beyond.

ANDREW MYA HAN (27 November 1931–31 May 2006) became the fourth archbishop of the Church and eleventh bishop of the diocese, serving from 1988 to 2001, including during the time of the province's change of name in 1989, when it became the Church of the Province of Myanmar.

(d) Archbishops of the Church of the Province of Myanmar (CPM)

ANDREW MYA HAN (27 November 1931–31 May 2006) was in post when the Church became the Church of the Province of Myanmar in 1989, serving until 2001. Archbishop Mya Han played a prominent role in the Karen peace process and was also a popular published poet.

SAMUEL SAN SI HTAY (1943–14 November 2018) became the fifth archbishop of the Church of the Province of Myanmar and twelfth bishop of Yangon (Rangoon) in 2001, serving until 2008. He distinguished himself for his ecumenical work between Christian denominations and also for improving the Church's international links.

STEPHEN THAN MYINT OO (born 1958) is the current and sixth archbishop of the Church of the Province of Myanmar and the thirteenth bishop of Yangon.

(e) Sources and Further Reading on Burma's Bishops

Anderson, Gerald H., ed. *Biographical Dictionary of Christian Missions*. Grand Rapids, MI: W. B. Eerdmans, 1999.

Chisholm, Hugh, ed. "Cotton, George Edward Lynch." In *Encyclopedia Britannica 7* (11th ed.), 255. Cambridge: Cambridge University Press, 1911.

Hawes, Christopher J. *Poor Relations: The Making of a Eurasian Community in British India, 1773–1833*. London: Routledge, 2013.

Hughes, Derrick. *Bishop Sahib: A Life of Reginald Heber*. Worthing, UK: Churchman Publishing, 1986.

Le Bas, Charles Webb. *The Life of the Right Reverend Thomas Fanshawe Middleton, Late Lord Bishop of Calcutta*. 2 vols. London: Rivington, 1831.

Milman, Frances Maria. *Memoir of the Rt. Rev. Robert Milman DD, Lord Bishop of Calcutta and Metropolitan of India, with a Selection from his Correspondence and Journals*. London: John Murray, 1879.

Nichols, Alan. *Dancing with Angels: The Life Story of Stephen Than, Archbishop of Myanmar*. Moreland: Acorn Press, 2015.

Tyndale-Biscoe, John. *For God Alone: The Life of George West, Bishop of Rangoon*. Oxford: Amate Press, 1984.

Appendix 3
List of Ethnic Groups and Subgroups in Burma

The task of listing Burma's indigenous ethnic groups and estimated 135 subgroups has long been recognized as a controversial exercise. The figure of 135 is quite well-established (see below) and has found broad acceptance, including with government agencies, but it has also been the subject of debate. A 2005 article appearing in the *Shan Herald* (see below) and on the now-defunct Shan Land website (www.shanland.org) disputed the ethnic groups and subgroups calculations, calling out ideological and political motivations behind the estimate. It was claimed, for example, that the number of Burman (Bamar) subgroups has been manipulated in order to add up to nine, the traditional Burman lucky number.

The 2005 article also challenged the fact that the name of each umbrella group—Chin, Kachin, Karen, and so forth—reappears within the list of subgroups itself, as if they were a kind of chief subgroup or dominant subgroup within that set. This suggestion of a hierarchy among subgroups is misleading and could be interpreted as politically charged, while the "umbrella" names of the major groups—Chin, Kachin, Karen, and so on—serve in reality as generic terms. The groupings are just that—an imperfect method of collating associated and related social groups according to ethnic characteristics.

In some cases, the name of a subgroup may also correspond to the name of a language group, and that language may not be exclusive to the subgroup of the same name. This means that members of different subgroups may be united by a common language whose name the subgroups themselves do not share. This could throw the conventional calculation into further doubt and raises the question of whether linguistic groupings would provide a more useful basis for categorization. (The *Shan Herald* article is now archived at https://web.archive.org/web/20140105075611/http://www.shanland.org/index.php?option=com_content&view=article&id=4965:135-counting-races-in-burma&catid=115:opinions&Itemid=308).

It is also important to consider the integration into Burmese society, after many generations, of ethnic groups that are not strictly speaking indigenous. These groups mostly originated, historically, from the bordering countries of India, China, and modern-day Bangladesh as well as the more distant Nepal, Pakistan, and Sri Lanka. Furthermore, there is the complex question of Caucasian, Celtic, European, Jewish, and Levantine ethnicities. None of these feature in the conventional listings of indigenous ethnic groups and subgroups.

Of the formal published attempts to list the groups and subgroups, Min Naing's *National Ethnic Groups of Myanmar* (see bibliography) has been very influential, being used by Myanmar government sources (see, e.g., https://www.embassyofmyanmar.be/ABOUT/ethnicgroups.htm). Min Naing's work draws in part,

APPENDIX 3

apparently, on a 1960 Burma Ministry of Culture document called *National Races of Burma*. The most widely accepted list includes the following ethnic groups, followed by the lists of subgroups, each in alphabetical order:

Ethnic Groups

(a) The Burman [Bamar] group consists of 9 subgroups.
(b) The Chin group consists of 53 subgroups.
(c) The Kachin group consists of 12 subgroups.
(d) The Karen [Kayin] group consists of 11 subgroups.
(e) The Karenni [Kayah] group consists of 9 subgroups.
(f) The Mon group has no subgroups.
(g) The Rakhine group consists of 7 subgroups.
(h) The Shan group consists of 33 subgroups.

Subgroups

(a) The Burman [Bamar]
Subgroups: Beik, Burman [Bamar], Dawei, Ganan, Hpon, Kadu, Salone, Yabein, Yaw

(b) The Chin
Subgroups: Anu, Anun, Asho [Plains], Awa Khami, Chin, Dai [Yindu], Dim, Gunte [Lyente], Gwete, Haulngo, Ka-Lin-Kaw [Lushay], Kaung Saing Chin, Kaungso, Khami, Khawno, Kwangli, Kwelshin, Lai, Laizao, Lawhtu, Laymyo, Lhinbu, Lushei [Lushay], Lyente, Magun, Malin, Matu, Meithei [Kathe], Mgan, Mi-er, Miram [Mara], Naga, Ngorn, Oo-Pu, Panun, Rongtu, Saing Zan, Saline, Sentang, Taishon, Tanghkul, Tapong, Tay-Zan, Thado, Tiddim [Hai-Dim], Torr, Wakim [Mro], Zahnyet [Zanniet], Za-How, Zizan, Zo, Zo-Pe, Zotung

(c) The Kachin
Subgroups: Atsi, Dalaung, Duleng, Guari, Hkahku, Jinghpaw, Kachin, Lashi [La Chit], Lisu, Maru [Lawgore], Rawang, Taron

(d) The Karen [Kayin]
Subgroups: Bwe, Karen [Kayin], Kayinpyu, Mon Karen [Mon Kayin] [Sarpyu], Monnepwa, Monpwa, Paku, Pa-Le-Chi, Sgaw, Shu [Pwo], Ta-Lay-Pwa

(e) The Karenni [Kayah]
Subgroups: Bre [Ka-Yaw], Gheko, Karenni [Kayah], Ka-Yun [Padaung], Kebar, Manaw, Manu Yin Baw, Yin Talai, Zayein

(f) The Mon
Mon (no subgroups)

APPENDIX 3

(g) The Rakhine
Subgroups: Daingnet, Kamein, Kwe Myi, Maramagyi, Mro, Rakhine, Thet[a]

(h) The Shan
Subgroups: Danaw, Danu, Eik-swair, Eng, Hkun, Intha, Kaw [Akha-E-Kaw], Khamti Shan, Khamu, Kokant, Kwi, Lahu, Maingtha, Man Zi, Maw Shan, Palaung [Ta'ang], Pale, Pa-Oh, Pyin, Shan, Shan Gale, Shan Gyi, Son, Tai-Lay, Tai-Lem, Tai-Loi, Tai-Lon, Taungyo, Wa, Yao, Yin Kya, Yin Net, Yun [Lao]

Notes

Introduction
1. Kelly, *Peeps at Many Lands*, 3.
2. Rogers, *Land Without Evil*, 29–31.
3. Rogers, *Burma*, xxx.
4. Orwell, review of *The Spirit of Catholicism* by Karl Adam, 79–80.
5. Babson, "Province of Myanmar (Burma)," 406.
6. Fleming, *Hidden Plight*, 1.
7. Ibid.
8. Rogers, *Burma*, xxix.
9. Ibid., xiii.
10. Saw Maung Doe, "Critical Appraisal of Christian Education," 23.
11. Lim and Dengthuama, "Overview of Christian Missions in Myanmar," 2.
12. Koepping, "India, Pakistan, Bangladesh, Burma / Myanmar," 11.

Chapter 1
1. Short, *On Burma's Eastern Frontier*, 11; compare West, *World That Works*, 10: "Tickle the earth and it laughs to harvest."
2. J. Thompson, *Forgotten Voices of Burma*, ix.
3. West, *Jungle Folk*, ix.
4. M. Smith, *State of Strife*, 11; see also M. Smith, *Burma*, 32; Popham, *Lady and the Peacock*, 277; Duncan, *Civilizing the Margins*, 163.
5. C. H. Chard in Rangoon Diocesan Association (RDA), *Quarterly Paper* 1 (February 1897): 9–10.
6. McLeish, *Christian Progress in Burma*, 15.
7. Titcomb, *Personal Recollections of British Burma*, 63.
8. Evers, "On the Trail of Spices," 66.
9. Hoskins, "Unjealous God?," S302.
10. Pieris, "Political Theologies in Asia," 258.
11. Ibid., 262.
12. Owen, *Emergence of Modern Southeast Asia*, 115–16.
13. Bell, "State and Civil Society," 425.
14. Pieris, "Political Theologies in Asia," 261–63.
15. Ngô-Đình-Thục, "Misericordias Domini in Aeternum Cantabo," 9–10.
16. Pieris, "Political Theologies in Asia," 256.
17. Evers, "On the Trail of Spices," 68.
18. C. H. Chard in RDA, *Quarterly Paper* 1 (February 1897): 6.
19. W. C. B. Purser, *Christian Missions in Burma*, 86.
20. Ibid.
21. C. R. Purser, *Burma*, 46.
22. W. C. B. Purser, *Christian Missions in Burma*, 87.
23. Ibid., 87–88.
24. Ibid.
25. Ibid., 91.
26. Wayland, *Memoir*, 260.
27. *Maulmain Almanac, Directory, and Diary for 1852*, 88; see also *Maulmain Almanac, Directory, and Diary for 1853*, 58.
28. D. E. Smith, *Religion and Politics in Burma*, 71.
29. J. M. Strachan in RDA, *Quarterly Paper* 1 (February 1897): 18.
30. C. H. Chard in ibid., 7–9.
31. J. M. Strachan in ibid., 18.
32. Ken's interesting life is related at length in several old books, including *The Life of Thomas Ken, Bishop of Bath and Wells*, part 1, by A. Layman (pseudonym of John Lavicount Anderdon).
33. *Maulmain Almanac, Directory, and Diary for 1853*, 132.
34. Rogers, *Land Without Evil*, 28.
35. J. M. Strachan in RDA, *Quarterly Paper* 1 (February 1897): 18.
36. RDA, *Burma News* 190 (Autumn 1960): 8.
37. J. M. Strachan in RDA, *Quarterly Paper* 1 (February 1897): 18.

38. Ibid.
39. O'Connor, *Three Centuries of Mission*, 6.
40. Ibid., 7–8.
41. J. M. Strachan, RDA, *Quarterly Paper* 1 (February 1897): 18.
42. O'Connor, *Three Centuries of Mission*, 72.
43. Pieris, "Political Theologies in Asia," 258.
44. Ibid., 259.
45. Ibid.
46. Bell, "State and Civil Society," 430.
47. O'Connor, *Three Centuries of Mission*, 99–100.
48. Ibid.
49. Pieris, *Asian Theology of Liberation*, 76.
50. Rogers, *Burma*, 129.
51. Pieris, "Political Theologies in Asia," 256.
52. Ibid.
53. Koepping, "India, Pakistan, Bangladesh, Burma / Myanmar," 11.
54. Pieris, "Political Theologies in Asia," 259.

Chapter 2

1. Owen, *Emergence of Modern Southeast Asia*, 87–89.
2. Evers, "On the Trail of Spices," 68.
3. Marks, *Forty Years in Burma*, 12.
4. W. C. B. Purser, *Christian Missions in Burma*, 86.
5. Ibid.
6. Marks, *Forty Years in Burma*, 12.
7. C. R. Purser, *Burma*, 46.
8. RDA, *Quarterly Paper* 3 (August 1897): 53.
9. The full story is related in Wayland, *Memoir*, 260.
10. C. H. Chard in RDA, *Quarterly Paper* 1 (February 1897): 6.
11. Ibid., 6–7.
12. *Maulmain Almanac, Directory, and Diary for 1853*, 134.
13. Ibid., 132.
14. Ibid., 85, 94, 108.
15. O'Connor, *Three Centuries of Mission*, 58.
16. C. H. Chard in RDA, *Quarterly Paper* 1 (February 1897): 7.
17. See A. M. Knight in his foreword to W. C. B. Purser, *Christian Missions in Burma*, vi.
18. Marks, *Forty Years in Burma*, viii.
19. Ibid., 2–3.
20. W. C. B. Purser in ibid., 4.
21. Saw Maung Doe, "Critical Appraisal of Christian Education," 46.
22. Marks, *Forty Years in Burma*, 15.
23. C. H. Chard in RDA, *Quarterly Paper* 1 (February 1897): 7.
24. Marks, *Forty Years in Burma*, 3.
25. RDA, *Quarterly Paper* 10 (June 1899): 27.
26. O'Connor, *Three Centuries of Mission*, 7.
27. Ibid., 72.
28. J. M. Strachan in RDA, *Quarterly Paper* 1 (February 1897): 17.
29. Babson, "Province of Myanmar (Burma)," 407.
30. RDA, *Quarterly Paper* 10 (June 1899): 28.
31. C. H. Chard in RDA, *Quarterly Paper* 1 (February 1897): 7.
32. Marks, *Forty Years in Burma*, 110–11.
33. Saw Maung Doe, "Critical Appraisal of Christian Education," 51.
34. RDA, *Quarterly Paper* 10 (June 1899): 28.
35. Ibid.
36. J. M. Strachan in RDA, *Quarterly Paper* 1 (February 1897): 17.
37. RDA, *Quarterly Paper* 10 (June 1899): 28.
38. C. R. Purser, *Burma*, 18.
39. RDA, *Quarterly Paper* 10 (June 1899): 28.
40. Marks, *Forty Years in Burma*, 41.
41. Ibid., 129.
42. Ibid., 52–59, 80–88, 129–30.
43. J. M. Strachan in RDA, *Quarterly Paper* 1 (February 1897): 17.
44. Ibid., 19.
45. M. Smith, *Burma*, 45.
46. Titcomb, *Personal Recollections of British Burma*, 63.
47. West, *Jungle Folk*, ix.
48. J. M. Strachan in RDA, *Quarterly Paper* 1 (February 1897): 19.
49. West, *Jungle Folk*, ix.
50. C. H. Chard in RDA, *Quarterly Paper* 1 (February 1897): 8.
51. J. M. Strachan in RDA, *Quarterly Paper* 1 (February 1897): 19.
52. M. Smith, *Burma*, 45.

53. D. E. Smith, *Religion and Politics in Burma*, 79.
54. J. M. Strachan in RDA, *Quarterly Paper* 1 (February 1897): 17.
55. Marks, *Forty Years in Burma*, 13.
56. C. H. Chard in RDA, *Quarterly Paper* 1 (February 1897): 9.
57. Ibid.
58. Ibid., 8.
59. J. M. Strachan in RDA, *Quarterly Paper* 1 (February 1897): 18.
60. C. H. Chard in RDA, *Quarterly Paper* 1 (February 1897): 8.
61. Marks, *Forty Years in Burma*, 88.
62. Ibid.
63. Ibid., 125.
64. Ibid., 125–26.
65. Ibid., 67-68.
66. W. C. B. Purser in ibid., 8–9.
67. Ibid.
68. Titcomb, *Personal Recollections of British Burma*, 72–73.
69. Marks, *Forty Years in Burma*, 126.
70. C. H. Chard in RDA, *Quarterly Paper* 1 (February 1897): 7.
71. Marks, *Forty Years in Burma*, 12.
72. D. E. Smith, *Religion and Politics in Burma*, 71.
73. O'Connor, *Three Centuries of Mission*, 64.
74. Ibid., 65.
75. Marks, *Forty Years in Burma*, 99–100.
76. Saw Maung Doe, "Critical Appraisal of Christian Education," 65.
77. Wilson, *Story of Fifty Years*, 14.
78. Orwell, *Burmese Days*, 68.
79. M. Smith, *Burma*, 45.
80. J. M. Strachan in RDA, *Quarterly Paper* 1 (February 1897): 17.
81. O'Connor, *Three Centuries of Mission*, 68–69.
82. Carter, *Bewitched by Burma*, 35.
83. Morris and Fermor-Hesketh, *Architecture of the British Empire*, 176.
84. RDA, *Quarterly Paper* 10 (June 1899): 28.
85. C. H. Chard in RDA, *Quarterly Paper* 1 (February 1897): 9.
86. Ibid., 9–10.
87. Orwell, *Burmese Days*, 68.
88. M. Smith, *Burma*, 45.
89. Wilson, *Story of Fifty Years*, 66–67.
90. Ibid.
91. *Maulmain Almanac, Directory, and Diary for 1853*, 132.
92. J. M. Strachan in RDA, *Quarterly Paper* 1 (February 1897): 18.
93. O'Connor, *Three Centuries of Mission*, 72.
94. Ibid.
95. J. M. Strachan in RDA, *Quarterly Paper* 1 (February 1897): 18.
96. Ibid.
97. M. Smith, *Burma*, 45.
98. Strachan in RDA, *Quarterly Paper* 1 (February 1897): 19.
99. M. Smith, *Burma*, 216, 322, 388.
100. Ibid.
101. Orwell, *Burmese Days*, 68.

Chapter 3

1. Carter, *Bewitched by Burma*, 2.
2. Ibid.
3. Marks, *Forty Years in Burma*, 6.
4. C. R. Purser, *Burma*, 68.
5. RDA, *Quarterly Paper* 7 (October 1898): 32.
6. RDA, *Quarterly Paper* 10 (June 1899): 28.
7. The full story was recounted by Archdeacon Chard in RDA, *Quarterly Paper* 1 (February 1897): 8.
8. Womack, "Contesting Indigenous and Female Authority," 543–59.
9. Saw Maung Doe, "Critical Appraisal of Christian Education," 50.
10. Ibid.
11. Chard in RDA, *Quarterly Paper* 1 (February 1897): 8.
12. Ibid.
13. RDA, *Quarterly Paper* 4 (November 1897): 85.
14. Saw Maung Doe, "Critical Appraisal of Christian Education," 51.
15. Titcomb, *Personal Recollections of British Burma*, 68.
16. See "News Notes" in RDA, *Quarterly Paper* 1 (February 1897): 22.
17. See "Sad News" in RDA, *Quarterly Paper* 1 (February 1897): 19.

18. The full story was recorded in RDA, *Quarterly Paper* 11 (September 1899): 64–65.
19. Ibid.
20. RDA, *Quarterly Paper* 6 (June 1898): 24.
21. Ibid., 24–25.
22. RDA, *Quarterly Paper* 6 (June 1898): 25.
23. W. C. B. Purser, *Christian Missions in Burma*, 1.
24. Ibid.
25. Titcomb, *Personal Recollections of British Burma*, 101.
26. C. R. Purser, *Burma*, 54.
27. RDA, *Quarterly Paper* 9 (March 1899): 12–14.
28. C. H. Chard in RDA, *Quarterly Paper* 1 (February 1897): 8.
29. Titcomb, *Personal Recollections of British Burma*, 46.
30. Strachan in RDA, *Quarterly Paper* 1 (February 1897): 19.
31. Titcomb, *Personal Recollections of British Burma*, 15.
32. RDA, *Quarterly Paper* 5 (March 1898): 3.
33. J. M. Strachan in RDA, *Quarterly Paper* 1 (February 1897): 19.
34. J. M. Strachan quoted in RDA, *Quarterly Paper* 3 (August 1897): 48.
35. Ibid., 49.
36. Ibid., 48–49.
37. Ibid., 49.
38. RDA, *Quarterly Paper* 15 (September 1900): 60.
39. Saw Maung Doe, "Critical Appraisal of Christian Education," 56–58.
40. C. R. Purser, *Burma*, 53–54.
41. RDA, *Quarterly Paper* 16 (December 1900): 77.
42. Annual Report of the RDA for 1946 in *Burma News* 159 (April 1947): 14.
43. Saw Maung Doe, "Critical Appraisal of Christian Education," 74.
44. Ibid., 59.
45. The story is related in Houghton, *Dense Jungle Green*, from page 19.
46. J. M. Strachan quoted in RDA, *Quarterly Paper* 3 (August 1897): 49.
47. West, *World That Works*, 25.
48. RDA, *Quarterly Paper* 6 (June 1898): 17–18.
49. C. R. Purser, *Burma*, 61.
50. West, *World That Works*, 12.
51. RDA, *Quarterly Paper* 10 (June 1899): 28.
52. Titcomb, *Personal Recollections of British Burma*, 33–34.
53. J. M. Strachan quoted in RDA, *Quarterly Paper* 3 (August 1897): 48.
54. RDA, *Quarterly Paper* 6 (June 1898): 28.
55. Ibid., 18.
56. Ibid.
57. Carter, *Bewitched by Burma*, 36.
58. R. S. Fyffe in RDA, *Quarterly Paper* 70 (June 1914): 356.
59. Carter, *Bewitched by Burma*, 59.
60. Ibid.; see also Titcomb, *Personal Recollections of British Burma*, 18.
61. RDA, *Quarterly Paper* 7 (October 1898): 32–33.
62. Ibid.
63. Titcomb, *Personal Recollections of British Burma*, 57.
64. RDA, *Quarterly Paper* 7 (October 1898): 33.
65. Ibid.
66. A. Salmon in RDA, *Quarterly Paper* 9 (March 1899): 6.
67. Ibid.
68. A. Salmon in RDA, *Quarterly Paper* 2 (May 1897): 32.
69. Ibid.
70. Carter, *Bewitched by Burma*, 128.
71. Lim and Dengthuama, "Overview of Christian Missions in Myanmar," 3–4.
72. RDA, *Quarterly Paper* 13 (March 1900): 9.
73. Ibid.
74. RDA, *Burma News* 151 (May 1939): 183.
75. RDA, *Quarterly Paper* 7 (October 1898): 32.
76. RDA, *Burma News* 151 (May 1939): 183.
77. Saw Maung Doe, "Critical Appraisal of Christian Education," 56–58.
78. J. M. Strachan in RDA, *Quarterly Paper* 1 (February 1897): 19.
79. Marks, *Forty Years in Burma*, 54.
80. Ibid., 55.

Chapter 4

1. Rangoon Diocesan Association (RDA), *Quarterly Paper* 10 (June 1899): 27.

2. J. M. Strachan quoted in RDA, *Quarterly Paper* 3 (August 1897): 48.
3. McLeish, *Christian Progress in Burma*, 17–18.
4. Marks, *Forty Years in Burma*, 83.
5. RDA, *Quarterly Paper* 9 (March 1899): 2–3.
6. RDA, *Quarterly Paper* 12 (December 1899): 75.
7. Ibid.
8. See entry "Lieutenant Cecil Gordon Salmon" at Imperial War Museum, https://www.iwm.org.uk/collections/item/object/205388218, accessed 17 October 2020.
9. RDA, *Quarterly Paper* 10 (June 1899): 33.
10. RDA, *Quarterly Paper* 12 (December 1899): 75.
11. RDA, *Quarterly Paper* 10 (June 1899): 33–34.
12. Saw Maung Doe, "Critical Appraisal of Christian Education," 72.
13. Annual Report of the RDA for 1946 in *Burma News* 159 (April 1947): 12.
14. W. C. B. Purser, *Christian Missions in Burma*, 93.
15. For a full description, see Annual Report of the RDA for 1939 in *Burma News* 152 (1939): 7–8.
16. D. E. Smith, *Religion and Politics in Burma*, 72.
17. A. M. Knight in W. C. B. Purser, *Christian Missions in Burma*, ix.
18. D. E. Smith, *Religion and Politics in Burma*, 76–77.
19. Ibid., 77.
20. A. M. Knight in W. C. B. Purser, *Christian Missions in Burma*, v.
21. Ibid., vii.
22. Carter, *Bewitched by Burma*, 35.
23. Rogers, *Burma*, 3.
24. RDA, *Quarterly Paper* 71 (September 1914): 395.
25. RDA, *Quarterly Paper* 74 (May 1915): 50.
26. Orwell, *Burmese Days*, 68.
27. Ibid., 67.
28. Marks, *Forty Years in Burma*, 36.
29. See entry "Lieutenant Cecil Gordon Salmon" at Imperial War Museum, https://www.iwm.org.uk/collections/item/object/205388218, accessed 17 October 2020.

30. RDA, *Quarterly Paper* 81 (January 1917): 274.
31. Ibid.
32. RDA, *Quarterly Paper* 82 (April 1917): 293.
33. RDA, *Quarterly Paper* 85 (January 1918): 3.
34. Annual Report of the RDA for 1946 in *Burma News* 159 (April 1947): 12–14.
35. McLeish, *Christian Progress in Burma*, 17.
36. Ibid., 17–18.
37. Ibid., 7.
38. W. C. B. Purser, *Christian Missions in Burma*, 1.
39. West, *World That Works*, 11.
40. McLeish, *Christian Progress in Burma*, 18.
41. Ibid.
42. Christian, *Modern Burma*, 205–7.
43. J. M. Strachan in RDA, *Quarterly Paper* 1 (February 1897): 18.
44. W. C. B. Purser, *Christian Missions in Burma*, 93.
45. Ibid., 94.
46. Ibid., 93.
47. R. S. Fyffe in RDA, *Quarterly Paper* 72 (December 1914): 427.
48. Marks, *Forty Years in Burma*, 126.
49. R. S. Fyffe in RDA, *Quarterly Paper* 72 (December 1914): 427.
50. RDA, *Quarterly Paper* 85 (January 1918): 10.
51. Ibid.
52. The story is recounted in RDA, *Quarterly Paper* 88 (October 1918): 88, and also in H. P. Thompson, *Into All Lands*, 639–40.
53. RDA, *Quarterly Paper* 88 (October 1918): 88–89; see also H. P. Thompson, *Into All Lands*, 639–40.
54. A number of books have been written about Father Jackson, including *An Ambassador in Bonds: The Story of William Henry Jackson, Priest, of the Mission to the Blind of Burma*, by his sister, Mary Chesmer Purser. Mrs. Purser had married Father Jackson's good friend Rev. W. C. B. Purser.
55. C. R. Purser, *Burma*, 58.
56. H. P. Thompson, *Into All Lands*, 641.

NOTES TO PAGES 75–90

57. RDA, *Burma News* 137 (January 1931): 452.
58. Petty, *Fact-Finders' Reports*, 580.
59. Rogers, *Burma*, 3.
60. Aung-Thwin, "Structuring Revolt," 297–317.
61. Rogers, *Burma*, 3–4.
62. Ibid.
63. RDA, *Burma News* 148 (May 1936): 112–13.
64. West, *World That Works*, 17–18.
65. Ibid., 22.
66. Dwight, "Rudyard Kipling's Poetry," 239.
67. J. M. Strachan in RDA, *Quarterly Paper* 1 (February 1897): 17.
68. Ibid.
69. Orwell, *Road to Wigan Pier*, 128.
70. Ibid.
71. Ibid.
72. Burgess, *Little Wilson and Big God*, 389.
73. C. H. Chard in RDA, *Quarterly Paper* 1 (February 1897): 7.
74. J. M. Strachan quoted in RDA, *Quarterly Paper* 3 (August 1897): 47.
75. Wilson, *Story of Fifty Years*, 40–41.
76. Ibid., 61.
77. C. R. Purser, *Burma*, 62.
78. Ibid., 62–64.
79. Marks, *Forty Years in Burma*, 136.
80. Ibid.
81. Ibid., 137.
82. Ibid.; emphasis added.
83. *Maulmain Almanac, Directory, and Diary for 1853*, 85.
84. Marks, *Forty Years in Burma*, 140.
85. RDA, *Quarterly Paper* 3 (August 1897): 46.
86. West, *World That Works*, 8.

Chapter 5

1. Orwell, *Burmese Days*, 67–68.
2. RDA, *Burma News* 151 (May 1939): 180.
3. Annual Report of the RDA for 1939 in *Burma News* 152 (1939): 1.
4. RDA, *Burma News* 151 (May 1939): 182.
5. Kelly, *Peeps at Many Lands*, 4.
6. Carter, *Bewitched by Burma*, 110–11, 221.
7. Annual Report of the RDA for 1939 in *Burma News* 152 (1939): 3.
8. Short, *On Burma's Eastern Frontier*, 47.
9. RDA, *Burma News* 151 (May 1939): 185.
10. Ibid.
11. Annual Report of the RDA for 1940 in *Burma News* 153 (May 1941): 3.
12. Short, *On Burma's Eastern Frontier*, 49.
13. West, *World That Works*, 8.
14. Annual Report of the RDA for 1940 in *Burma News* 153 (May 1941): 3.
15. Ibid., 4.
16. Ibid.
17. West, *World That Works*, 7.
18. Annual Report of the RDA for 1945 in *Burma News* 158 (April 1946): 7.
19. Annual Report of the RDA for 1941 in *Burma News* 154 (March 1942): 2.
20. Annual Report of the RDA for 1940 in *Burma News* 153 (May 1941): 5.
21. West, *World That Works*, 46.
22. Annual Report of the RDA for 1941 in *Burma News* 154 (March 1942): 2.
23. Ibid.
24. Ibid., 10.
25. Appleton, *War and After*, 18.
26. West, *World That Works*, 45.
27. Annual Report of the RDA for 1942 in *Burma News* 155 (April 1943): 3. A longer extract from the letter is relayed in Appleton, *War and After*, 19:
We have trekked 256 miles and are still 100 miles from the railhead in India. More often than not we live on one meal a day, of watery rice, as this is the only way we can make the supply go far. 60 per cent of us have tummy-trouble, sores, bad colds or fevers; 7 of our girls have malaria. We have had a very hard journey so far, steep precipitous mountain climbing in the pouring rain, through dense tropical jungle infested with wild animals; across dangerous rapids, walking through paddy fields and ditches waist-deep in water and ploughing through the jungle path often thigh-deep. God has indeed been with us at every step of our journey. On an average we do six miles a day. We have slept in the jungle without shelter, and with highly decayed corpses around us.... We are staying put in this village as (1) 300 Chinese bandits are trekking into Burma this way; (2) most of us feel we cannot walk on any more. We are all on the verge of physical collapse. Believe

me we cannot do any more. Most of the children are sans blanket, sans shoes, sans change of clothes. Trusting you will remember us in your prayers . . .

28. Appleton, *War and After*, 19.
29. Annual Report of the RDA for 1942 in *Burma News* 155 (April 1943): 1.
30. Ibid.
31. Ibid., 4.
32. See Ms. Bald's letter, reported in Appleton, *War and After*, 19.
33. Annual Report of the RDA for 1942 in *Burma News* 155 (April 1943): 7.
34. Carter, *Bewitched by Burma*, 178.
35. Annual Report of the RDA for 1942 in *Burma News* 155 (April 1943): 7.
36. Annual Report of the RDA for 1944 in *Burma News* 157 (April 1945): 11.
37. Ibid.
38. Appleton, *War and After*, 18.
39. Ibid., 19.
40. Annual Report of the RDA for 1945 in *Burma News* 158 (April 1946): 7.
41. Annual Report of the RDA for 1942 in *Burma News* 155 (April 1943): 1.
42. Ibid.
43. Annual Report of the RDA for 1943 in *Burma News* 156 (April 1944): 7.
44. Ibid., 1.
45. Archdeacon D. Moxon in Annual Report of the RDA for 1946 in *Burma News* 159 (April 1947): 7.
46. R. S. Fyffe in Annual Report of the RDA for 1946 in *Burma News* 159 (April 1947): 8.
47. Annual Report of the RDA for 1945 in *Burma News* 158 (April 1946): 5–6.
48. Saw Maung Doe, "Critical Appraisal of Christian Education," 91.
49. West, *World That Works*, 54.
50. Ibid., 46.
51. J. Thompson, *Forgotten Voices of Burma*, 3.
52. Marks, *Forty Years in Burma*, 36.
53. J. Thompson, *Forgotten Voices of Burma*, 3.
54. Appleton, *War and After*, 22.
55. Ibid., 23.
56. Ibid., 24–25.
57. Winn, *Going My Way*, 198.
58. Annual Report of the RDA for 1943 in *Burma News* 156 (April 1944): 7.
59. Ibid., 1.
60. Ibid.
61. RDA, *Burma News* 192 (1961): 10–11.
62. West, *World That Works*, 90.
63. Annual Report of the RDA for 1943 in *Burma News* 156 (April 1944): 7.
64. Ibid., 2.
65. Ibid., 3.
66. Ibid.
67. Koepping, "India, Pakistan, Bangladesh, Burma / Myanmar," 11.
68. Evers, "On the Trail of Spices," 66.
69. Rogers, *Burma*, 52.
70. Appleton in Annual Report of the RDA for 1944 in *Burma News* 157 (April 1945): 3.
71. Ibid.
72. Ibid.
73. See Christopher Tubbs's obituary, *Yorkshire Post*, 23 April 2010: https://www.yorkshirepost.co.uk/news/obituaries/christopher-tubbs-1-2571954, accessed 30 October 2020.
74. Carter, *Bewitched by Burma*, 187.
75. Annual Report of the RDA for 1944 in *Burma News* 157 (April 1945): 10.
76. Ibid., 11.
77. West, *World That Works*, 90.
78. Annual Report of the RDA for 1943 in *Burma News* 156 (April 1944): 7.
79. Appleton, *War and After*, 31.
80. Annual Report of the RDA for 1945 in *Burma News* 158 (April 1946): 3.
81. Ibid., 7.
82. Ibid.
83. Ibid.
84. H. P. Thompson, *Into All Lands*, 647–48.
85. Gruhl, *Imperial Japan's World War Two*, 102.
86. Annual Report of the RDA for 1945 in *Burma News* 158 (April 1946): 7.
87. Ibid.
88. Ibid., 3.
89. Ibid., 4.

Chapter 6

1. Carter, *Bewitched by Burma*, 190.
2. Ibid., 191.

3. Annual Report of the RDA for 1946 in *Burma News* 159 (April 1947): 12.

4. Carter, *Bewitched by Burma*, 187.

5. Ibid.

6. Ibid., 191–92.

7. Short, *On Burma's Eastern Frontier*, 135.

8. King George VI quoted in Annual Report of the RDA for 1945 in *Burma News* 158 (April 1946): 4.

9. Annual Report of the RDA for 1945 in *Burma News* 158 (April 1946): 8.

10. Ibid.

11. Ibid.

12. Koepping, "India, Pakistan, Bangladesh, Burma / Myanmar," 25.

13. Ibid., 25–26.

14. Annual Report of the RDA for 1946 in *Burma News* 159 (April 1947): 7.

15. Annual Report of the RDA for 1945 in *Burma News* 158 (April 1946): 9.

16. Ibid.

17. Appleton, *War and After*, 40.

18. Ibid., 43.

19. Ibid.

20. Ibid., 36.

21. Annual Report of the RDA for 1945 in *Burma News* 158 (April 1946): 9.

22. R. S. Fyffe in Annual Report of the RDA for 1945 in *Burma News* 158 (April 1946): 8.

23. Ibid.

24. Appleton, *War and After*, 37.

25. Ibid., 38.

26. R. S. Fyffe in Annual Report of the RDA for 1946 in *Burma News* 159 (April 1947): 3.

27. Saw Maung Doe, "Critical Appraisal of Christian Education," 96.

28. Appleton, *War and After*, 38.

29. Ibid., 43.

30. Annual Report of the RDA for 1945 in *Burma News* 158 (April 1946): 5–6.

31. H. P. Thompson, *Into All Lands*, 644–45; see also "Church News," *South Western Times* (Bunbury, Western Australia), 27 June 1946: 9.

32. Annual Report of the RDA for 1946 in *Burma News* 159 (April 1947): 3.

33. Saw Maung Doe, "Critical Appraisal of Christian Education," 96.

34. Ibid., 95.

35. H. P. Thompson, *Into All Lands*, 642.

36. O'Connor, *Three Centuries of Mission*, 106.

37. Annual Report of the RDA for 1946 in *Burma News* 159 (April 1947): 3.

38. Ibid., 10.

39. Ibid., 8.

40. Ibid.

41. Appleton in Annual Report of the RDA for 1946 in *Burma News* 159 (April 1947): 10.

42. Annual Report of the RDA for 1946 in *Burma News* 159 (April 1947): 10.

43. Ibid.

44. West, *World That Works*, 67.

45. Annual Report of the RDA for 1946 in *Burma News* 159 (April 1947): 10.

46. Carter, *Bewitched by Burma*, 194.

47. Ibid.

48. Ibid.—"Karens, Shans, Kachins, Indians and . . . [sic] I wonder whether [star] number five is for Chinese or English people." In fact it is unlikely that the Indians were considered one of the five peoples of Burma represented by the stars on the flag. The five peoples could have been interpreted as Karens, Shans, Kachins, Chins, and Karenni, which would still have excluded the Rakhine and Mon peoples and not even begun to address the issues of the Chinese, Indians, Anglo-Indians, and so forth.

49. Koepping, "India, Pakistan, Bangladesh, Burma / Myanmar," 11.

50. Titcomb, *Personal Recollections of British Burma*, 46.

51. H. P. Thompson, *Into All Lands*, 646.

52. West, *World That Works*, 28–29.

53. Ward, *History of Global Anglicanism*, 242.

54. Saw Maung Doe, "Critical Appraisal of Christian Education," 99.

55. Ibid., 136–38.

56. Rogers, *Burma*, 9.

57. Ibid., 8, 87.

58. D. E. Smith, *Religion and Politics in Burma*, 248.

59. Saw Maung Doe, "Critical Appraisal of Christian Education," 113.

60. RDA, *Burma News* 195 (Saint Andrew's 1963): 8.

61. Rogers, *Land Without Evil*, 33.

62. Saw Maung Doe, "Critical Appraisal of Christian Education," 11.
63. RDA, *Burma News* 195 (1963): 2–3.
64. RDA, *Burma News* 189 (1960): 7–8.
65. RDA, *Burma News* 192 (1961): 3.
66. Bishop Victor Shearburn in RDA, *Burma News* 190 (Autumn 1960): 4.
67. O'Connor, *Three Centuries of Mission*, 154–55.
68. Lim and Dengthuama, "Overview of Christian Missions in Myanmar," 13.
69. Ibid.
70. Rev. Canon Houghton in RDA, *Burma News* 209 (1970): 8.
71. Lim and Dengthuama, "Overview of Christian Missions in Myanmar," 7.
72. Saw Maung Doe, "Critical Appraisal of Christian Education," 13.
73. Ibid., 140–41.
74. Ward, *History of Global Anglicanism*, 242.
75. Ibid., 242–43.
76. Appleton, *War and After*, 38.
77. Saw Maung Doe, "Critical Appraisal of Christian Education," 22.
78. Appleton, *War and After*, 40.
79. Ibid.
80. Archbishop Francis Ah Mya's report in RDA, *Burma News* 210 (All Saints 1970): 3.
81. Ibid.
82. Annual Report of the RDA for 1946 in *Burma News* 159 (April 1947): 10.

Chapter 7

1. Goh, *Christianity in Southeast Asia*, 5.
2. Ibid., 6.
3. Lim and Dengthuama, "Overview of Christian Missions in Myanmar," 14.
4. Ibid.
5. Goh, *Christianity in Southeast Asia*, 6.
6. O'Connor, *Three Centuries of Mission*, 8.
7. Ibid.
8. Bell, "State and Civil Society," 425.
9. O'Connor, *Three Centuries of Mission*, 8.
10. Goh, *Christianity in Southeast Asia*, 6–7.
11. M. Smith, *Burma*, 45.
12. Marks, *Forty Years in Burma*, 12.
13. Goh, *Christianity in Southeast Asia*, 10.
14. Titcomb, *Personal Recollections of British Burma*, 26.
15. Ibid.
16. Pieris, "Political Theologies in Asia," 259.
17. Olson and Roberts, *Where the Domino Fell*, 55.
18. Keith, *Catholic Vietnam*, 177.
19. Appleton, *War and After*, 37–38.
20. Ibid.
21. Lim and Dengthuama, "Overview of Christian Missions in Myanmar," 3–4.
22. Marks, *Forty Years in Burma*, 87–88.
23. A. Salmon in RDA, *Quarterly Paper* 2 (May 1897): 34–35.
24. Ibid., 36.
25. RDA, *Quarterly Paper* 13 (March 1900): 9.
26. RDA, *Burma News* 151 (May 1939): 183.
27. RDA, *Quarterly Paper* 7 (October 1898): 32.
28. West, *World That Works*, 15–17.
29. Ibid.
30. Appleton, *War and After*, 36.
31. Pieris, "Political Theologies in Asia," 263.
32. Appleton, *War and After*, 36.
33. Chin Khua Khai, "Pentecostalism in Myanmar," 55–61.
34. Rogers, *Carrying the Cross*, 41–42.
35. Pieris, "Political Theologies in Asia," 261–62.
36. Ibid., 256–57.
37. Ibid.
38. Evers, "On the Trail of Spices," 66.
39. Pieris, "Political Theologies in Asia," 256–57.
40. Jarvis, *Carlos Duarte Costa*, 187.
41. Pieris, "Political Theologies in Asia," 257.
42. Lim and Dengthuama, "Overview of Christian Missions in Myanmar," 6.
43. Ibid.
44. Ibid., 13.
45. Ibid.
46. Christian Solidarity Worldwide, *Burma's Identity Crisis*, 64.
47. Rogers, *Carrying the Cross*, 27.
48. Lim and Dengthuama, "Overview of Christian Missions in Myanmar," 13.
49. Rogers, *Carrying the Cross*, 41.
50. Ngun Ling, "Does Dialogue Cancel Mission?," 8.

51. Ibid., 1–10; Ngun Ling, "Christ Through Our Neighbors' Eyes," 3–19.
52. Saw Maung Doe, "Critical Appraisal of Christian Education," 102.
53. Ibid.
54. Lim and Dengthuama, "Overview of Christian Missions in Myanmar," 6.
55. Sugden, "Report on GAFCON," 2—"GAFCON is not an alternative Anglican Communion because we are the true Anglican Church."
56. GAFCON, *The Way, the Truth and the Life*, 30–41.
57. O'Connor, *Three Centuries of Mission*, 7–8.
58. See Nicholas D. Okoh, archbishop of Bendel, Nigeria, in his preface to GAFCON, *The Way, the Truth and the Life*, 1.
59. Ibid.
60. Ibid., 28.
61. Ibid.
62. See Canon Marie Rowley-Brooke, "'Willfully Schismatic' Movement Supports Submission of Women to Men," *Irish Times*, 3 July 2018, https://www.irishtimes.com/opinion/wilfully-schismatic-movement-supports-submission-of-women-to-men-1.3551424.
63. Lim and Dengthuama, "Overview of Christian Missions in Myanmar," 5.
64. Koepping, "India, Pakistan, Bangladesh, Burma / Myanmar," 31–32.
65. Ibid.
66. Ibid., 31.
67. Ibid., 25.
68. West, *World That Works*, 67.
69. Rogers, *Burma*, 87.
70. Ibid., 129.
71. Christian Solidarity Worldwide, *Burma's Identity Crisis*, 14.
72. Ibid.
73. Lim and Dengthuama, "Overview of Christian Missions in Myanmar," 6.
74. Ibid.
75. Marks, *Forty Years in Burma*, 73.
76. Houghton, *Dense Jungle Green*, 93.
77. O'Connor, *Three Centuries of Mission*, 184.
78. Lim and Dengthuama, "Overview of Christian Missions in Myanmar," 14.
79. Ibid., 14–15.

80. Appleton, *War and After*, 37.
81. Lim and Dengthuama, "Overview of Christian Missions in Myanmar," 17.
82. Ibid., 22.

Chapter 8

1. Diocese of Yangon, https://yangon.anglicanmyanmar.org, accessed 18 October 2020.
2. This figure of approximately 22 percent is for Christians of all denominations across the eleven states of Southeast Asia, compared to approximately 37 percent Muslims (all denominations) and approximately 21 percent Buddhists (all denominations)—see ARDA (Association of Religion Data Archives): https://www.thearda.com/internationaldata/regions/profiles/Region_16_1.asp, accessed 28 October 2020.
3. Koepping, "India, Pakistan, Bangladesh, Burma / Myanmar," 11.
4. Ibid., 31.
5. Evers, "On the Trail of Spices," 66.
6. Koepping, "India, Pakistan, Bangladesh, Burma / Myanmar," 25.
7. West, *World That Works*, 67.
8. Koepping, "India, Pakistan, Bangladesh, Burma / Myanmar," 25.
9. Ibid., 26.
10. Rogers, *Burma*, 103.
11. Fleming, *Hidden Plight*, 1.
12. Ibid.
13. Christian Solidarity Worldwide, *Burma's Identity Crisis*, 14.
14. Ibid., 6.
15. Fleming, *Hidden Plight*, 1.
16. Appleton, *War and After*, 37.
17. Nichols, *Dancing with Angels*, 1.
18. Koepping, "India, Pakistan, Bangladesh, Burma / Myanmar," 26.
19. Christian Solidarity Worldwide, *Burma's Identity Crisis*, 6.
20. Rogers, *Carrying the Cross*, 10.
21. Fleming, *Hidden Plight*, 1.
22. Rogers, *Carrying the Cross*, 18.
23. Rogers, *Burma*, xxix.
24. Fleming, *Hidden Plight*, 21.
25. Koepping, "India, Pakistan, Bangladesh, Burma / Myanmar," 25.

26. Christian Solidarity Worldwide, *Burma's Identity Crisis*, 52–53.
27. The CPM's current dioceses consist of Yangon, Hpa-an, Taungoo (or Toungoo), Mandalay, Myitkyina, Sittwe, and the missionary dioceses of Pathein and Pyay (Prome).
28. Fleming, *Hidden Plight*, 6–7, 11.
29. Rogers, *Carrying the Cross*, 10.
30. Ibid., 31.
31. Carter, *Bewitched by Burma*, 59, 98.
32. RDA, *Burma News* 189 (1960): 7–8.
33. Carter, *Bewitched by Burma*, 165.
34. Ibid., 164.
35. Ibid., 138.
36. A. T. Houghton in RDA, *Burma News* 209 (1970): 8.
37. RDA, *Burma News* 146 (May 1934): 69.
38. Houghton, *Dense Jungle Green*, 93.
39. Ibid., 64.
40. O'Connor, *Three Centuries of Mission*, 141.
41. Ibid., 212.
42. For more on this, see USPG, https://www.uspg.org.uk/worldwide/myanmar, accessed 18 October 2020.
43. Kyaw Ye Lynn and Clare Hammond, "'They're Fearless': The Women Battling to Free Myanmar from Meth," *Guardian*, 7 May 2020, https://www.theguardian.com/global-development/2020/may/07/theyre-fearless-the-women-battling-to-free-myanmar-from-meth.
44. BNI Online, "KNO: UNODC Should Support Kachin Community's Anti-Drug Efforts," 10 July 2019, https://www.bnionline.net/en/news/kno-unodc-should-support-kachin-communitys-anti-drug-efforts.
45. Yola Verbruggen, "Pat Ja San: A Controversial Mission," *Myanmar Times*, 21 March 2016, https://www.mmtimes.com/in-depth/19566-pat-ja-san-a-controversial-mission.html.
46. Emily Fishbein, "Fighting Addiction in Kachin State," *Frontier Myanmar*, 2 July 2019, https://frontiermyanmar.net/en/fighting-addiction-in-kachin-state.
47. BNI Online, "KNO."
48. Babson, "Province of Myanmar (Burma)," 406.
49. Koepping, "India, Pakistan, Bangladesh, Burma / Myanmar," 32.
50. Nichols, *Dancing with Angels*, 1.
51. Ibid., 3–4.
52. Ibid., 4–5.
53. Saw Maung Doe, "Critical Appraisal of Christian Education," 8.
54. These are estimates based on interviews with current and former students and staff.
55. Saw Maung Doe, "Critical Appraisal of Christian Education," 10.

Afterword

1. C. R. Purser, *Burma*, 5.
2. Rogers, *Burma*, xxx.
3. Babson, "Province of Myanmar (Burma)," 406.
4. J. M. Strachan in Rangoon Diocesan Association, *Quarterly Paper* 1 (February 1897): 17.
5. C. R. Purser, *Burma*, 47.
6. Lim and Dengthuama, "Overview of Christian Missions in Myanmar," 13.
7. Orwell, review of *The Spirit of Catholicism* by Karl Adam, 79–80.
8. RDA, *Quarterly Paper* 85 (January 1918): 10.
9. West, *World That Works*, 16–17.
10. Ibid., 21.
11. Marks, *Forty Years in Burma*, 69.
12. Saw Maung Doe, "Critical Appraisal of Christian Education," 56–58.
13. O'Connor, *Three Centuries of Mission*, 92.
14. Rogers, *Burma*, xxx.
15. Christian Solidarity Worldwide, *Burma's Identity Crisis*, 64.
16. Ibid.
17. Rogers, *Carrying the Cross*, 15.
18. Kyaw Lin Htoon, "Two Children Among Five Kachin Civilians Killed by Shelling in Northern Shan," *Frontier Myanmar*, 1 September 2019, https://frontiermyanmar.net/en/two-children-among-five-kachin-civilians-killed-by-shelling-in-northern-shan. The actual number of children killed was three.
19. Christian Solidarity Worldwide, *Burma's Identity Crisis*, 10.
20. Ibid.
21. Marks, *Forty Years in Burma*, 6.

22. Charles Raven, "Authentic Anglicanism and False Fears," GAFCON, 28 January 2020, https://www.gafcon.org/news/authentic-anglicanism-and-false-fears: "The charge that GAFCON is a *breakaway or separatist* group is not supported by the evidence. It is a movement of *reform and revitalization* which has enabled faithful Anglicans to remain within the Communion, especially in North America and Brazil. While being clear that participation in its common life is based upon fidelity to the biblical gospel, not merely upon historic ties, the Jerusalem Statement and Declaration of 2008 says quite unequivocally that 'Our fellowship is not breaking away from the Anglican Communion'" (emphasis added).

Bibliography

Anderson, Gerald H., ed. *Biographical Dictionary of Christian Missions*. Grand Rapids, MI: W. B. Eerdmans, 1999.

Appleton, George. *The War and After*. Westminster, UK: Society for the Propagation of the Gospel in Foreign Parts, 1946.

Aung-Thwin, Maitrii [Michael Arthur]. "Structuring Revolt: Communities of Interpretation in the Historiography of the Saya San Rebellion." *Journal of Southeast Asian Studies* 2, no. 39 (2008): 297–317.

Babson, Katherine E. "The Province of Myanmar (Burma)." In *The Oxford Guide to The Book of Common Prayer: A Worldwide Survey*, edited by Charles Hefling and Cynthia Shattuck, 406–10. Oxford: Oxford University Press, 2006.

Bell, Daniel M., Jr. "State and Civil Society." In *The Blackwell Companion to Political Theology*, edited by Peter Scott and William T. Cavanaugh, 423–38. Oxford: Blackwell, 2004.

Brennan, Michael G. *George Orwell and Religion*. London: Bloomsbury, 2017.

Burgess, Anthony. *Little Wilson and Big God*. London: Vintage, 2012.

Carter, Anne. *Bewitched by Burma: A Unique Insight into Burma's Complex Past*. Kibworth Beauchamp, UK: Matador, 2012.

Chin Khua Khai. "Pentecostalism in Myanmar: An Overview." *Asian Journal of Pentecostal Studies* 5, no. 1 (2002): 51–71.

Christian, John Leroy. *Modern Burma*. Berkeley: University of California Press, 1942.

Christian Solidarity Worldwide. *Burma's Identity Crisis: How Ethno-religious Nationalism Has Led to Religious Intolerance, Crimes against Humanity and Genocide*. New Malden, UK: Christian Solidarity Worldwide, 2019.

Crick, Bernard. *George Orwell: A Life*. Harmondsworth, UK: Penguin, 1982.

Duncan, Christopher R., ed. *Civilizing the Margins: Southeast Asian Government Policies for the Development of Minorities*. Ithaca: Cornell University Press, 2004.

Dwight, Winthrop E. "Rudyard Kipling's Poetry." *Yale Literary Magazine* 58, no. 5 (1893): 239–42.

Evers, Georg. "'On the Trail of Spices': Christianity in Southeast Asia." In *The Oxford Handbook of Christianity in Asia*, edited by Felix Wilfred, 65–79. Oxford: Oxford University Press, 2014.

Fleming, Rachel. *Hidden Plight: Christian Minorities in Burma*. Washington, DC: US Commission on International Religious Freedom, 2016.

GAFCON (Global Anglican Future Conference) Theological Resource Team. *The Way, the Truth and the Life: Theological Resources for a Pilgrimage to a Global Anglican Future*. London: Latimer Trust, 2008.

Goh, Robbie B. H. *Christianity in Southeast Asia*. Singapore: Institute of Southeast Asian Studies Publications, 2005.

Gros, Jeffrey, Thomas F. Best, and Lorelei F. Fuchs, eds. *Growth in Agreement III: International Dialogue Texts and Agreed Statements, 1998–2005*. Geneva: WCC Publications, 2007.

Gross, Miriam, ed. *The World of George Orwell*. London: Weidenfeld and Nicolson, 1972.

Gruhl, Werner. *Imperial Japan's World War Two: 1931–1945*. New Brunswick, NJ: Transaction Publishers, 2007.

Hanson, Ola. *The Kachins: Their Customs and Traditions*. Cambridge: Cambridge University Press, 2012. First published by American Baptist Mission Press, 1913.

BIBLIOGRAPHY

Hawes, Christopher J. *Poor Relations: The Making of a Eurasian Community in British India, 1773–1833*. London: Routledge, 2013.

Heikkila-Horn, Marja-Leena. "Identity Politics and Ethnicity: Chin Christian Churches and Cross Planting." Mahidol University International College, n.d.

Hooton, W. S., and J. Stafford Wright. *The First Twenty-Five Years of the Bible Churchmen's Missionary Society (1922–1947)*. London: Bible Churchmen's Missionary Society, 1947.

Hoskins, Janet Alison. "An Unjealous God? Christian Elements in a Vietnamese Syncretistic Religion." *Current Anthropology* 55, no. S10 (2014): S302–S311.

Houghton, A. T. *Dense Jungle Green, the First Twelve Years of the B.C.M.S. Burma Mission*. London: Bible Churchmen's Missionary Society, 1937.

Hughes, Derrick. *Bishop Sahib: A Life of Reginald Heber*. Worthing, UK: Churchman Publishing, 1986.

Jarvis, Edward. *Carlos Duarte Costa: Testament of a Socialist Bishop*. Berkeley: Apocryphile Press, 2019.

Keith, Charles. *Catholic Vietnam: A Church from Empire to Nation*. Berkeley: University of California Press, 2012.

Kelly, R. Talbot. *Peeps at Many Lands: Burma*. London: Adam and Charles Black, 1908.

Kennedy, David J. *Eucharistic Sacramentality in an Ecumenical Context: The Anglican Epiclesis*. Abingdon, UK: Routledge, 2008.

Koepping, Elizabeth. "India, Pakistan, Bangladesh, Burma / Myanmar." In *Christianities in Asia*, edited by Peter C. Phan, 9–44. Chichester, UK: Wiley-Blackwell, 2011.

Kyaw Win. *My Conscience: An Exile's Memoir of Burma*. Eugene, OR: Resource, 2016.

Lim, Theodore, and Dengthuama. "An Overview of Christian Missions in Myanmar." *Global Missiology* 3, no. 13 (2016): http://ojs.globalmissiology.org/index.php/english/issue/view/167.

Lowis, C. C. *Census of India, 1901*. Vol. 12, *Burma*. Part 1, *Report*. Rangoon: Office of the Superintendent of Government Printing, 1902.

Markham, Ian S., J. Barney Hawkins IV, Justin Terry, and Leslie Nuñez Steffensen, eds. *The Wiley-Blackwell Companion to The Anglican Communion*. Chichester, UK: Wiley-Blackwell, 2013.

Marks, John Ebenezer. *Forty Years in Burma*. Edited by W. C. B. Purser. London: Hutchinson, 1917.

The Maulmain Almanac, Directory, and Diary for 1852. Maulmain: American Mission Press, 1851.

The Maulmain Almanac, Directory, and Diary for 1853. Maulmain: American Mission Press, 1852.

The Maulmain Almanac for 1850. Maulmain: American Mission Press, 1849.

McLeish, Alexander. *Christian Progress in Burma*. London: World Dominion Press, 1929.

Min Naing. *National Ethnic Groups of Myanmar*. Yangon: Swiftwinds Books, 2000.

Morris, Jan, and Robert Fermor-Hesketh. *Architecture of the British Empire*. New York: Vendome Press, 1986.

Ngô-Đình-Thục, Pierre Martin. "'Misericordias Domini in Aeternum Cantabo': Autobiography of Mgr. Pierre Martin Ngô-dinh-Thục, Archbishop of Huế." *Einsicht* (special edition), Munich: Una-Voce-Gruppe Maria, August 1982: 1–93.

Ngun Ling, Samuel. "Christ Through Our Neighbors' Eyes." *Rays* 2 (2010): 3–19.

———. "Does Dialogue Cancel Mission? Revisiting Church's Mission in the Context of Interreligious Dialogue." *Missio Dei* 1 (2007): 1–10.

Nichols, Alan. *Dancing with Angels: The Life Story of Stephen Than, Archbishop of Myanmar*. Moreland: Acorn Press, 2015.

O'Connor, Daniel, et al. *Three Centuries of Mission: The United Society for the Propagation of the Gospel, 1701–2000*. London: Continuum, 2000.

Olson, James S., and Randy Roberts. *Where the Domino Fell: America and Vietnam 1945 to 1990*. New York: St. Martin's Press, 1991.

Orwell, George. *Burmese Days*. Modern Classics edition with a new introduction. London: Penguin, 2009.

———. Review of *The Spirit of Catholicism* by Karl Adam (1932). In *The Collected Essays, Journalism and Letters of George Orwell*, vol. 1, edited by Sonia Orwell and Ian Angus, 79–80. London: Secker and Warburg, 1968.

———. *The Road to Wigan Pier*. London: Secker and Warburg / Octopus, 1980.

Owen, Norman G., ed. *The Emergence of Modern Southeast Asia: A New History*. Honolulu: University of Hawai'i Press, 2005.

Petty, Orville Anderson, ed., for Laymen's Foreign Missions Inquiry. *Fact-Finders' Reports: IV India-Burma (Volume 4 of Supplementary Series)*. New York: Harper and Brothers, 1933.

Phan, Peter C., ed. *Christianities in Asia*. Chichester, UK: Wiley-Blackwell, 2011.

Pieris, Aloysius, SJ. *An Asian Theology of Liberation*. London: T&T Clark, 1988.

———. "Political Theologies in Asia." In *The Blackwell Companion to Political Theology*, edited by Peter Scott and William T. Cavanaugh, 256–70. Oxford: Blackwell, 2004.

Popham, Peter. *The Lady and the Peacock: The Life of Aung San Suu Kyi*. New York: Experiment, 2013.

Preston, Ronald H. *Religion and the Persistence of Capitalism*. London: SCM Press, 1979.

Purser, C. R. *Burma*. Westminster, UK: Society for the Propagation of the Gospel in Foreign Parts, 1929.

Purser, Mary Chesmer. *An Ambassador in Bonds: The Story of William Henry Jackson, Priest, of the Mission to the Blind of Burma*. 2nd ed. Westminster, UK: Society for the Propagation of the Gospel in Foreign Parts, 1933.

Purser, W. C. B. *Christian Missions in Burma*. Westminster, UK: Society for the Propagation of the Gospel in Foreign Parts, 1911.

Rangoon Diocesan Association (RDA). *Burma News*, nos. 125–210 (1928–70).

———. *Quarterly Paper*, nos. 1–124 (1897–1927).

Rees, Richard. *George Orwell: Fugitive from the Camp of Victory*. London: Secker and Warburg, 1961.

Rogers, Benedict. *Burma: A Nation at the Crossroads*. London: Ebury, 2012.

———. *Carrying the Cross: The Military Regime's Campaign of Restriction, Discrimination and Persecution Against Christians in Burma*. New Malden, UK: Christian Solidarity Worldwide, 2007.

———. *A Land Without Evil*. Oxford: Monarch, 2004.

Sandison, Alan. *The Last Man in Europe: An Essay on George Orwell*. London: Macmillan, 1974.

Saw Maung Doe, Mark. "A Critical Appraisal of Christian Education in the Diocese of Yangon: With a Special Focus on the Contribution of U Tun (1955–2003)." PhD thesis, Oxford Centre for Mission Studies, University of Wales, 2008.

Short, Stanley W. *On Burma's Eastern Frontier*. London: Marshall, Morgan and Scott, 1945.

Small, Christopher. *The Road to Miniluv: George Orwell, the State, and God*. London: Victor Gollancz, 1975.

Smith, Donald Eugene. *Religion and Politics in Burma*. Princeton: Princeton University Press, 2015. Originally published 1965.

Smith, Martin. *Burma: Insurgency and the Politics of Ethnicity*. London: Zed Books, 1991.

———. *State of Strife: The Dynamics of Ethnic Conflict in Burma*. Policy Studies 36. Washington, DC: East-West Center, 2007.

South, Ashley. *Ethnic Politics in Burma: States of Conflict*. London: Routledge, 2008.

South Western Times (Bunbury, Western Australia). "Church News," 27 June 1946, 9.

Sugden, Chris. "Report on GAFCON." June 2018.

Taylor, D. J. *Orwell: The Life*. London: Vintage, 2004.

Thompson, H. P. *Into All Lands: The History of the Society for the Propagation of* the Gospel in Foreign Parts, 1701–1950. London: SPCK, 1951.

Thompson, Julian. *Forgotten Voices of Burma*. London: Ebury, 2010.

Titcomb, Jonathan H. *Personal Recollections of British Burma and Its Church Mission Work*. London: Wells Gardner, Darton, 1880.

Tyndale-Biscoe, John. *For God Alone: The Life of George West, Bishop of Rangoon*. Oxford: Amate Press, 1984.

Ward, Kevin. *A History of Global Anglicanism*. Cambridge: Cambridge University Press, 2006.

Wayland, Francis. *A Memoir of the Life and Labors of the Rev. Adoniram Judson DD*. 2 vols. Boston: Phillips, Sampson, 1853.

West, George Algernon. *Jungle Witnesses*. Westminster, UK: Society for the Propagation of the Gospel in Foreign Parts, 1948.

———. *The World That Works*. London: Blandford Press, 1945.

West, George Algernon, with D. C. Atwool. *Jungle Folk*. Westminster, UK: Society for the Propagation of the Gospel in Foreign Parts, 1933.

———. *Jungle Friends*. Westminster, UK: Society for the Propagation of the Gospel in Foreign Parts, 1933.

Wilfred, Felix, ed. *The Oxford Handbook of Christianity in Asia*. Oxford: Oxford University Press, 2014.

Wilson, Elizabeth. *The Story of Fifty Years of the Young Women's Christian Association of India, Burma and Ceylon*. Calcutta: Association Press (YWCA), 1925.

Winn, Godfrey. *Going My Way*. New York: Hutchinson, 1948.

Womack, William. "Contesting Indigenous and Female Authority in the Burma Baptist Mission: The Case of Ellen Mason." *Women's History Review* 17, no. 4 (2008): 543–59.

Index

Ah Mya, Francis (bishop)
  background and election, 109, 112–13, 113
  career as bishop and archbishop, 113–14, 117, 120, 190
  views, aims and objectives, 114, 115, 118, 119
  war record, 96, 108
Andaman and Nicobar Islands, 53–54, 88–89, 100–101
Anglicanism
  Anglican Church in North America (ACNA), 136, 138, 149
  Anglo-Catholicism, 19, 135, 156, 157
  "atheists of empire", 20–21, 109
  charismatic and Pentecostal worship, 130, 138–39, 162
  continuing Anglican movement, 138, 149
  crisis in, 147, 178–79, 179–80
  in England, 150
  Fellowship of Confessing Anglicans (FCA), 136, 149
  GAFCON, 6, 136–38, 149
  Global South (conservative group), 136–37, 149
  High Church tradition in, 18–19, 124, 137
  in other parts of Asia, 138–39, 148, 150
  realignment, 149–50, 179–80
animism. *See* spirit beliefs
Aung Hla, John (bishop), 96, 108, 112–13, 190
Aung San, 76, 94, 99–100, 110–11
Aung San Suu Kyi, 152

Bamar. *See* Burman (Bamar) ethnic group
Baptists
  advantages enjoyed by, 51, 59, 71–72, 173
  arrival in Burma, 26
  Judson College, 107
  in Kachin state, 156
  and Karen controversy, 44–45
  wartime exile of, 97
Bible Churchmen's Missionary Society (BCMS), 52–53, 86, 163–64
Bishop's College (Calcutta), 28, 74, 188
British East India Company (BEIC), 14–15, 174
Buddhism
  and anti-Christianism, 21, 41, 66, 117
  and anti-colonialism, 21, 66, 82–83
  converts from, 45, 55, 62, 73–74, 174
  and independence movement, 75, 82–83
  and nationalism, 66, 75, 82, 117, 153
  perceptions of, 16–18, 23, 34, 129, 175
  political instrumentalization of, 21, 140–41, 177
  and social status, 133
  as state religion, 114, 140
  theology, 143–44
Burma
  census returns, 62, 70
  customs and traditions of, 128–29
  ethnic diversity in, 1, 2, 3, 9, 48–49, 54–55
  geography and natural hazards of, 8, 43, 57, 59
  health and social problems of, 164–66, 177
  languages of, 2, 36, 50–53, 54, 158–59, 179
  and national identity, 112, 158
  perceptions of, 31–32, 39, 41, 129, 175, 176
  population of, 1, 9
  religious diversity in, 2, 3, 22–23, 70, 133, 173
Burma, history of
  ancient history and social structure, 8–9, 10
  Anglo-Burmese Wars: First, 24; Second, 24, 28, 30; Third, 24, 38, 49, 62
  colonization, 24–25
  first Christian missionaries, 15–16
  independence and nationalist movements, 67, 94, 104–5
  national independence, 112, 132
  recent events, 152
  renamed Myanmar, 5, 120, 160–61
  under Japanese occupation, 92–96, 99–100
Burma, interethnic tensions in
  ethnic groups and British military service, 76, 95
  expulsions and deportations, 115, 116, 117
  persecution of minorities, 151
  postwar animosity, 105–6, 110–11, 121, 122, 140–41
Burma Christian Council (BCC). *See* Myanmar Council of Churches (MCC)

INDEX

Burma Council of Churches (BCC). *See* Myanmar Council of Churches (MCC)
Burman (Bamar) ethnic group
    and Buddhism, 133
    and colonization, 25
    and nationalism, 153

Catholicism. *See* Roman Catholicism
Chin ethnic group
    beliefs and customs of, 50, 130, 177
    and colonization, 25
    at Panglong conferences, 110
    and Pentecostalism, 130
    perceptions of, 50
    revolt of, 115
    subgroups of, 52, 53, 177
Chinese Christians, 33, 36, 49, 72, 116
Christianity in Burma
    Christian unity and ecumenism, 72–73, 106–7, 121–22
    criticisms of, 130–31, 134, 141, 179
    denominations of, 15, 35, 48, 71, 75, 125, 126; relations between, 56, 157, 176
    dialogue with Buddhism, 73–74, 107, 140–44
    as example to non-Christians, 67
    intolerance and persecution of Christians, 3–4, 15, 26, 151–53, 177, 178
    as "lesser evil," 81, 84
    perceived as a Western religion, 123–24, 141, 145, 146
    as political theology, 124–25, 130, 141
    spread of, 70–71
Church of England in Burma (1824–1930)
    Additional Clergy Society (ACS), 32, 38, 39
    attitudes and prejudices within, 60–61, 68–69
    complicity in colonialism, 39, 61, 134
    emphasis on education, 72, 125–26, 175, 176
    missionaries: desirable attributes of, 59, 63–64; first missionaries in Burma, 26–27;
    hardships endured by, 43, 45–46, 57, 59; skills of, 50, 51, 55, 59, 60
    and mixed ethnicity congregations, 54–55
    and orphans, 80–81, 83–84
    and social outreach, 43, 59, 175, 176
Church of India, Burma, and Ceylon (CIBC) in Burma (1930–1947)
    becomes Church of India, Pakistan, Burma, and Ceylon (CIPBC), 112
    creation and perceptions of, 75, 83
    and first native archdeacons, 108
    identity of, 98, 102
    and openness to Buddhism, 107
    postwar projects and uncertainties in, 107–8
Church of India, Pakistan, Burma and Ceylon (CIPBC) in Burma (1947–1970)
    and censorship, 117
    creation of, 112
    dissolution of, 118, 119, 147–48, 148–49
    first native bishops of, 109, 112–13
    growth of, 116
    and lay leadership, 118, 120
    missionaries, expulsion of, 116, 117, 132, 164
    and regional differences, 116, 122
Church Missionary Society (CMS), 32, 52, 86
Church of the Province of Burma (CPB) 1970–1989
    becomes Church of the Province of Myanmar (CPM), 120
    creation of, 119–20, 147
Church of the Province of Myanmar (CPM) 1989–
    and censorship, 161
    ethnic minorities and mixed congregations in, 156, 157, 162
    identity and language, 158–59
    leadership and election of bishops, 163
    liturgy, 166
    membership, 147
    role within Anglicanism, 147
Colonialism in Burma
    attitudes and prejudice, 77–78, 78–79, 83
    challenged by Second World War, 94, 102
    changing stance on religion, 66, 82
    described as despotism, 37–38, 39, 40–42
    as "lesser evil," 81, 84
    objectives of, 11–13
    perceived benefits of, 3, 19, 39, 40–42
    religious ideals of, 14, 18, 19, 22, 123–24
    religious neutrality of, 16, 17, 25, 34, 36–37, 39, 125
    and sexual conduct, 78–81, 83–84, 174
    and sympathy for the Anglican Church, 66–67, 125
Cotton, George E. L. (bishop), 30, 45, 189
Crosslinks. *See* Bible Churchmen's Missionary Society

East India Company. *See* British East India Company (BEIC)

First World War, 68–70, 129
Fyffe, Rollestone Sterritt (bishop)

background and consecration, 67, 189–90
views and opinions, 55, 72, 110

Holy Cross Theological College (HCTC)
closures due to unrest, 112, 113
foundation and opening, 76–77
postwar reopening, 103
at present, 49, 168–69
Houghton, Alfred T. (bishop designate), 53, 88, 141, 164

Johnson, Ralph (bishop), 32, 189
Judson, Adoniram, 26–27, 142

Kachin ethnic group
and colonization, 25
denominations of, 156
first missions to, 52–53
identity and language of, 159, 177
Kachin Independence Organization (KIO), 158, 160
at Panglong conferences, 110–11
perceptions of, 53
revolt of, 112, 115
Karen (Kayin) ethnic group
annual conferences of, 47–48
and church leadership, 162–63, 176
and colonization, 9–10, 25
ethnic defense organizations and revolt of, 111, 112
legends, customs, and traditions of, 33, 48
mass conversion of, 33, 38, 44–48, 176
at Panglong conferences, 110–11
Karenni (Kayah) ethnic group, 25, 177
Kayah. *See* Karenni (Kayah) ethnic group
Kayin. *See* Karen (Kayin) ethnic group
Knight, Arthur Mesac (bishop), 64, 65–66, 66, 189

Marks, John Ebenezer
admitting non-Christians to schools, 35
background and arrival in Burma, 28–29, 32
language knowledge, 36
rapport with King Mindon, 29, 35
Middleton, Thomas F. (bishop), 28, 188
Milman, Robert (bishop), 30, 45, 189
Mindon, King, 29, 34, 35, 31
missionaries. *See* Church of England in Burma (1824–1930); Church of India, Pakistan, Burma and Ceylon (CIPBC) in Burma (1947–1970); Roman Catholicism
Mon ethnic group, 25, 111, 112
Myanmar. *See* Burma

Myanmar Council of Churches (MCC), 97, 114, 140, 157
Myanmar Institute of Theology (MIT), 134, 168, 169

nats or *nat* worship. *See* spirit beliefs
Ne Win (military leader), 114–15, 115–16, 117
Nu (prime minister), 41–42, 112, 114

Ordination
of Burmans, 74, 182
of Chins, 52, 183, 185
of Kachins, 183
of Karens, 32, 182, 183
of Tamils, 33, 49, 182
of women, 138, 139–40, 149, 150
Orwell, George, 2, 39, 77, 78–79, 81, 84

Panglong conferences, 109–11, 121, 151
Pat Jasan (Christian anti-drugs movement), 165–66

Rakhine ethnic group, 25, 111
Rangoon
Anglican cathedral, 38, 63, 65–66, 104
foundation of Diocese of, 30–31, 62
Roman Catholic cathedral, 63, 65
university, 103
Rangoon Diocesan Association (RDA), 85–86, 108–9
Rohingya ethnic group, 3, 153–56
Roman Catholicism
and colonization, 10, 12–14, 13
missionaries, 15–16, 72, 174
perceptions of, 14–15, 71–72, 72
relative proportions in Burma, 71
schools, 72

Saya San Rebellion, 75–76
Second World War
Andaman and Nicobar Islands, 88–89, 100–101
army chaplains, 92, 99, 103–4
the Church in exile, 96–97
evacuation of mainland Burma, 90–92
exacerbation of ethnic tensions, 94–95, 97–98, 102
initial impact of the war in Burma, 85–86, 87
Japanese objectives in, 87, 89, 94
and local clergy, 95–96
Shan ethnic group
and colonization, 25
Palaung (subgroup), 55, 111

INDEX

Shan ethnic group (*continued*)
   at Panglong conferences, 110–11
   perceptions of, 50
   Shan Federal Movement and revolt of, 115
Shearburn, Victor G. (bishop)
   advocacy of local leadership, 114
   arrival in Burma and background, 113, 190
   expulsion and retirement, 117, 190
   projects and innovations, 113–114
Society for Promoting Christian Knowledge (SPCK), 18, 30, 32, 46
Society for the Propagation of the Gospel in Foreign Parts (SPG)
   arrival and expansion in Burma, 28, 32, 37
   character of, 18, 28, 29, 40–41, 135
   evolution of methods, 120, 164–65
   numbers of missionaries, 63, 64, 67
   and Second World War, 86
Southeast Asia
   acceptance and development of Christian identities, 124, 126–27, 137–38, 144
   and cosmic religious outlook, 20–21, 23
   countries of, 10–11
   introduction of Christianity to, 10–12, 123, 127
   and origins of the Second World War, 85, 87
   religions of, 10–12, 11, 19–20, 21, 127, 147
spirit beliefs, 34–35, 51, 58–59, 60, 128–29
Strachan, John M. (bishop)
   arrival and impact, 38
   attitudes and cultural understanding, 33, 39, 40, 56, 78
   ethnic missions and pastoral visits, 49, 50, 54, 57
   retirement and death, 64, 189
   views on Church growth, 32, 41, 62, 64

Tamil Christians, 33, 48–49, 71–72, 92
Telugu Christians, 49, 71–72
Than Myint Oo, Stephen (bishop), 136, 152, 167–68
Theology, third-world, 131–32, 133
Theology of liberation, 132–33

Thibaw, King, 31, 40, 62
Titcomb, Jonathan H. (bishop)
   advocacy of local leadership, 112
   attitudes and cultural understanding, 34, 36
   consecration, arrival and career in Burma, 30, 32, 38
   debilitating accident and resignation, 31, 57, 189
   ethnic missions and pastoral visits, 49, 53, 54, 57
Translations
   of the Bible, 51, 52, 160–61
   of Prayer Book, 29, 46, 51, 52, 114
Tubbs, Norman Henry (bishop)
   advocacy of local leadership, 75
   background, 74–75, 190
   retirement, 77, 190
   on Second World War, 88
   sons, 99, 104

United Society for the Propagation of the Gospel (USPG). *See* Society for the Propagation of the Gospel in Foreign Parts (SPG)
United States Commission on International Religious Freedom (USCIRF), 151

West, George A. (bishop)
   arrival in Burma, 113
   attitudes and policies, 70, 81, 104, 107, 109
   background and consecration, 77, 190
   near-fatal road accident, 88
   retirement, 113, 190
   wartime leadership, 96–97, 99
Winchester, Diocese of, 30–31
Winchester Brotherhood, 55, 67
Women's Mission Association (WMA), 37, 139
World War One. *See* First World War
World War Two. *See* Second World War

Young Men's Buddhist Association (YMBA), 67, 75
Young Women's Christian Association (YWCA), 37, 39, 79, 139

CPSIA information can be obtained
at www.ICGtesting.com
Printed in the USA
BVHW030317090122
625753BV00001B/20